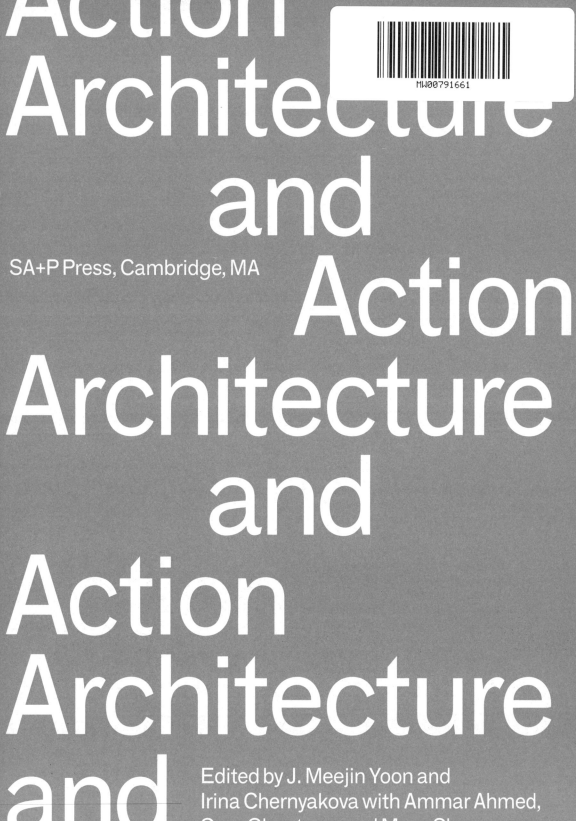

Action
Architecture
and
Action
Architecture
and
Action
Architecture
and
Action

SA+P Press, Cambridge, MA

MW00791661

Edited by J. Meejin Yoon and
Irina Chernyakova with Ammar Ahmed,
Sam Ghantous, and Maya Shopova

Architecture and Action: Design and Research in the
MIT Department of Architecture

Editors
J. Meejin Yoon, Irina Chernyakova

Assistant Editors
Ammar Ahmed, Sam Ghantous, Maya Shopova

Design
MTWTF, NY

Layout
Editorial Team

Copyediting
Editorial Team, Patsy Baudoin, Susan Spilecki

Proofreading
Editorial Team, Lucas Freeman

Publisher
SA+P Press

ISBN
978-0-9981170-6-5

Library of Congress Control Number: 2018952116

Distributed by The MIT Press, Cambridge, Massachusetts,
and London, England.

Printing
CONTI Tipocolor, Florence, Italy

Course descriptions and syllabi were provided by the instructor of the course
or studio; project and thesis texts were provided by the students. All texts have
been edited by the editorial team. Visual material was provided by the author
unless stated otherwise. All previously published texts include the original
publication credits.

Contact
Massachusetts Institute of Technology
School of Architecture and Planning
Department of Architecture
77 Massachusetts Avenue
Room 7-337
Cambridge, MA 02139
arch@mit.edu

Contents

Setting Agendas
J. Meejin Yoon

When William R. Ware, the first Professor of Architecture at MIT, outlined in 1865 that it was the aim of the school to "ensure that the Architecture of the future shall be worthy of the future," he brought to bear a deep sense of responsibility on the faculty, students, and discipline.[1] This timeless mission statement, both optimistic and succinct, created a unique context for a school of architecture within an institute of technology. Since then, the pedagogical experiment that is MIT Architecture, with its discipline groups of engineers, artists, historians, theorists, computer scientists, urbanists, and architects has brought both a critical and constructive lens to MIT's mission to solve the world's great challenges. This critical perspective allows for an expanded awareness—a recognition that problems have contexts, that one's solutions can be another's problems, and a solution can be a problem in and of itself. This perspective enables an active reimagining of contexts in order to ultimately intervene and transform them. Both are important disciplinary actions; both are essential for *world-building* in the real world.

Every few years, the scholarship, research, and creative production of the faculty and students in the Department of Architecture at MIT is curated into a publication referred to as the *Agendas in Architecture* series. From *Uncertain Futures* to *Testing to Failure*, these publications not only reflect the topical questions of the time, but they reveal underlying and enduring concerns and commitments. These concerns are obsessive, critical, analytical, speculative, probing, anti-aesthetic, and yet at times beautiful, compelling, and vexing. Over the past few years we have seen an intensified appetite for disciplinary "plus"—not extra-disciplinarity for novelty's sake but conscious and conversant in the concerns and debates outside our discipline in order to better engage, impact, and act in the world. To that extent, MIT Architecture operates as an amalgam of labs, studios, networks, and fieldworks to create a broad platform for critical thinking, soul searching, and risk taking.

The following pages reflect our conversations with one another, with the discipline, and with broader audiences. From social justice, to racial equity, to displacement, to climate change, to representation, to geometry, to archives, to authorship, to nuclear waste, to utopia, the work of students and faculty represented in *Architecture and Action* highlights these critical and constructive acts. Future-making requires us to not only be "concerned with how things *ought* to be" but to make concrete steps that will enable us to construct those futures.[2] In *Architecture and Action* we share our way of articulating positions, advancing research, and ultimately taking action, not only to be worthy of the future but to position a future to which we can contribute.

1   William R. Ware, *An Outline of a Course of Architectural Instruction* (Boston: John Wilson and Sons, 1866).
2   I borrow the term "future-making" from Nick Montfort, *The Future* (Cambridge, MA: MIT Press, 2017). Herbert A. Simon defines design in his seminal book *The Sciences of the Artificial*: "The natural sciences are concerned with how things are.... Design, on the other hand, is concerned with how things ought to be, with devising artifacts to attain goals." See *The Sciences of the Artificial* (Cambridge, MA: MIT Press, 1968), 114–115.

Modifying Action

In conceiving this volume of the Department's *Agendas* series, *Architecture and Action*, we sought to reflect on how agency and action are conceptualized and realized by students and faculty—from the types of acts that count as architecture, to the sites, scales, and speeds at which they take place. How do students and faculty understand, embrace, or distribute agency, whether in pedagogy or practice, on campus or off? And how does this understanding translate to action? *Architecture and Action* brings together work through the prism of these questions. Acknowledging that action is not a linear directive, we seek to modify the term, long associated with confident and imposing acts and problem-solving attitudes. What about the slow work of collaboration, of dealing with the mess of matters, or at times, staying still? Thinking through reciprocal ideas of agency and action necessitates looking not just at intentions and outcomes, but also at quotidian minor acts, duration, scalability, contingencies, and circulation.

   Architecture and Action is organized into five Acts: Instrumental, Material, Collective, Environmental, and Discursive. Each is treated as both a theme and an approach to category, scale, and intent. As most projects could be read through multiple entry points by this framing, the organization of work within each chapter aims to highlight tensions and create dialogue.

   "Instrumental Acts" begins with acts of urgency—immediate responses and interventions—that spark · reflection and long-term inquiry. In "Material Acts," we look closely at the heavy entangled mess of matter to understand material desires, potentials, and consequences. Here projects are resourceful: they hack modes of production, imagine new afterlives for refuse, or project into the future to help us see our current habits in a new light. Acknowledging the numerous actors involved in any act of architecture, "Collective Acts," brings together practices and projects that embrace anonymity, collaboration, and decentralized modes of production. Projects focus on new forms and programs, expanding from small-scale installations to cross-institutional collaborations. "Environmental Acts" contends with our troubled relationship to land and territory and with looming effects of environmental change. The projects document current values, challenge permanence, embrace indeterminacy, and suggest common tools across disciplines to address these questions. "Discursive Acts" revisits our central inquiries: how are these conversations framed at MIT? How do we discuss these questions? We leave you with projects premised on pedagogy as action and focused on ways to retool naturalized modes of thinking, learning, and producing work.

　　In the spirit of the *Agendas* series, we embrace the multiplicity of ways people make things happen. As a site of knowledge-building, we dwell in the space between cultivating utopia and practicing dissent. Propositions are always in and of the real world while also serving as representations of proposed futures. The ideas are presented as questions: How is our discipline acting, acted upon, and how might it act otherwise? What can our work enable? Cutting through the assembly of work in this way allows us to see how the personal, the political, and the institutional are intertwined and how the students and faculty here produce work in strategic and perceptive ways.

　　Architecture and Action is a stocktaking, a proclamation, and an invitation. It allows for a critical assessment of the work happening at MIT Architecture. We pause to collect discussions, reinterpret, and debate what we have done in order to plant new inquiries. We acknowledge and amplify the seriousness with which students see challenges, probe consequential issues, and the ways they use the academic setting to test, speculate, and make space for thoughtful work. The diversity of projects, interests, and approaches gathered illuminates, to us, how the environment and pedagogy here can enable students to understand that their work can produce effects through numerous forms, and to think about their work with an eye to what is possible today and what will take generations to enact.

Here at MIT, we have the privilege to choose the questions and work we take on. It is through this work, regardless of the form it takes, that we can negotiate our hopes and imagine the necessary transformations to instigate change, both in the academy and profession. Architecture, in the multitude of ways positioned in this book, is an instrument to understand, visualize, discuss, and think, and sometimes to do nothing, or to critique, enable, and transform. We remain optimistic.

On behalf of the editorial team,
Irina Chernyakova

Instrumental
Acts
Instrumental
Acts
Instrumental
Acts
Instrumental
Acts
Instrumental
Acts

How do students and faculty make statements, take positions, start conversations, and intervene in debates? How do they conceptualize agency and produce actions? By what means, and with which tools?

From posters to editorials, physical devices to ceremonial events, we begin with seemingly small acts. From inventing a fictional architecture collective to think through discourse on disinvestment, to visualizing a difficult and evolving situation to understand and engage a political crisis, to testing new mediums and telling old stories, this Act draws together projects that think through the tension between the desire to act quickly and the decision to resist the problem-solving tendencies of the profession.

The projects gathered here also activate the space of speed and reaction, of making one's voice heard, of mobilizing peers, and leveraging institutions. They imagine new ways of working and find ways to implement these ideas on campus and off. Organizational capacities and acts that leverage privilege are instruments every bit as much as the instruments of drawing, image-making, research, scholarship, practice, and writing. Students speak up; with small acts, they try to change the course of the conversation.

Students and faculty bring their concerns and preoccupations into the studio; they test potential and limits of artistic and architectural interventions. They assume a variety of attitudes, from earnest to cynical, realistic to optimistic—and deploy pragmatic and speculative tools in the likes of performances, plug-ins, manifestos, gizmos, narratives, drawings, courses, and conversations.

Importantly, this collection serves as more than a catalog of techniques. These are strategic, site-specific, and deliberate interventions—a repertoire of arguments and tactics. Each action articulates a position on a potential means of engagement. Each is a means to produce an effect.

FLAGLIFE
Laura Serejo Genes
November 7–9, 2016

ON IMMIGRATION AND HUMANIST VALUES
Nasser Rabbat
MIT Faculty Newsletter
March/April 2018

OUR CITY, WHAT RUINS
Martin Elliott
MArch Thesis
Advisor: Joel Lamere
Fall 2017

This thesis presents the work of a small collective, Anatopia. It formed amidst the fallout of the financial crisis in early 2009, out of frustration with the continued failures of city government, local institutions, and architectural practice to address the politics of the time.

The collective worked in partnership with foundations and not-for-profit entities who represented local interests. Anatopia's mission was to advocate on behalf of local residents and marginalized communities in the pursuit of resource accessibility, wealth accumulation, and racial and social justice. Their practice sought to dismantle the methods, norms, and structural biases on which architectural production is typically predicated.

They approached their work in a non-hierarchical manner. In their documentation, urban plans hold the same amount of space as a documentary photograph, a polemical collage, a model, or a legal document. Their aim was to highlight the ways architects could leverage their agency towards an expanded field. They wrote:

Leaks, demolitions, vacancy, and ruins. "Our City, What Ruins" is a phrase we use to describe the conditions of urban life at the time of our practice. One third of the land lay vacant, transformed into blight, and targeted for demolition. The city was the world's flagship destination for wonders of the modern-day ruin. We declared the largest federal bankruptcy in the nation's history, and our democratically elected officials were on their way to prison. It was clear the ruined landscape was a metaphor for a failing system. Our work willingly drops the connotations associated with the ruins, the blight that surrounds them, and the human bodies who still call the city home.

Our practice was born out of an observed social need: a collectively-led spatial justice practice that was willing to work both nefariously and legally, on the psyche and on the land, on damaged histories and new futures. We advocate for an expanded agency of the architect, especially in the domains of divestment and subtraction.

Our body of work explores spatial and socioeconomic tactics relating to the rebranding of the body, community wealth-building, and emancipatory infrastructures; our work takes the form of drawings, models, slides, legal documents, and literature. Just as our practice worked to unravel the failed bureaucracy that helped produce Our City, we ask: What Ruins?

KINETIC SPEAKERS AND SONIC COMMONS
Rainar Aasrand, Jessica Adams, Nicolás Kisic Aguirre, Andrea Carrillo, Walker Downey, Martin Elliott, Kyle Joba-Woodruff, Alexander Lefell, Samantha Adler de Oliveira, Alexander Souvannakhot
Seminar: Art, Culture and Technology (ACT)
Instructors: Sam Auinger, Jan St. Werner
Spring 2017

The Kinetic Speaker is a collectively designed and built circular speaker wheel; it stems from an effort to design, build, and play objects with historical and theoretical depth and to perform and diffuse sound in completely new ways. The students staged a performance on March 15, 2017 in ACT's Cube and Lobby 10 with drummer John Colpitts (Laurie Anderson, Man Forever) and Jon Whitney (Brainwashed.com). The multimedia choreographed performance provided a dynamic embodied experience for performers and listeners. Listen and view excerpts from the performance: mitsoundcreations.tumblr.com.

THE ECOLOGY OF TRUTH: A SCOPING DEVICE FOR REFLECTING ON THE INSTITUTE
Samuel Schneider
MArch Thesis
Advisor: Azra Akšamija
Spring 2018

The spaces we inhabit influence the way we experience our surroundings, but this causal relationship is much weaker than designers and architects like to imagine. The Ecology of Truth investigates these weak effects as a mesoscope, a device designed to interrogate the spaces and relationships between the microscopic and the macroscopic.

The work draws on the aesthetic of the laboratory at MIT—both transparent and reflective—visible, yet inaccessible. The Ecology of Truth derives its aesthetic influence from the solipsistic world of architectural language, blending it with scopic histories that run throughout the development of modern science. If the project has a single inspiration, it is the Wunderkammer, also known as the cabinet of curiosities—the idea that a unified curation of its contained objects reassembles their spatial lives, turning "real" objects into a mythic, often singular narrative of the world—a miniature ecological prism, with various competing truths.

The life of the work is dynamic: moving around the Institute, it captures scientific curios bound for the trash, repurposing them as a narrative gallery of failed *objets-types*—modern tools transformed into contingent objects of contemporary space. While on the move, the cabinet turns eyes, and hopefully some of the minds behind those puzzled glances.

Photo: Sam Muller

POWER LUNCH
Stephanie Lee/MIT NOMAS (National Organization of Minority Architecture Students)
Spring 2017

Power Lunch, an off-the-record female-led conversation series, brought together students and faculty to discuss the experiences of women in architectural practice, academia, urban planning, and activism. Power Lunch created the time and space amid the regular lecture series cycle to explore what it means to be a woman in architecture and to highlight narratives and experiences that are too often either dismissed or pushed aside. The goal of the series was to address head-on the myth that women's rights—and, by extension, other social movements—and architectural design are incompatible.

Stephanie Lee, "Power Lunch," *The Site Magazine*, May 7, 2018, http://www.thesitemagazine.com/read/power-lunch.

PROPS
Lucy Siyao Liu, Matthew Bohne
Fall 2016–ongoing

PROPS is a weekly paper of images. *PROPS* disregards disciplinary boundaries and proposes an alternative visual atlas of juxtapositions. *PROPS* is an expanded archive of work by image makers, image collectors, and accidental image connoisseurs.

Issue 02: *Workspace Spacestation*
Text: Christianna Bonin

As a historian and critic of architecture and art, images provide my lifeblood, my daily bread, my paycheck, my creative fodder. Books, streets, interiors, museums, sketchbooks, Pinterest, theaters, billboards, archives, factories, facades, films, clothing. Images rattle me awake. They make me question my presuppositions. They are

springboards to ideas I rarely foresee. They are Trojans in my head, rustling up the experiences I wish I could forget. I print them, save them, share them, debate them, cut them out, pin them up, rip them apart. I seek and find images in my surroundings. I interrogate the ways that artists and architects have perceived their worlds and represented future ones. I write histories of image-making and image-makers.

For me, images are more than a painting on a wall or a photograph of a building. They are graphic and verbal; optical and mental; above all, they are perceptual. Anytime I sit down to write about a work of art or architecture, I struggle to put into words—to make a verbal image—of something that has already been expressed (perhaps more perfectly) in another graphic medium. Why bother to translate between different kinds of images? Because I believe that language can produce a discourse or reveal a state of affairs that can be tested against other representations. Just the same, I have faith in the pithiness and eloquence of graphic images. Sometimes, no words are needed.

AGENCY—ACTION
Azra Akšamija, Caroline A. Jones, Ana Miljački; Irina Chernyakova, J. Meejin Yoon
Conversation
Fall 2018

1002 INVENTIONS: ART AND DESIGN IN THE AL AZRAQ REFUGEE CAMP
Future Heritage Lab: Azra Akšamija, Melina Philippou; Omar Al-Darwish, Muteeb Awad Al-Hamdan, Rejan Ashour, Zeid Madi, Raafat Majzoub, Mohammad Yaghan, CARE Jordan
Spring 2017–ongoing

1002 Inventions is a documentation of everyday life in the Al Azraq Refugee Camp in Jordan through the lens of fascinating creations designed by Syrian refugees. The ingenuity and resourcefulness of Al Azraq creations reveal the cultural, emotional, and architectural needs of refugees within a context of scarcity, war trauma, and struggle for a future. The photo series, taken by the Al Azraq journal team in collaboration with the Future Heritage Lab, documents a wide range of artworks, design inventions, shelter modifications, and paintings. The photographs are accompanied by stories written by a group of twenty young authors from the camp. Both the photographs and stories were created through educational workshops organized by the lab in Al Azraq, introducing skills of photography, creative writing, and critical exchange.

The photos and stories will become part of a book titled *1002 Inventions*. The title references the work of Arab scholar Al-Jazari (1136–1206), who wrote one of the most important twelfth-century treatises on mechanical engineering and automata in the Islamic tradition. The book celebrates the ongoing forms of innovation of Arab communities and highlights the role of art, architecture, and design as the antidote to war and destruction. Refugee inventions demonstrate how art, architecture, and design inspire hope and underpin innovation in a humanitarian context. The book suggests a method for a culturally-sensitive approach to humanitarian architecture informed by the resilience and creativity of displaced communities. *1002 Inventions* aims to inform the competencies of humanitarian design today and offer new modes for cultural preservation amidst conflict and crisis.

Images
P 40–42: Zeid Madi, Nabil Sayfayn, and Al Azraq Journal Team Members: Hussain Al-Abdullah, Jamil Hameidy, Yassin Al-Yassin, Mohammad Al-Qo'airy, and Mohammad Al-Mez'al.

Project
1002 Inventions was first produced for Amman Design Week 2017. Concept: Azra Akšamija; Development: Azra Akšamija, Melina Philippou, Omar Al-Darwish, Zeid Madi, Nabil Sayfayn; Production Photos: Zeid Madi, Nabil Sayfayn (Future Heritage Lab), Hussain Al-Abdullah, Yassin Al-Yassin, Mohammad Al-Qo'airy, Mohammad Al-Mez'al (Al Azraq Journal Team members); Stories: Hana'a Ahmed, Kifah Akeel, Hussein Al-Abdallah, Hasan Al-Abdallah, Hatem Al-Balkhy, Wa'el Al-Faraj, Nagham Alsalha, Heba Caleh, Mohammed Al-Hamedy, Ahma Al-Hassan, Jar Al-Naby Abazaid, Yassin Al-Yassin, Mustafa Hamadah, Jameel Homede, Abdulkarim Ihsan, Ahmad Khalaf, Rawan Maher, Mohammed Mizail, Jameel Mousli, Mohammed Shaban (authors from Al Azraq Camp, ages 14–25); Editors: Azra Akšamija (Chief Editor), Omar Al-Darwish, Zeid Madi, Melina Philippou (Future Heritage Lab), Muteeb Awad Al Hamdan (Al Azraq Camp), Mohammad Yaghan (Advisor in Amman, German-Jordanian University).

GROWING CHANGE/NORTH CAROLINA
Group Project: Alexander Bodkin, John Fechtel, Stephanie Lee, Milan Outlaw, Joseph Swerdlin
Spring 2017–ongoing

Group Project was founded by students in the Departments of Architecture and Urban Studies and Planning. We work with nonprofits and community organizations to navigate the process of transforming decommissioned prisons into radical, socially minded spaces for their communities. Across the United States, there is a growing inventory of government-owned closed prisons that could be redeveloped into sites of responsible economic and community growth. Working primarily in disinvested areas, Group Project connects local nonprofits and community organizations who need permanent spaces with governments that own decommissioned buildings. We use our planning and architectural expertise to translate the organization's mission into a compelling and feasible adaptive reuse proposal.

DISPATCHES FROM THE TRANSIENT CITY
Grigori Enikolopov
MArch Thesis
Advisor: Timothy Hyde
Fall 2016

Unprecedented levels of migration, displacement, and expulsions mark the contemporary moment. With the increase of protracted conflicts and environmental crises, the numbers of displaced persons fleeing war, famine, disease, or poverty has now surpassed levels seen previously only after WWII.

The spatial technologies that surround this mass movement of persons have been inadequately explored and represented. A new form of urbanism is emerging—not static cities of migration, but conduit cities of populations in motion. This new form of transient urbanism will not replace the static city. Instead it is superimposed upon the existing city; it emerges from its obsolete artifacts.

The city of Athens, Greece, a gateway into Europe and confluence on the migrant route from the Middle East, is taken as a case study for architectural speculations into the ways transience alters the experience of cities. Athens poses numerous difficulties and opportunities as the state's ability to formulate meaningful action is challenged by the ongoing government-debt crisis that began in 2009. Another consequence of the crisis is the hollowing out of the city center: vacant building stock increased to the tens of thousands, reports journalist Yiannis Baboulias.

This thesis takes the form of a manifesto that aims to replace the camp imaginary with correspondences from the transient city. The proposal projects not a utopian vision of the future but a provisional project already in the process of becoming. Drawing is used as a tool to heighten and amplify the transformations already underway.

AMERICAN SANCTUARY: ARCHITECTURE AND (IN)JUSTICE
Noora Aljabi
MArch Thesis
Advisor: Azra Akšamija
Fall 2018

The United States has a long history of harsh and discriminatory immigration policies, which has often been in tension with those who believe in the nation's promise to take in the "tired, … poor, … huddled masses." This tension has led to a growing Sanctuary movement across the country as people have joined together to protect their undocumented neighbors from the increasingly severe deportation tactics of Immigration and Customs

Enforcement (ICE). As part of this movement, several states, counties, and cities around the country have declared themselves "sanctuaries" and have limited their cooperation with federal government efforts to enforce immigration law.

Although the notion of sanctuary in the United States has centered on immigration policies, it should also be considered as an architectural and spatial phenomenon. The spaces in which ICE raids take place, such as the home, the workplace, and the courthouse, have been complicit in allowing for the transgression of rights during immigration arrests. There is a need for architectural interventions to resist this injustice.

Through the exploration of multiple narrative outcomes of raids at the home, the workplace, and the courthouse, this thesis aims to demonstrate the capacity of architecture to change a sequence of events, while also recognizing the unpredictability of design decisions. This approach tests the limits of architectural agency in resisting injustice as part of the Sanctuary movement—not by providing solutions, but rather by speculating on the many ways that architecture can participate in producing social change by engaging with law and other disciplines.

SEPTEMBER 55
Deniz Tortum, Nil Tuzcu, Çağrı Zaman
Fall 2017

September 55 is a ten-minute virtual-reality documentary of the Istanbul Pogrom, a government-initiated organized attack on the minorities of Istanbul on September 6–7, 1955. This interactive installation places the viewer in a photography studio in the midst of the pogrom, allowing one to witness the events from the perspective of a local shop owner. Drawing on the photographic archive of Maryam Şahinyan (1911–1996) and Osep Minasoglu (1929–2013), Armenian photographers who lived in Istanbul at the time, the installation materializes an extinct space. The wall in the virtual studio that exhibits Şahinyan's photographs exhibits a documentation of the raids and their aftermath in the physical space.

EPIC ARCHITECTURE: BARCELONA AND THE THEATER OF ESTRANGEMENT
Option Studio
Instructor: Cristina Goberna Pesudo
Spring 2018

Taking Bertolt Brecht's "epic theater" as primary reference, Epic Architecture encourages students to address current polemical issues in the discipline and the city. This studio explores the design of theaters in contested areas of Barcelona to address current architectural, cultural, and political affairs in the city. The aim is to create architectural artifacts that render problems visible rather than aim to resolve them; raise questions rather than exhibit good intentions; and, create an effect of estrangement rather than a pragmatic response. Could such moments of revelation transform users into critical observers of architecture and reality?

Since its invention, theater has served as a mirror to society. Theater spaces have evolved in size, visibility, respectability, capacity, and monumentality as political, social, and cultural conditions changed around the world. The theater, at all times, has operated as a social condenser. Barcelona has an exceptionally rich tradition of theater, from opera palaces such as the Liceu, cabarets in the former red district of El Raval, popular venues in El Parallel or avant-garde experimental venues from the 1960s—all have played witness to politics of the day. Today, Barcelona is a stage for other reasons: it has suffered terrorist attacks, witnessed the rise of nationalism, extreme police violence, and the imprisonment of its political representatives. As a space of cultural friction as well as a disciplinary thermometer, the typology of the theater is a potential agent for disciplinary and political provocation.

THEATER OF THE PNEU CIRCUS
Dalma Földesi, Jung In Seo

The Theater of the Pneu Circus is a speculative urban proposal for a set of inflatables presented as a play and a short film, set in Barcelona. The Pneu Circus follows in the footsteps of Barcelona's long, and long-forgotten, history of circus. We continue in the tradition of the Teatro Circo Olympia in the Ronda de Sant Pau, a circus that brought together acrobats, clowns, zarzuela, political activists, and trade unions. Like the Circo Ecuestre, a traveling circus stationed in the middle of the Plaça de Catalunya for almost twenty years, with its tents overtaking the vista from Las Ramblas, our circus lives in inflatable domes that can be requested and quickly assembled on demand.

We invite you to four current performances:
    The Zarzuela Circus!
    Barcelona's Greatest Clown!
    The Speakeasy Burlesque!
    The Pinhole Peep Show!

The Pneu Circus is a global circus company that aims to empower citizens by leveraging the legal status of art performances to fight oppression.

Our circuses, as temporary, inflatable spectacles, are designed as media instruments for citizens, providing a means of representation beyond mass media.

We decided to make Barcelona our next destination in response to the poor quality of the city's media circus. Especially during protests, media and legal restrictions have heavily censored and flattened public opinion. As members of the Pneu Circus Company, we invite you to use our performance spaces to evade Barcelona's restrictive media laws, counteract the manipulation of mass media, and defy instructions given to you by populist leaders. Our pneumatic architecture is an ephemeral sanctuary of free expression. Our soft membrane provides an immaterial wall in the face of media oppression.

THE THEATER OF CRUELTY
Anne Graziano, Mackenzie Muhonen

The theater as we know it is inadequate and irrelevant. We must rescue theater from its servitude to the observer, from its subjugation to written text. We must destroy the line between actor and observer. We must create a true spectacle. We must create an impossible Theater of Cruelty in the name of the lost culture of the city!

An order of operations can be exercised on any unsuspecting interior: a set of four theaters, scalable and reconfigurable entities, can ease a new actor into a deep state of exorcism, creating a renewed spectacle. A renovated tableau for organic expression. These four theaters—the waitress cafe, the cabaret, the bar, and the concert hall—revive the lost cultural memory of our city.

The Theater of Cruelty must create temptations for subconscious anarchy. It must seduce the actor, through architecture, through a sequence of intensified architectural encounters. Imagine: The actor is moved from waitress cafe, to cabaret, to bar, to concert hall. Each space more shocking, more tempting than the last. The stage in each space seduces; it operates as the threshold to move into the next space of immersion. The stage eases the actor into steeper gradients of performative engagement. It is the rhythm of the Theater of Cruelty, the harmony, which enacts a new language. This succession lulls the intoxicated subject along a punctuated flow of perceptions. One image merges into the next, and dimensions of time and space wax and wane …

This is the Theater of Cruelty, with its phantasmagoric immersions unfolded for full comprehension. Read these spaces as an instruction set, as a kit of parts, to be enacted on unsuspecting architectures. Read these as a virus that invades the city. Read these as a code for new zoning, for a new urban condition. Read these as an architectural tradition, an unearthed knowledge, to be enacted by you, the actor.

THEATERS OF AGONISTIC ENCOUNTERS
Carlos Casalduc, Milap Dixit, Dijana Milenov

Increasing nationalism has urgent economic and social implications for people in Catalonia and Spain. The Spanish government suspended Catalonia's parliament after it held a referendum and declared independence last year. Its subsequent repression is symptomatic of the failure of representative institutions—they absorb dissent rather than act as a forum.

In this context, people have lost trust in their representative institutions. Everyday lives are increasingly detached from shrinking political commitments. During the anti-austerity movement (15-M), hundreds of citizen "parliaments" formed all over Spain. However, these formations did not have an architectural manifestation. The physicality of a building can help social movements to acquire legibility.

The theater, as a spatial type, has the capacity to elicit specific modes of agonistic encounter. We propose a family of theaters that function as cultural institutions and spaces for enabling agonistic encounters. Each of the theaters corresponds to a part of Barcelona's urban morphology: Eixample blocks, the narrow streets of El Raval, the courtyards of Gràcia blocks, and the cafés with outdoor seating. The structures, attached to hot air balloons, are mobile and move freely through the city. They aggregate to form linear theaters that occupy an entire street, transforming the street into a forum. The space of politics becomes interiorized within the street; the street becomes a tool to recuperate agonism in public life.

THE THEATER OF DISCOMFORT:
THE PLANET AS A FESTIVAL, THE CITY AS A PLAYGROUND, THE THEATER AS A CLUB
Stratton Coffman, Aaron Powers

ACT 1: The Barcelona Chamber of Commerce, in partnership with Ryanair, would like to introduce you to Super-Club, Barcelona's hottest new party venue. Open twenty-four hours, seven days a week, and located directly on the city's busiest tourist mega-artery, La Rambla, in the center of its party hub, Super-Club has it ALL! Equipped to meet all the needs, desires, and urges of the typical party tourist.

The Barcelona Heritage Foundation, with support from the Barcelona City Council, invite you to Super-Theater, Barcelona's foremost venue for the consumption of authentic cultural productions. Located in the city's preserved medieval-era core, on the border between El Raval and the Gothic Quarter, Super-Theater transports you to a world of preserved artistic integrity.

ACT 2: According to our Office of Tourism, the influx of tourists into our city—supported by budget airline companies like Ryanair—has hollowed out our housing market, turning over apartments to vacation rental companies like Airbnb. This has led to inflated rental prices that displace longtime residents. Moreover, and more insidiously, these practices have commodified our public space, transformed it into a generic playground with services that cater to tourists over residents. Consider, as an example, La Rambla, the city's second most visited attraction. Once a hub of political parties and civic organizing, now La Rambla is the home to only 120 full-time residents, out of the thousands of apartments on this street.

We have recently acquired a trio of Superinstruments to accelerate these entrenched urban dynamics, to bring about a wave of internal discomfort among these populations of tourists and, in doing so, temporarily repel them from our city. These untested experimental tools will be used in a series of short-term installments to create irresistible tourist attractions, namely a Super-Club and a Super-Theater, that in turn set up moments of conflict between the two venues and produce experiences of unbearable discomfort. In this way, the Superinstruments will breed rumors and mistrust that temporarily reduce the number of tourists visiting Barcelona.

ACT 3: Hi fans, I just heard from my vlog friend about this club in Barcelona. It was like the best time of her life until she realized she couldn't hear the music anymore and thought her eardrums had burst. She stayed in this place for two days straight. I don't know if it sounds terrible or fucking rad. I might have to put Ibiza on hold this year and go check it out.

Epilogue, Year 2021: Word spread of these bad times, opening a destructive-creative spiral of intrigue, as some pass on Barcelona to party it up in Amsterdam or visit the Vienna State Opera.

Others venture to experience this novelty for themselves. As the city continues to swell with tourists, more Superinstruments are installed in cultural spots like the main flamenco venue on La Rambla or the notorious cabaret, El Molino. In their growing overuse, the Superinstruments breed new attractions and risk domesticating their own power, ever on the verge of absorption into the industry they are designed to resist.

TECHNOPOLITICS, CULTURE, INTERVENTION
Arindam Dutta
Seminar: History, Theory and Criticism
Fall 2018 (first taught Fall 2011)

Much of what goes in the name of technological thinking invokes an economistic understanding of politics as caused largely by scarcity. There is not enough (take your pick: energy, free speech, communication, food, healthcare, etc.) to go around, the thought goes, technology can act as "disruptor" to effectuate new supply chains, or alternatively, in cases where old ways of functioning might themselves be seen as the cause of existing inefficiencies or stagnation, to upend these systems by forging new pathways or circuits. Politics, in other words, is a "problem," stemming from inefficiencies in this system or the other, and technological invention and intervention must be thought of as its substitute. "Architecture or revolution? Revolution can be avoided," in Le Corbusier's famous phrase, or to quote from Mark Zuckerberg's manifesto *The Hacker Way*: "Code wins arguments." (This before Facebook was itself hacked in the course of the 2016 United States presidential election.)

Caroline Jones and I conceived of Technopolitics, Culture, Intervention in response to a tacit demand. Surrounded by technological production of all kinds, MIT students in art and architecture had deeply felt the need for a course in critical theory that helped them confront their own see-sawing about technology: from cultic enthusiasm to abnegatory cynicism (MIT has had an enduring "primitivist" tradition). Working with examples from architecture, art, history, theory, and philosophy, we fashioned the course to provide students with robust critical tools that allow them to think of technology and politics not as alibis or substitutes for each other, but rather going hand in hand. Politics or problems as cognized by technological firms or thinkers may not have technological solutions or fixes, if at all a solution is something to be desired. Conversely, technology fosters violence as much as it does reconciliation, alienation as much as community, and great degrees of poverty as well as wealth. Technology produces its own politics as much as politics uses technology of different kinds to shift the nature of power.

Using this basic premise, students work through reading, discussion, and writing to build both conceptual understanding as well as critical tools to help them negotiate their professional futures and everyday terrain. In class discussion, movies, popular cultural references, institutional history, and gossip are mixed in with difficult thinkers such as Martin Heidegger, Donna Haraway, and Michel Foucault; students are encouraged to develop familiarity with radical art and architecture, to take up questions revolving around bodies, systems, labor, the environment, territory, and so on. Case studies assist the class in building a repertoire of formal strategies, arguments and counter-arguments, a good test for which has been the graduating thesis, where students are often challenged with the task of inventing sites, contexts, and critiques ex nihilo.

TAKING STOCK
Zain Karsan
MArch Thesis
Advisor: Sheila Kennedy
Fall 2017

This thesis is sited in a near and uncertain future in the Rust Belt of the United States. Its title refers to three interrelated conditions: industrial technology, material culture, and architectural agency. "Taking" refers to the act of taking control and reclaiming agency; "stock" describes the vast potential of industrial sites as materially, technologically, and architecturally fertile ground.

New figures emerge in the city of industrial abandonment and decline. This is the story of the material monks, who, garbed in the protective cloaks of their foundry, take back their material agency to mine cities of rust, to comb through the dross around them. They come from a world of quotidian obsolescence, but they bring with them a new assessment of stock. Their resistance materializes in a set of machine hacks. By taking stock of the tools of their foundry and the materials that surround them, the monks construct their monastery. With each hack they devise, they transform waste into building material.

They are troubled by the scale of the undertaking and the impossibility of completing their task, for nothing can escape the scrutiny of their attention or the scope of their salvages. They accept that their work will never finish, and like Sisyphus, hack and rehack, endlessly recycling material and technology. They never escape the furnace that melts down their machine parts, or the hopper that takes and redistributes their crushed and dismantled assemblies.

GEOSTORIES: ANOTHER ARCHITECTURE FOR THE ENVIRONMENT
DESIGN EARTH: Rania Ghosn, El Hadi Jazairy
Geostories
Fall 2017

OTHER MASKS
William O'Brien Jr./WOJR
Spring 2017

The body of work shown in the exhibition, *Other Masks*, stems from an ongoing project titled Mask House, which offers a grieving man a hidden space of refuge in the woods. Included in the exhibition is a range of artifacts that explore the periphery of architectural representation; while orthographic drawings and a scale model provide the work with an architectural center of gravity, pieces such as a stone bas-relief and seven sculptural masks engage the overlapping domain of art.

Other Masks situates the artifact of the mask within the context of the discipline of architecture. An artifact is an object of intrigue that elicits close readings and analyses, which in turn may reveal evidence of its culture and its use. A close reading of an artifact involves examination of all of its physical characteristics, including its figural, structural, material, and decorative features. This study is done not only with the aim of identifying the cultural significance of the particular object, but also with the broader aspiration of understanding the rituals and values of the users of the object, and those of its makers. The most curious of artifacts are those whose features invoke multiple, competing interpretations of their cultural significance.

For WOJR, the making of architecture is the making of artifacts. To think about the design of a work of architecture as such is to regard the acts of making form and reading form as simultaneous and inseparable. Being attuned to architecture in this particular way has led to a practice that is invested deeply, if not wholly, in the agency of architectural form as the medium through which cultural commentary is conveyed.

Other Masks was on view at Balts Projects in Zurich, Switzerland, April 12–May 14, 2017. This exhibition was made possible through the generous support and fabrication of Quarra Stone.

NOT WRITING
Sarah Rifky
ArteEast Quarterly
Fall 2016

FLAGLIFE
Laura Serejo Genes

At 4:30 pm on Monday, November 7, 2016, the Reserve Officer Training Corp (ROTC) at MIT will lower the United States flag flying by the athletic fields. An alternate flag will be raised in its place. This alternate flag will fly for the entirety of Election Day and will be lowered on Wednesday, November 9, 2016.

Please come raise the flag if you identify with *any* of the following.

If you:

A. Are (for whatever reason) not voting in the 2016 Presidential Election
B. Were born in America
C. Have been granted DACA
D. Like the color combination: red, white & blue
E. Have one or more passports
F. Checked-in at Standing Rock
G. Have been detained
H. Have never left the country
I. Have been tricked to work for free
J. Worked for minimum wage
K. Like Canada more than Mexico, or vice-versa
L. Want to learn Arabic
M. Speak Arabic
N. Want to do good
O. Want to do better
P. Have been in more synagogues than churches
Q. Have ever wanted to raise a flag
R. [Reserved]
S. Have been subject to additional security screening
T. Have a favorite President
U. Would like the opportunity to kneel during the national anthem
V. Believe in rivalry
W. Feel surveilled
X. Cut corners
Y. Wish you had more time to yourself
Z. Have better things to do
AA. Believe "the flag represents a living country and is itself considered a living thing" (4 U.S.C. § 8(j))

Participate in an act of arbitrary solidarity before the 2016 Presidential Election.

All participants will have a hand in the ceremony. The event will start exactly at 4:30 pm EST, sunset, at the flagpole behind Henry Steinbrenner Stadium (follow the path past the Z-Center) and will not last longer than half an hour.

There will be live music.

Those who wish to participate are encouraged to report to the flagpole by 4:25 pm EST, on Monday, November 7, 2016.

RSVP encouraged, but not by any means required.

The flag raising is free and open to the public.

Thanks to the contributions of MIT Media Lab computational law researcher Dazza Greenwood, the authenticity of this flag and provenance of this event will be immutably and publicly verifiable through distributed global blockchain technology. For more information, see: law.MIT.edu/FlagLife.

This project has been made possible by funding from the Program in Art, Culture & Technology.

-#-#-#-
In witness of this flag and the flag raising event, we the seven people undersigned, publicly declare our names:
1. Dazza Greenwood
2. Gediminas Urbonas
3. Mason Gohl
4. Nicolás Kisić Aguirre
5. Rio Fischer
6. Neil Sanzgiri
7. Angel Chen

This email invitation was sent by Laura Serejo Genes to students, faculty, and staff in the MIT Program in Art, Culture and Technlogy and the Department of Architecture on November 4, 2016.

ON IMMIGRATION AND HUMANIST VALUES
Nasser Rabbat

Immigration (*hijra*) in the Islamic consciousness is first and foremost an act of liberation. The Prophet Muhammad migrated from his native city, Mecca, to the city of Yathrib (later named Madina) to escape persecution and preserve his faith. So crucial was that journey to the formation of the budding religion that it marked the beginning of the Islamic calendar, which was moreover named after it (First Hegira year = 622 CE).

Immigration remained a valiant undertaking for centuries to come. It animated great movements of oppressed individuals and communities across vast distances to protect their faith and have a chance to live freely, as happened after the Spanish *Reconquista* in the fifteenth century, when both Spanish Muslims and Jews immigrated to North African and Ottoman cities, or after the Russian colonial expansion in the Caucasus in the late nineteenth century, which forced countless Circassian Muslims to move to the Middle East. The term *hijra* survives today in various Islamic languages: a *muhajir* in Pakistan, for instance, is an individual who had fled India after Partition in 1947 and relocated to the new Islamic country.

The importance of this redemptive act should have resonated within the American psyche, Americans having been reared on the stories of religiously persecuted communities from the old continent, especially Britain, finding refuge in the New World. Pilgrims, Puritans, Quakers, Huguenots, Mennonites, Amish, and Jews were all oppressed faith groups who fled Europe in the sixteenth, seventeenth, and eighteenth centuries to seek their religious freedom in the United States. The same could be said about larger groups of non-conformists, including the more numerous English Catholics, Scottish Presbyterians, and German and Swedish Lutherans who came in the eighteenth and nineteenth centuries. The lessons of religious discrimination that these immigrants brought with them have inspired some of the most fundamentally humanistic principles expressed in the First Amendment to the Constitution, namely "Congress shall make no law respecting an establishment of religion, or prohibiting the free exercise thereof ..." In this definitive act of separating church and state while respecting freedom of worship, the United States set the path for other liberal democracies to follow.

It is thus both perplexing and depressing to witness the confusion caused by President Trump's executive orders, popularly known as the "Muslim Ban." The disappointment stems less from the virulent rhetoric used by President Trump and his inner circle of conservative advisors, who never hid their demagogic intentions, against all immigrants. It is rather directed at the American political and intellectual classes who should be much more alert to the dangers the "Muslim Ban" represents to the core values of the American civil system and its Constitutional safeguards.

Both in its first fiasco version and its second supposedly measured one, the Ban pretends to be merely a preventive procedure aimed at plugging holes in the already excessive visa vetting system and protecting the borders of the United States from "Islamist terrorists." But, besides the false pronouncements it makes about terrorism and the exclusively Islamic identity of its perpetrators, the Ban actually undermines the fundamental principles of equality before the law, freedom of belief, non-discrimination, and separation of church and state, all enshrined in the Constitution, in addition to its contemptuous disregard for the requisite input from the two other branches of government: the legislative and the judiciary.

As expected, reactions to the Ban from academic, cultural, and political institutions on the whole have been critical. Many have condemned it for its legal overreaching or, more often, for its undeniable harm to the proper functioning of their operation, while noticing its overall corrosive effect on liberal American values. This is at least how one can read the slew of statements issued by universities, museums, and academic associations after the Ban's first iteration (no similar outcry occurred after the second). The letter sent to President Trump on February 3, 2017 by forty-eight top United States university presidents, including President L. Rafael Reif of MIT, for instance, states that the order "threatens both American higher education and the defining principles of our country." It continues to assert that the Ban

… specifically prevents talented, law-abiding students and scholars from the affected regions from reaching our campuses. American higher education has benefited tremendously from this country's long history of embracing immigrants from around the world. Their innovations and scholarship have enhanced American learning, added to our prosperity, and enriched our culture.

All these objections are valid, and all reflect the concerns of these distinguished signatories. But the universities' letter, and other countless similar ones, misses the big picture. The assault embedded in the "Muslim Ban" is not just directed against students and researchers from specific countries, or Muslims, or even refugees in general. It is a trial balloon in a concerted, ideologically motivated effort aimed at a set of values that together make up the fiber of our American democracy.

This should be clear to anyone watching the unfolding of the Trump administration's appointments, policies, and public statements. Notwithstanding his smokescreen-like and seemingly impulsive tweets, President Trump is systematically and resolutely implementing all of his campaign promises, no matter how outlandish they might have seemed when first uttered. He is doing that by issuing one executive order after another aimed at dismantling the achievements of his predecessor and by shrewdly placing likeminded people in leading positions, who will help him realize the radical changes in our political system he wants, each in their tried and tested area. Thus, for example, we have an Education Secretary who does not believe in public schools, an Attorney General who is highly critical of the gains in civil rights over the last 50 years, a Housing and Urban Development (HUD) Secretary who wants to reduce public housing, and an Administrator of the Environmental Protection Agency (EPA) who is skeptical of climate change, and who publicly doubted that carbon dioxide is a primary contributor to global warming. We also have clear indications that the Trump administration is planning to drastically reduce funding for the National Institutes of Health (NIH) and to totally eliminate the National Endowment for the Arts (NEA), the National Endowment for the Humanities (NEH), the Institute of Museum and Library Services (IMLS), and the Corporation for Public Broadcasting (CPB).

There is a distinct pattern here that is not to be taken lightly or blamed on the erratic methods of governing that the Trump administration seems to have adopted. The pattern is ideological and it is not just neoliberal, advancing the private over the public in every domain, as many commentators have observed. In its anti-scientific, anti-intellectual, anti-factual, discriminatory, and isolationist stances, it is anti-humanist to the core.

By anti-humanist, I do not mean the values of European Enlightenment as established around the same time as the drafting of the American Constitution and later much criticized. I mean universal humanism as it has evolved through tremendous struggles all over the world to redress the wrongs wrought on all disenfranchised people everywhere.

This is the humanism that was inscribed in a number of international documents, most notably the Universal Declaration of Human Rights (1948), adopted after the atrocities of World War II, the European Convention on Human Rights (1950), and its updated and enlarged version, The Charter of Fundamental Rights of the European Union (2000), which explicitly takes into account the "changes in society, social progress and scientific and technological developments."

This is also the humanism that defines the spirit behind all of our federal, scientific, and cultural endowments threatened with funding cuts nowadays, and underlies the mission of American higher education despite recent shifts toward a more entrepreneurial orientation. It is the humanism that we—educators, scholars, researchers, scientists, and intellectuals—ought to relentlessly reaffirm, promote, and defend.

"On Immigration and Humanist Values" was first published in the *MIT Faculty Newsletter* 24 no. 4 (March/April 2017), http://web.mit.edu/fnl/volume/294/rabbat.html.

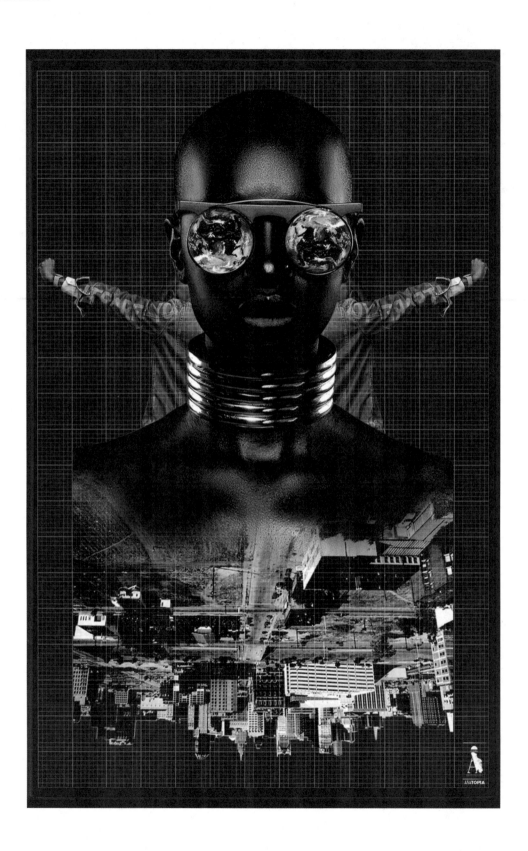

25

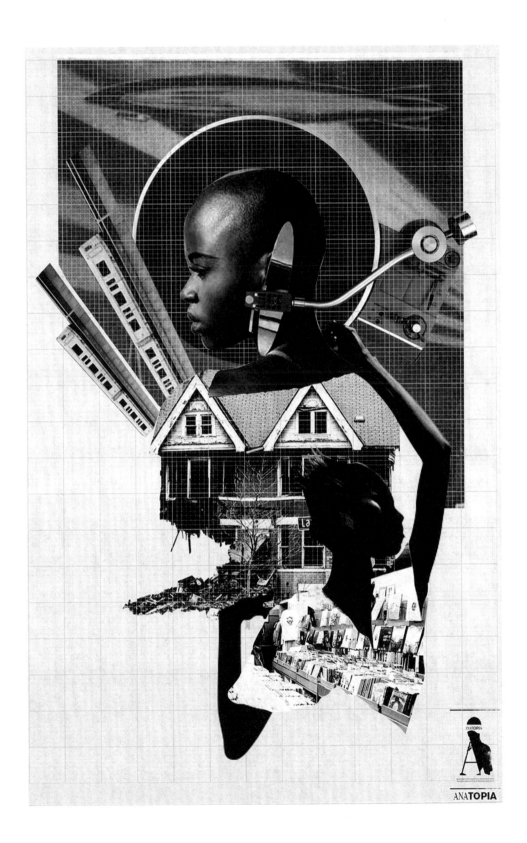

KINETIC SPEAKERS AND SONIC COMMONS
Rainar Aasrand, Jessica Adams, Nicolás Kisic Aguirre, Andrea Carrillo, Walker Downey, Martin Elliott, Kyle Joba-Woodruff, Alexander Lefell, Samantha Adler de Oliveira, Alexander Souvannakhot

THE ECOLOGY OF TRUTH: A SCOPING DEVICE FOR REFLECTING ON THE INSTITUTE
Samuel Schneider

omen were
eview?

5 6 7 8 9+
5 6 7 8 9+
5 6 7 8 9+
5 6 7 8 9+
5 6 7 8 9+
5 6 7 8 9+
5 6 7 8 9+
5 0 7 0 9+
5 6 7 8 9+
5 6 7 8 9+
5 6 7 8 9+
5 6 7 8 9+
5 6 7 8 9+
5 6 7 8 9+
5 6 7 8 9+

How many woman-run
architecture firms can
you think of?

(circle one)

0 1 2 3 4 5 6 7 8 9+
0 1 2 3 4 5 6 7 8 9+
0 1 2 3 4 5 6 7 8 9+
0 1 2 3 4 5 6 7 8 9+
0 1 2 3 4 5 6 7 8 9+
0 1 2 3 4 5 6 7 8 9+
0 1 2 3 4 5 6 7 8 9+
0 1 2 3 4 5 6 7 8 9+
0 1 2 3 4 5 6 7 8 9+
0 1 2 3 4 5 6 7 8 9+
0 1 2 3 4 5 6 7 8 9+
0 1 2 3 4 5 6 7 8 9+

How many wor
on your syllab

(circle one)

0 1 2 3 4
0 1 2 3 4
0 1 2 3 4
0 1 2 3 4
0 1 2 3 4
0 1 2 3 4
0 1 2 3 4
0 1 2 3 4
0 1 2 3 4
0 1 2 3 4
0 1 2 3 4
0 1 2 3 4

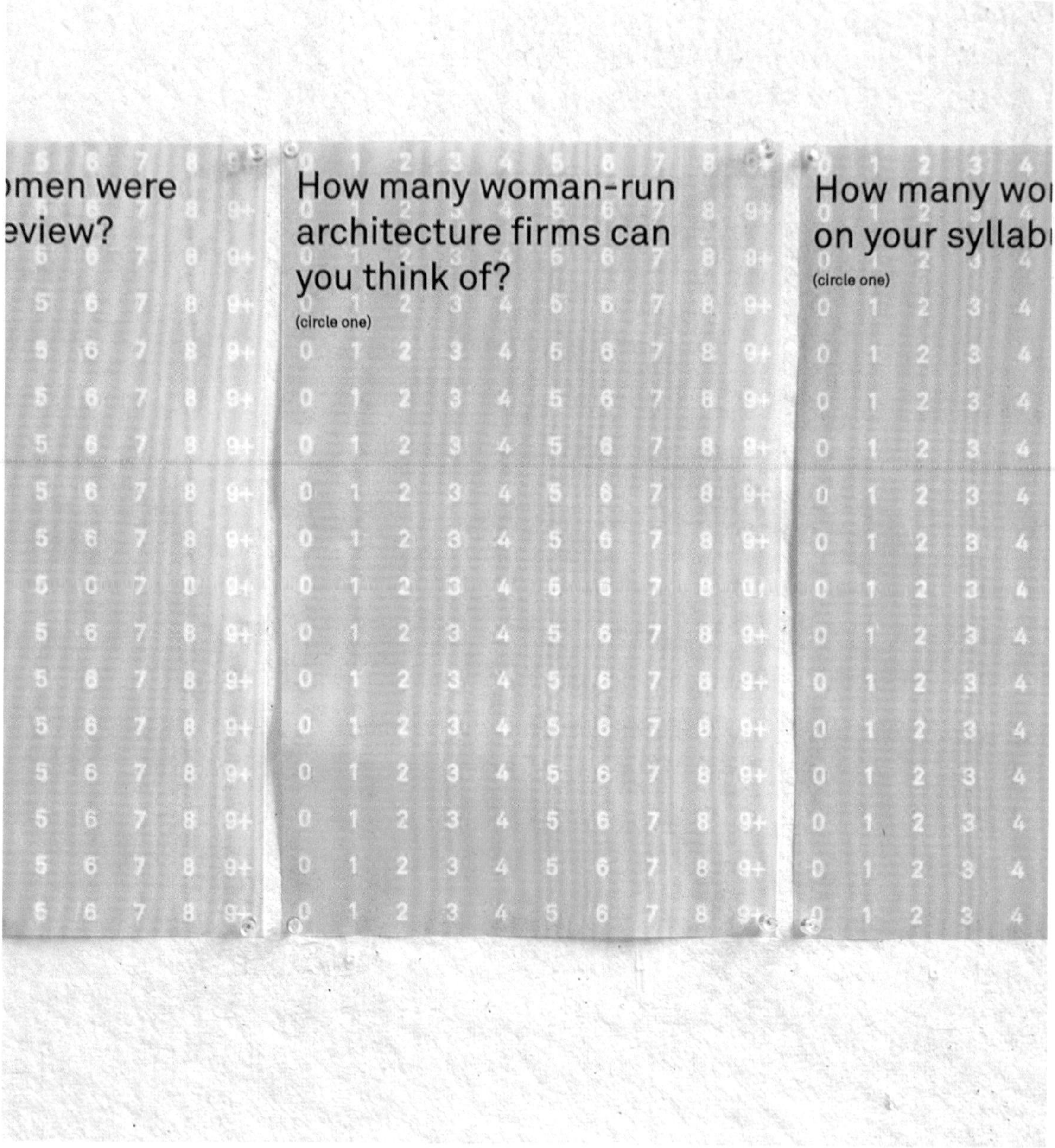

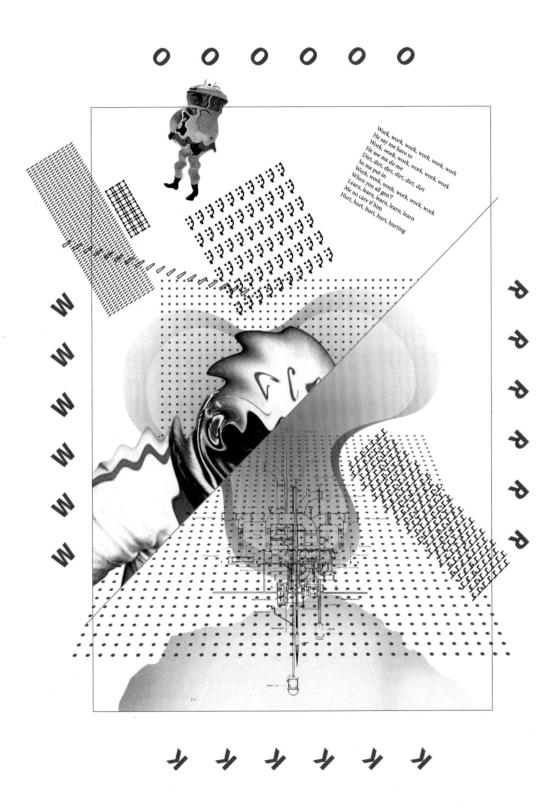

Work, work, work, work, work, work
He say me have to
Work, work, work, work, work, work
He see me do me
Dirt, dirt, dirt, dirt, dirt
So me put in
Work, work, work, work, work, work
When you all gon'?
Learn, learn, learn, learn, learn
Me no care if him
Hurt, hurt, hurt, hurt, hurting

Irina Chernyakova and J. Meejin Yoon
(IC and JMY)
The theme for this volume became very clear to us in November 2017; the numerous discussions with students, among the faculty, in conversations small and large, private and public, signaled that there was a need to more explicitly discuss how student and faculty understand and position the agency of their own work. As vocal participants then, could you reflect upon the role of pedagogy and spaces of education in this moment?

Ana Miljački (AM)
I'll start far out, the night that Trump won. I had my Critical Precedents class the following day. I had been worried about this, I thought inevitable moment, the whole semester. I kept thinking: "It's coming," and we are going to have a class the day after. Having heard the news, I spent the night thinking, "How do I talk to my students now? What is there to say? What is the point of what we do here, in school?" The only thing that seemed important was to share the way that I narrate my job to myself. I am here at MIT in order to cultivate a kind of utopia— to cultivate values among the students that, in some clear sense, are in opposition to what the election results seem to stand for. That seemed important. We ended up discussing what brought us all here and how we understood our task. We have to continue discussing our various contemporary predicaments in ways that enable politically important work, work that allows for debates to happen, that allows for difference to happen, and that enables us to think of our agency in the world in a variety of ways.

We have different modalities of teaching at MIT. There are certainly labs and workshops that catapult students into various forms of action in the world, but I also think it's extremely important that we have tables around which we can reflect upon the world together, and with our students, think about who are these future artists and architects that we are producing? How are we preparing them for futures that we, by definition, cannot imagine with any precision?

Caroline A. Jones (CAJ)
The kind of utopia that you mention is a collective discussion of how to imagine that future world. It's not: "We don't know what's going to happen," and forget about it. It's: "We don't know what's going to happen, so let's imagine what we want to happen," right? And there is agency in that, already.

AM
Absolutely. This is the way that I think of the agency of the school in the contemporary moment, and therefore of its faculty.

CAJ
Let's talk about the kinds of actions that happened here, mostly motivated by students in the Department of Urban Studies and Planning (DUSP), but the recognition that we formed a community and that the community itself is an action—that was so powerful for me. You need to consistently take actions to build, sustain, and support that community, particularly in an age of putatively "social" network platforms. Students themselves demanded that we get together in person, to cry, commiserate, and discuss. These were very important gestures that helped me, personally—and that sense of the students themselves, together with us teachers as part of a larger world is very important. MIT is absolutely in the world—we are in the belly of the beast. That was amply demonstrated by our community in the days immediately following the election, and our community as a school began suddenly to be extremely palpable.

AM
Some of our students said that they don't necessarily know how to act politically, yet. They have for the most part grown up in the Obama version of this country. Some have not had the chance to encounter the historical force of politics. We, their teachers, whether we like it or not, model political behavior in the schools. This is not just about what I teach in class (or anyone else), it's about how we precisely deal with the magnitude of political change, and its meaning, in our day-to-day interactions.

Azra Akšamija (AA)
It's a really tricky zone. There are students who are already very sensitive to various cultural contexts and politics, and they just need some sharpening. Others come from gated communities; they are smart but naïve to the cruelty of the world. I've also encountered students who are trained to think in the neoliberal model. There is an institutional politics that is ingrained in some students.

I have seen some shifts in the student work. Some are actively getting out and looking for problems in the real world to address. Yet there is still a disconnect and a question: How do we link issues on the ground with new technologies and resources? And what is the meaning of all this stuff? Why are we making all this stuff?

And so, partly, it is on us to do some learning with the students. Most importantly, we need to take action without being reactionary. We need to create with students a vision of some kind of better future.

AM
Maybe this helps me sleep better, but I believe that our own department represents at least a small world of cultural and moral consciousness in the larger Institute; that as the oldest school of architecture in an institute of engineering and technology, we are also the school that has the longest history of critiquing techno-optimism and the kind of blind faith in progress. Many of our most memorable Master of Architecture (MArch) theses operate in this realm.

CAJ
But we've also been the school that has been the longest involved in implementing techno-optimism, and we can't dissociate ourselves from that history.

AM
That's true.

CAJ
If we are the students' benevolent interlocutors, we have to pay attention to the actions they are taking. Students recognize that politics begin at home, that MIT has not divested from fossil fuels, for example. We've had the founding of a minority architects chapter for the first time; we've had members of the HTC group enter directly into governance at MIT, becoming student representatives at the highest level of the Institute. They are trying to have a voice in decisions on student housing.

I think we have witnessed the emergence of a generation that once again understands that action can begin right where you live. That's really powerful and very moving. As teachers, we offer critical voices and our kind of critical conscience, but I don't want to leave that in the intellectual realm. These students are burning midnight oil to become a part of actual change in the communities that we've built together.

AM
I think there has also been a lot of interest and organizing around the question of gender and racial equity. There's a group of students, including our NOMAS chapter, who initiated a project to work directly with an NGO in North Carolina to remake a prison. To me, it's exciting that our students are organizing, but even more, that they're finding venues to produce change in the world.

CAJ
I think our responsibility goes back to what Azra was saying; in our teaching, we are not only addressing the technocrats from MIT. Even if there are diehard technocrats, we are embedding ourselves in them, infecting them with a reflective and critical practice. I'm tempted to channel Donna Haraway: the modest witness. I'm tempted to modify agency, to modify action, sort of saying tender agency, exploratory action, or intra-action, to quote Karen Barad.

We're in a very, very important moment where action itself has to be leveraged from the tiniest points of contact. Our gestures need to be modified and made permeable and open. Somehow, the discourse of the expert, which MIT has mastered for over 150 years, has to be made more modest, more dialogical, more generous, even as it becomes more urgent. We have the tools for it; there are all these mechanisms (stakeholder meetings, field conditions) for engaging and producing something new out of that encounter.

AA
And we need to make space for students to have that freedom. In order to produce meaningful work, you need to have some time to "go out," to contemplate, and to think. In a way, we have all been hamstering, the faculty and the students. The working speed at MIT is limiting the freedom of both thought and action. We have the tools, but we don't have the time.

I remember when I taught a first-year course with Joan Jonas; she was very hands-off. Students were frustrated, asking: "Why is she not teaching us? Where is the lecture?" And then, after a month of frustration, they started to create awesome sculptures and performances; she would then get in and start massaging the work. It was brilliant. The students needed that moment of boredom, and we just don't give them that.

CAJ
Yes! But that pedagogical silence is very hard for us to achieve. Tolerating silence, understanding that you can't listen if you're talking—these are important pedagogical actions.

IC and JMY
How do you see these issues playing out in studios, in student work, and practice? Through what forms?

AM
What's amazing about this particular moment in time in architectural pedagogy is that we are capable of conceiving agency in architecture on so many different levels. The architectural object is but one of the venues through which one produces effects in

the world. There are many other ways of engaging the world, and I think our students are absolutely tuned into this. And the hope is that in working together we will find, maybe recover, that sense of architecture's capacity to be also politically effective, despite the problematic world in which we live—in which it has been very easy for architects to think that they have no political agency.

JMY

It seems that the "architectural object" is of less concern. Student work focuses on the narrative, the scene-setting; there's always a protagonist or antagonists that carry the narrative. Students take on the re-imaging of context in the project. But there is also a kind of environmental agency in focusing on the performative aspects, as opposed to the formal and iconic.

AM

Yes—the world has always been entangled; we are better able to understand and describe some of those entanglements. A narrative strategy perhaps allows for and forces us to make sense of those entanglements.

I think we (students, pedagogues, and scholars) are much more aware, and even able, to articulate the way in which political and economic processes intermingle with others to produce architecture. It's not only about architecture and its users, it's about architecture and the various disciplines and forces that come together to materialize a piece of architecture. Given this increased understanding of the real politico-aesthetic complex, there is no easy way to claim neutrality.

AA

I also see many students get caught up in the narrative as the translation from the narrative into the object. Perhaps this comes from losing trust in the agency of material culture. Yet there is a lot of agency in the aesthetic of the object, its ability to transfer meanings, to incite certain actions, to be evidence of presence.

In the example of Bosnia, from my own research, the destruction of heritage and the removal of monuments—graves, buildings, digging out foundation stones of buildings, the removal of meaningful objects that embody people and values—people completely identify themselves with objects of material culture. These objects are a kind of evidence of existence.

In Bosnia, during the 1990s war for example, the architecture was subject to a form of symbolic torture. Buildings were destroyed during religious holidays as a form of celebration, all to enhance the suffering of the targeted population. The destruction did not hurt the stone, but it did hurt the people. So, there is something so powerful in the cultural and symbolic meaning embedded in the material.

CAJ

Well, it may hurt the stone. One of the interesting things about the agency of iconoclasm is that often the iconoclast provides more belief to the object than the person whose religion it ostensibly represented. So, notions of agency are often ascribed to objects by people who haven't used them, which is another conundrum of reception, of history.

AM

But I think what you are identifying, the kind of narrative, and maybe lack of faith in the material artifact, is also a product of the contemporary circulation of images in the world in which both the real artifacts and the imagined narratives have been granted the same status and relevance by the simple laws of distribution. The images will circulate, and those that circulate more will win in the general imaginary. It's obvious now how one might produce effects through producing images that circulate. It's less obvious how one might produce effects through producing built work.

CAJ

Although, some of the most interesting studio projects that I've seen have had very evocative interfaces. And they are not models of the building. I remember Tyler Stevermer's small, hand-held wood object that had hair coming out of it. Was it even a "model" as such? I no longer remember how this belonged to his narrative, but I will never forget that object.

Part of my work, as a historian, is always to underscore how the meanings of objects do not travel with them. They fan out, they meet the desires of the viewer, user, receiver. And it's very hard to predict the agency of that object, but agency it has. Without Tyler's object, I would have no memory of encountering this very strange, almost surrealist thing. And as I probe that memory, I recall that its uncanniness was part of his architectural approach to the discourse of the "posthuman"—he was recalling, in this haptic prosthesis, that we were organic chimeras of cells and hair.

Similarly, students have been exploring multi-sensory, multi-modal approaches to architecture that resonate with some art-world rebellions against the white cube. They are asking, "What does it smell like? Could a building be programmed to have a sort of atmosphere?" So, yes, the objects speak of a narrative that we, the user, encounter or have to construct to make sense of this bewildering experience. And I think the students could get better at using that ambiguity. The object does not reduce to the text. The text cannot explain fully the object. These are two completely different modes that, nonetheless, each have a kind of agency, but will never foreclose the making of meanings in other ways. Agency is distributed, and that is what I want to articulate: agency is multiply-distributed among bodies, texts, buildings, and things.

AA

That's a question in some of the work of artists coming from our program (Art, Culture and Technology), especially those working in public space. A lot of the socially engaged work is dependent on the presence of artists mediating the whole experience: What happens when these people leave? And what's responsibility of the artist/architect in introducing these social spaces in the world? In some projects, like that of alum Matthew Mazzotta, for example, the work functions without him. He doesn't need to talk about it—the community takes it on; it actually shifts something within the space. His intention is to transfer ownership to the community, and it incites these processes. So, it's interesting to think about the ways in which things operate in the world.

AM

How do you explain, or how do you articulate, what an artist or architect's expertise or agency is in the situation that you're describing? What is it that they do that would qualify it as art or architecture?

AA

Well, we debate—some people claim to create social relations, and that's the whole point of their art or architecture, so the object itself doesn't matter.

CAJ

So, we create a space for art to be safe, a space of culture. We can claim it is just representation; it is not the real thing, no actual guns will be fired. Azra, you've gone into a refugee camp where a funding organization, or a government representative, or a foreign combatant would not be able to get in. So, art is kind of an aegis, too.

AA

Yes, there, or here at MIT, it opens doors. In postwar Bosnia, no one would talk to a historian, but they would talk to an artist. I was able to get information from people through that lens.

CAJ

In that respect, the architect would be very different because they would be asked: "Are you part of a development organization?" Artists are presumed to be "innocent" of capital in ways that architects are not.

AA

Right. "On whose behalf are you working?" This discussion between ethics and aesthetics in art practice, and where art should have its role, is so interesting. Architecture is less affected by this dilemma because the utilitarian dimension of architecture is less contested. With art it's different. Do you troubleshoot social agencies that are not doing the work properly? You see the problem, you want to address it.

CAJ

There has been for so long this space of argument about whether artists should be required to have an ethic, to have a positionality, to be aware of that, to be conscious and articulate about that, or whether art should be precisely that space which is preserved from these struggles and these strivings. And both of those have never stopped, and are completely active today.

AA

It is kind of a false dichotomy. There are so many different ways in which you can make that critical point and be disruptive. And so, that's, again, the agency of design, where you can create a sense of discomfort, antagonism, and provocation in many different ways so that you can balance both the ethics and aesthetics depending, of course, on the audience.
    I don't have a problem antagonizing humanitarians, but I do have a problem antagonizing refugees because I don't want to inflict additional trauma. But I am still pushing the boundaries in subtle ways, for example by creating encounters between refugee youth and students from different backgrounds, collaborations with unveiled Muslim women, or with female engineers.

JMY

In that context, Azra, in the work that you're doing, do you find that objects have as much agency as the process you're engaged in, and your being there?

CAJ

To interject: the object is also a mediator, it's a third term, it's something in between you two.

AA

Exactly. So, what is the skill of an artist, of an architect coming in? And this is not to pretend that they don't have any skills. To create and design things in a collaborative manner allows everyone to pitch in their skills and perspectives. Of course, in the refugee camp, we from MIT bring in our own biases and we come from a more powerful position. It is important to acknowledge these asymmetrical hierarchies, and to deal with them consciously and sensitively. But this should not prevent us from collaborating. It is critical that we not impose our own agenda, but rather that we generate a creative exchange through artistic mediators, architectural mediators, or design mediators.

CAJ
The point being, just to clarify, that they are being entrained to design something. You're giving tools, and a format, and a set of skills, and then this object is the mediator of this encounter.

AA
Yes. But I am also trained by them. Everyone is teaching and learning something in this process. If it's successful, then it is something that people take on. If it's not, it was a nice conversation. But there is a possibility to copy and learn from the collectively envisioned models. So, for people who have been deprived of their imagination—where we can help decolonize someone's mind—the key is to actually imagine, visualize, and make a thing happen. The response is usually: "Wow, I can actually make this mechanism out of cardboard." It's evidence of someone's personal agency, ingenuity, of what is possible. Then, people can build on that.

CAJ
So in that context, ideas themselves have agency. The idea that something could change in material to another purpose is itself an agential event.

IC and JMY
Would you share more about your own current work? What's your next action? Has your own work shifted in recent years?

AM
I have been trying to find a way to open up both pedagogical and institutional spaces at MIT for researching and acting through the medium of architectural exhibition, broadly conceived. To that end, I am finally launching the Critical Broadcasting Lab. It will begin its existence through three workshops that together constitute this semester's Agit Arch Experiments. We start with a conversation on citizenship with the curators of the United States Pavilion in Venice 2018, and work from that constellation of issues toward other urgent questions

and frustrations that the participants in the workshop have with contemporary politics and the way in which architecture does or doesn't have agency within those realms.

For me, what's important about the broadcast as a format, whatever medium it ultimately takes, is that it allows audiences and interventions of various kinds. It's not clear where it might push buttons, but it could produce effects in discourse, in policy. It could force a pedagogical question, or push a boundary in the cultural environment of the school. Broadcast conceived this way also provides us a way to express something that may not be as easily or as quickly transmitted in a building—though buildings too, broadcast. My dream is that the Critical Broadcasting Lab will become a platform from which to intervene intelligently within the contemporary media-image complex of architectural discourse and beyond. And on top of the Agit Arch Experiment, the lab has launched its first project, an oral history on two forms of refusal—to take on a commissions and to take a fellow architect to court for IP issues—titled: "I Would Prefer Not To."

AA
I'm working on the creation of future heritage by people who will organize themselves around that heritage, particularly in sites where it seems nothing is possible. I'm interested in people who create art as a way to survive, and to bring their lessons to a public setting. We're also working with collections from Western museums to copy and disseminate information about heritage.

I am also continuing my work on the Bosnian genocide. We just acknowledged the 22nd anniversary of the genocide in Srebrenica, but it's the only one that's recognized as such. There were so many massacres during the 1990s war in Bosnia. Today, a whole community of survivors is living in an apartheid-like situation, governed by those who tortured them, who killed their families, who were not convicted. I think we survivors have a voice: we need to tell our stories of how we actually survived this war; what made people overcome their personal and collective tragedy; and how people are reconnecting today through art. We need to communicate that there is hope in that hopeless situation. I think the lessons are really valuable in light of what might come here or to Europe, as countries are banning immigration and turning to nationalism. Much can be learned from Bosnia for the future of Europe. So, I'm thinking about what we can actually do to prevent future wars.

CAJ

At this precise moment, I'm concerned with the remnant humanism of the term agency; I want to see non-human things—entities, microbes, whatever—as having some kind of agency that we need to acknowledge if we're going to survive as a species.

Otherwise, I'm working with Peter Galison on a new project—it is a weird project because it has neither art nor architecture. Those intentional and aesthetic operations aren't doing it for us. We're trying to take our tools and bring them to the question: What is an operative image? We're looking at the interface of activists and people who call themselves accidental activists: they stumble upon a technical or even robotic image that reveals staggering environmental harm, and they vector it into viral agency via networked platforms. The efficacy comes when a regulation changes and monetized extraction or dumping stops. And our fantasy is, this little book will be in the back pocket of a messenger and she's biking around Manhattan thinking about the world that she's inheriting and needs to change. That's our ideal audience: it is the potential activist, the accidental activist, the operative citizen or inhabitant of the planet. The vectored image is a meta-action for future action.

1002 INVENTIONS: ART AND DESIGN IN THE AL AZRAQ REFUGEE CAMP

Future Heritage Lab: Azra Akšamija, Melina Philippou; Omar Al-Darwish, Muteeb Awad Al-Hamdan, Rejan Ashour, Zeid Madi, Raafat Majzoub, Mohammad Yaghan, CARE Jordan

مكانٌ توقفَ فيه الزمان
رَهينُ الأسْر إلا أنه على قَيدِ الحياة
جزءٌ صغير مِن العالم ينبض بالحياة
هُنا الكرامةُ يُحظى بها
ألْهَمَهَ التراث
قاهراً النقص و العوز
لتتجاوز راحتك
أنْ تَعيشَ ذكرياتٍ عنْ وَطَنْ
أن تَبْقى إنسان

placed in a timeless place
trapped, yet alive
a living part of the world
here, dignity is invented
inspired by heritage
overcoming scarcity
to exceed your comforts
living memories of home
still human

Co-written in Arabic and English by Hana'a Ahmed,
Muteeb Awad Al-Hamdan, Azra Akšamija, Omar
Dahmous, Omar Darwish, Raed Suleiman

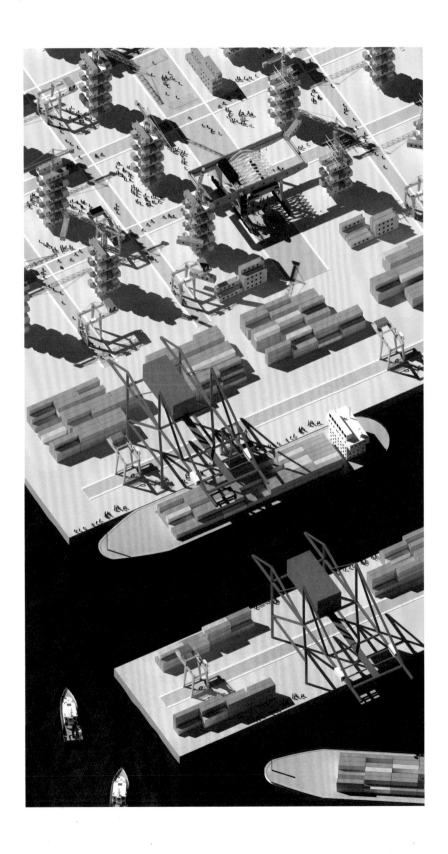

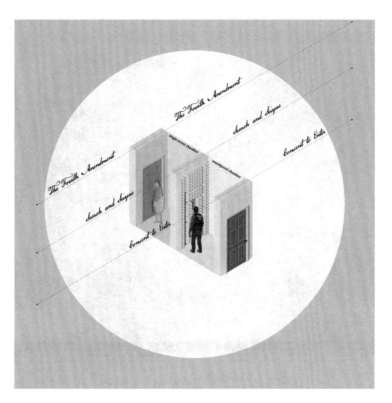

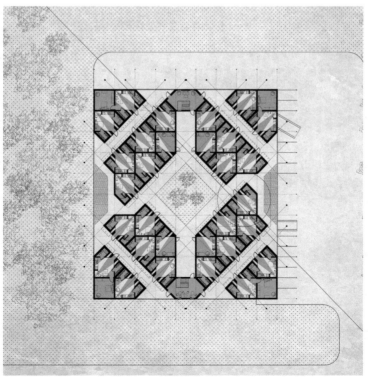

47

recording of   first person experience

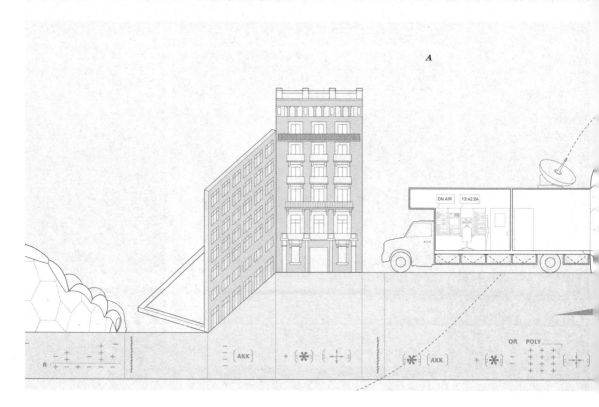

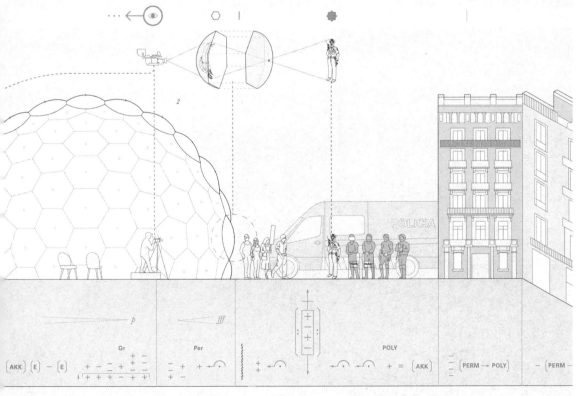

THE THEATER OF CRUELTY
Anne Graziano, Mackenzie Muhonen

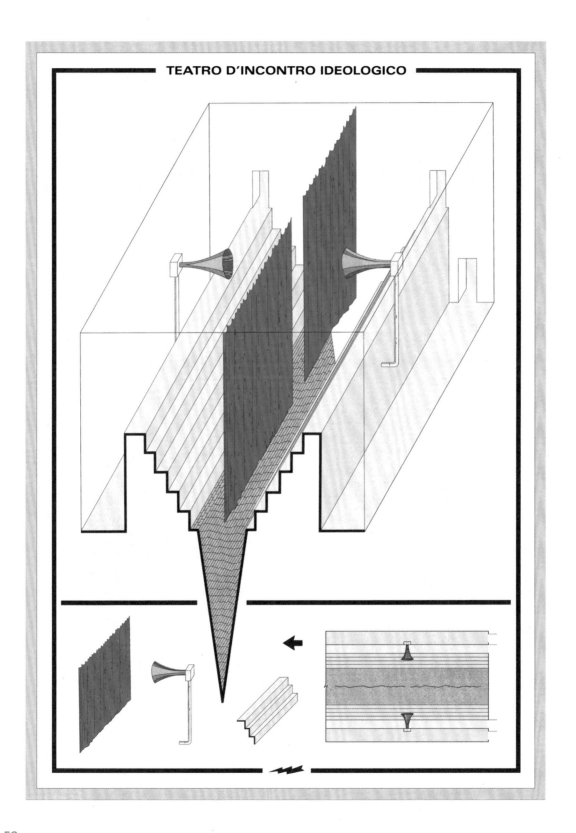

THEATERS OF AGONISTIC ENCOUNTERS
Carlos Casalduc, Milap Dixit, Dijana Milenov

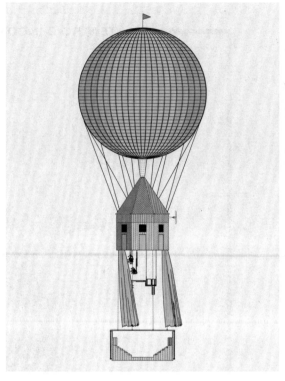

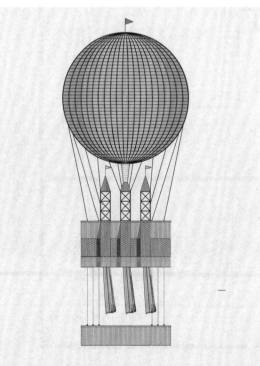

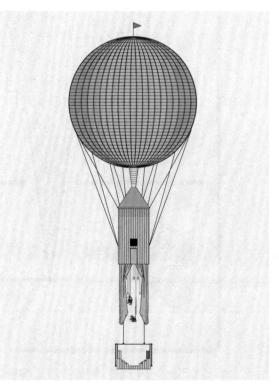

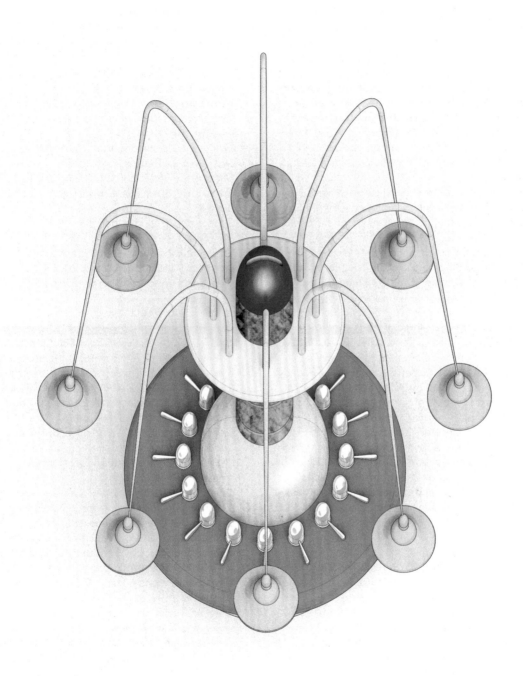

STINK HYDRANT

TECHNOPOLITICS, CULTURE, INTERVENTION
Arindam Dutta

Twentieth and twenty-first-century architecture is defined by its rhetorical subservience to something called "technology." Architecture relates to technology in multiple forms: as the organizational basis of society, as production system, as formal inspiration, as mode of temporization, as communicational vehicle, and so on. Managerial or "systems-based" paradigms for societal, industrial, and governmental organization have routinely percolated into architecture's considerations, at its various scales from the urban to the domestic, of the relationships of parts to wholes.

Architectural literature is filled with a surfeit of both metaphorical and literal embraces of what architects consider technology: these range from the utopian to the cartoonish, to the faux-philosophical, to the inadvertently religious, often to the seriously deluded. Can architecture's relationship to technology go beyond the semiotic and the metaphorical? To answer this sort of question, it would be important to consider what one means by the term technology, and then subsequently some of the key ways in which questions of technology have been absorbed into architectural, and more generally, other forms of cultural (art, cinematic, etc.) practice. The course is designed to augment the architectural student's literacy in critical forms of technological thought and their history in architecture and art.

Particularly important here is technology's claim for greater "humanization," and the manner in which architecture and art theories respond to this sort of claim. The course will investigate how technology produces the human, and conversely, how humans have "linked up" with ongoing technoscientific regimes.

Movies and Shows
- *The Belly of an Architect* (Peter Greenaway, 1987)
- *Blade Runner* (Ridley Scott, 1982)
- *Crash* (David Cronenberg, 1997)
- *Silence of the Lambs* (Jonathan Demme, 1991)
- *Hannibal* (Ridley Scott, 2001)
- *Matrix* (Larry and Andy Wachowski, 1999)
- *Gattaca* (Andrew Niccol, 1997)
- *The Texas Chainsaw Massacre* (Tobe Hooper, 1974)
- *Pi* (Darren Aronofsky, 1998)
- *The Alien Legacy: Alien* (Ridley Scott, 1979)
- *Aliens* (James Cameron, 1986)
- *Alien 3* (David Fincher, 1992)
- *Alien Resurrection* (Jean-Pierre Jeunet, 1997)
- *Prometheus* (Ridley Scott, 2012)
- *Covenant* (Ridley Scott, 2017)
- *Rise of the Planet of the Apes* (Rupert Wyatt, 2011)
- *The Ister* (David Barison, Daniel Ross, 2004)
- *I, Robot* (Alex Proyas, 2004)
- *I Am Legend* (Francis Lawrence, 2007)
- *2 or 3 Things I Know About Her* (Jean-Luc Godard, 1967)
- *Battlestar Galactica* (Series 2004–2009)
- *Orphan Black* (Series 2013–2017)
- *Ghost in the Shell* (Mamoru Oshii, 1995)
- *Ghost in the Shell 2: Innocence* (Mamoru Oshii, 2004)
- *Concussion* (Peter Landesman, 2015)
- *Her* (Spike Jonze, 2013)
- *Frozen/Jídù hánl ng* (Wang Xiaoshuai, 1997)
- *Memento* (Christopher Nolan, 2000)
- *Mad Max: Fury Road* (George Miller, 2015)

The Selves of Automata
- Otto Mayr, *Authority, Liberty and Automatic Machinery in Early Modern Europe* (Baltimore: Johns Hopkins University Press, 1986). Selections: 3. The Clockwork Universe; 7. Imagery of Balance and Equilibrium; 9. Self-Balancing Political Systems; 10. Self-Regulation in Economic Thought.
- René Descartes, "Sixth Meditation: The Existence of Material Things, and the Real Distinction between Mind and Body," in *Meditations on First Philosophy* (Cambridge: Cambridge University Press, 1996).
- Julien Offray De La Mettrie, "Machine Man," in *Machine Man and Other Writings* (Cambridge: Cambridge University Press, 1996).
- Georges Canguilheim, "Machine and Organism," in *Incorporations*, eds. Jonathan Crary and Sanford Kwinter (New York: Zone Books, 1992).
- "Prosthesis," special issue, *Ottagono*, no. 96 (September 1990). Articles: Adrian Forty, Jacques Guillerme, Georges Teyssot, Anthony Vidler, and Mark Wigley.
- Browse: Jean-Claude Beaune, "The Classical Age of Automata: An Impressionistic Survey from the Sixteenth to the Nineteenth Century," in *Fragments for a History of the Human Body, Part 1*, eds. Michel Feher, Ramona Naddaff and Nadia Tazi (New York: Zone Books, 1989).

Organicism

- Donna Haraway, "The Elements of Organicism," in *Crystals, Fabrics, and Fields: Metaphors of Organicism in Twentieth-Century Developmental Biology* (New Haven: Yale University Press, 1976).
- Herbert Simon, "Understanding the Natural and the Artificial Worlds," in *The Sciences of the Artificial* (Cambridge, MA: MIT Press, 1969).
- Maurice Merleau-Ponty, Second Course, "The Concept of Nature, 1957–1958: Animality, the Human Body, and the Passage to Culture," in *Nature, Course Notes from the Collège de France*, notes by Dominique Séglard, trans. Robert Vallier, (Evanston, Ill: Northwestern University Press, 2003).
- Philip Ritterbush, "Organic Form: Aesthetics and Objectivity in the Study of Form in the Life Sciences," in *Organic Form: The Life of an Idea*, ed. G. S. Rousseau (London: Routledge and Kegan Paul, 1972).
- Oliver Botar, "The Biocentric Bauhaus," in Charissa N. Terranova and Meredith Tromble, eds., *The Routledge Companion to Biology in Art and Architecture* (London: Routledge, 2016).
- William A. Braham and Jonathan A. Hale, eds., *Rethinking Technology: A Reader in Architectural Theory* (New York: Routledge, 2006)

Bodies

- Michel Foucault, "Open Up a Few Corpses," in *The Birth of the Clinic: An Archaeology of Medical Perception*, trans. A. M. Sheridan Smith (New York: Vintage Books, 1994).
- Robin Middleton, "Sickness, Madness and Crime as the Grounds of Form" *AA Files*, no. 24 (Autumn 1992).
- Thomas Keenan, "Getting the Dead to Tell Me What Happened," in *Forensis: The Architecture of Public Truth* (Berlin: Sternberg Press, 2015).
- Giorgio Agamben, *Homo Sacer: Sovereign Power and Bare Life*, trans. Daniel Heller-Roazen (Stanford, CA: Stanford University Press, 1998). Selections from Part 3: "The Camp as Biopolitical Paradigm of the Modern": 1. Biopolitics and the Rights of Man; 2. Life that Does not Deserve to Live; 3. The Camp as the 'Nomos' of the Modern.
- Ronald Rael, "Borderwall as Architecture: The Divided States of North America," in *Borderwall as Architecture: A Manifesto for the U.S.-Mexico Boundary* (Los Angeles, CA: University of California Press, 2017).
- Browse: The Senate Committee on Intelligence, "The Detention of Abu Zubaydah and the Development and Authorization of the CIA's Enhanced Interrogation Techniques," in *The Senate Intelligence Committee Report on Torture: Committee Study of the Central Intelligence Agency's Detention and Interrogation Program* (New York: Melville House, 2014).
- Eyal Weizman, "Walking Through Walls: Soldiers as Architects in the Israeli-Palestinian Conflict," *Radical Philosophy* 136, no. 8 (March 2006).
- Charles Heller and Lorenzo Pezzani, "Liquid Traces: Investigating the Deaths of Migrants at the EU's Maritime Frontier," in *Forensis: The Architecture of Public Truth* (Berlin: Sternberg Press, 2015).
- Frances Ashcroft, *Life at the Extremes: The Science of Survival* (Los Angeles: University of California Press, 2000).
- Films: *Concussion* (Peter Landesman, 2015); *The Persecution and Assassination of Jean-Paul Marat as Performed by the Inmates of the Asylum of Charenton Under the Direction of the Marquis de Sade* (*Marat/Sade*) (Peter Brook, 1967).

Biopolitics

- Giorgio Agamben, "What is an Apparatus?" in *What is an Apparatus? and Other Essays*, trans. David Kishik and Stefan Pedatella (Stanford, CA: Stanford University Press, 2009).
- Alain Corbin, *The Foul and the Fragrant: Odor and the French Social Imagination* (Cambridge, MA: Harvard University Press, 1986). Selections: 9: The Stench of the Poor; 10: Domestic Atmospheres (142–175).
- Timothy Mitchell, "Can the Mosquito Speak?" in *Rule of Experts: Egypt, Techno-Politics, Modernity* (Berkeley, CA: University of California Press, 2002).
- Beng-Huat Chua, "Public Housing and Political Legitimacy," in *Political Legitimacy and Housing: Singapore's Stakeholder Society* (London: Routledge, 1997).
- Anne McClintock, "Imperial Leather: Race, Cross-dressing and the Cult of Domesticity," in *Imperial Leather: Race, Gender and Sexuality in the Colonial Context* (New York: Routledge, 1995).
- Omnia El Shakry, "Rural Reconstruction: The Road to a New Sanitary Life," in *The Great Social Laboratory: Subjects of Knowledge in Colonial and Postcolonial Egypt* (Stanford, CA: Stanford University Press, 2007).
- Joseph S. Alter, "Gandhi's Body, Gandhi's Truth: Nonviolence and the Biomoral Imperative of Public Health," in *The Journal of Asian Studies* 55, no. 2 (May 1996).

- Adriana Petryna, "Biological Citizenship," in *Life Exposed: Biological Citizens After Chernobyl* (Princeton: Princeton University Press, 2002).
- David Gissen, *Subnature: Architecture's Other Environments* (Princeton: Princeton Architectural Press, 2009).

Technology/Technique/Tectonics

- Martin Heidegger, "The Question Concerning Technology," in *The Question Concerning Technology and Other Essays*, trans. William Lovitt (New York: Harper and Row, 1977).
- Martin Heidegger, "Building Dwelling Thinking," in *Poetry, Language, Thought*, trans. Albert Hofstadter (New York: Perennial, Harper Collins, 2001), 141–160.
- Branko Mitrovic, "Phenomenology and Hermeneutics," in *Philosophy for Architects* (New York: Princeton Architectural Press, 2011).
- Jeff Malpas, "Geography, Biology, and Politics," in *Heidegger and the Thinking of Place: Explorations in the Topology of Being* (Cambridge, MA: MIT Press, 2017).

Cyborg Collectives

- Karl Marx, "Wage Labor and Capital," in *Karl Marx: Selected Writings*, ed. David McLellan (Oxford: Oxford University Press, 1977).
- Anson Rabinbach, "The Political Economy of Labour Power," in *The Human Motor: Energy, Fatigue and the Origins of Modernity* (Berkeley: University of California Press, 1990).
- Friedrich Engels, "The Part Played by Labour in the Transition from Ape to Man," in *Dialectics of Nature* (Moscow: Progress Publishers, 1934, 1972).
- Donna Haraway, "A Cyborg Manifesto: Science, Technology, and Socialist-Feminism in the Late Twentieth Century," in *Simians, Cyborgs and Women: The Reinvention of Nature* (New York: Routledge, 1991).
- Richard Biernacki, "The Control of Time and Space," in *The Fabrication of Labor: Germany and Britain, 1640–1914* (Los Angeles, CA: University of California Press, 1997).
- Caroline A. Jones, "Frank Stella, Executive Artist," in *Machine in the Studio* (Chicago: University of Chicago Press, 1998).
- Anthony Vidler, "Homes for Cyborgs," in Christopher Reed, *Not At Home; The Suppression of Domesticity in Modern Art and Architecture* (London: Thames and Hudson, 1996).
- Juliet Koss, "Bauhaus Theater of Human Dolls," *The Art Bulletin* 85, no. 4 (December 2003): 724–745.

Reproductivity

- John Danaher and Neil McArthur, *Robot Sex* (Cambridge, MA: MIT Press, 2017): Selection: 1. Litzka Strikwerda, "Legal and Moral Implications of Child Sex Robots"; 2. Steve Peterson, "Is it Good for Them Too? Ethical Concern for the Sexbots"; 3. Joshua D. Goldstein, "Was it Good for You Too? The New Natural Law Theory and the Paradoxical Good of Sexbots"; 4. Sven Nyholm and Lily Eva Frank, "From Sex Robots to Love Robots: Is Mutual Love with a Robot Possible?"
- Paul B. Preciado, *Testo-Junkie: Sex, Drugs and Biopolitics in the Pharmacopornographic Era* (New York: Feminist Press, 2013). Selections: 1. Your Death; 2. The Pharmacopornographic Era; 4. History of Technosexuality; 6. Technogender; 8. Pharmacopower.
- Stoya, "Graphic Depictions, Scene 3," in *Philosophy, Pussycats and Porn* (Los Angeles, CA: Stoya Inc, 2018).
- Matthew Connelly, "The Population Establishment," and "Controlling Nations," in *Fatal Misconception: The Struggle to Control World Population* (Cambridge, MA: Belknap/Harvard, 2008).
- Farida Akhter, "A Brief History of the External Intervention (sic) into the Reproductive Behaviour of a Society," in *Depopulating Bangladesh: Essays on the Politics of Fertility* (Dhaka: Narigrantha Prabartana, 2005).
- Browse: Fabio Gramazio and Matthias Kohler, *Architectural Design 229–Made by Robots: Challenging Architecture at a Larger Scale* (London: Academy Press, 2014).

Systems

- Slava Gerovitch, "Cyberspeak: A Universal Language for Men and Machines," in *Newspeak to Cyber Speak: A History of Soviet Cybernetics* (Cambridge, MA: MIT Press, 2002).
- Christian Bonnefoi, "Louis Kahn and Minimalism," in *Oppositions* 24 (Spring 1981).
- Peter D. Eisenman, "Aspects of Modernism: Maison Dom-ino and the Self-Referential Sign," *Oppositions* 15/16 (Winter/Spring 1979).
- Alise Upitis, "Machines, Humans, Mental Pathology, and Christopher Alexander, 1959–1965," in *Nature Normative: The Design Methods Movement, 1944–1967*, Unpublished Dissertation, Department of Architecture, MIT, September 2008.
- Caroline A. Jones, "Hans Haacke 1967," in *Hans Haacke 1967* (Cambridge: MIT List Visual Art Center, 2011).

- Eden Medina, *Cybernetic Revolutionaries: Technology and Politics in Allende's Chile* (Cambridge, MA: MIT Press, 2011). Selections: 3. Designing a Network; 4. Constructing the Liberty Machine.
- Felicity Scott, "DISCOURSE, SEEK, INTER-ACT: Urban Systems at MIT," in *A Second Modernism: MIT, Architecture, and the "Techno-Social" Moment,* ed. Arindam Dutta (Cambridge, MA: MIT Press, 2012).
- Benjamin H. Bratton, "User Layer," in *The Stack: On Software and Sovereignty* (Cambridge, MA: MIT Press, 2015).
- Jose Luis Blanco et. al., "Seizing Opportunity in Today's Construction Technology Ecosystem," *McKinsey & Company*, 2018, www.mckinsey.com/industries/capital-projects-and-infrastructure/our-insights/seizing-opportunity-in-todays-construction-technology-ecosystem.

Territory

- Michel Foucault, "Space, Knowledge, and Power," in *Power*, ed. James D. Faubion, *Essential Works of Michel Foucault*, Vol. 3 (New York: The New Press, 2000).
- Henri Lefebvre, "Social Space," in *The Production of Space*, trans. Donald Nicholson-Smith (Cambridge, MA: Blackwell, 1991).
- Deborah Cowen, *The Deadly Life of Logistics: Mapping Violence in Global Trade* (Minneapolis: University of Minnesota Press, 2014). Selections: 2. The Rise of Supply Chain Security; 4. The Geo-Economics of Piracy.
- Stefano Liberti, "Geneva: The Financiers of Arable Land," in *Land Grabbing: Journeys in the New Colonialism*, trans. Enda Flannelly (New York: Verso, 2013).
- Nikita Sud, "From Land to the Tiller to Land Liberalization: The Political Economy of Gujarat's Shifting Land Policy," in *Modern Asia Studies* 41, no. 3 (May 2007): 603–637.
- Gavin Shatkin, *Cities for Profit: The Real Estate Turn in Asia's Urban Politics* (Ithaca, NY: Cornell University Press, 2017). Selections: 3. Planned Grab: Capitalizing on Land Dualism in New Order Jakarta; 5. Chongqing: The State Capitalist Growth Machine.
- Dallas Rogers, "New Discursive Code: Internet, Libertarianism, Upload, Download," in *The Geopolitics of Real Estate: Reconfiguring Property, Capital and Rights* (London: Rowman and Littlefield, 2017).
- Llerena Guiu Searle, *Landscapes of Accumulation: Real Estate and the Neoliberal Imagination in Contemporary India* (Chicago: University of Chicago Press, 2016). Selections: 5. Transparency and Control; 6. Developers' Quest for Credibility and Capital.

Environment

- Sandra D. Mitchell, "Science: How We Investigate the World," and "Policy: How We Act in the World," in *Unsimple Truths: Science, Complexity and Policy* (Chicago: University of Chicago Press, 2009).
- Paul N. Edwards, "Simulation Models and Atmospheric Politics, 1960–1992," and "Signal and Noise: Consensus, Controversy, and Climate Change," in *A Vast Machine: Computer Models, Climate Data, and the Politics of Global Warming* (Cambridge, MA: MIT Press, 2010).
- Farida Akhter, "Climate Change and Population," *UBINIG*, November 25, 2009, http://www.ubinig.org/index.php/home/showAerticle/3/english.
- Centre for Science and Environment, "Mediocre Model," and "Race to the Bottom," in *Poles Apart, Global Environmental Negotiations, Part 2* (New Delhi: Centre for Science and Environment, 2001).
- Kate Ervine, "The Global Political Economy of Carbon," and "Trading Carbon to Cool the World?" in *Carbon* (Cambridge, UK: Polity, 2018).
- Troy Vettese, "To Freeze the Thames: Natural Geo-Engineering and Biodiversity," *New Left Review* 111 (May–June 2018).
- Mike Davis, "Taking the Temperature of History: Le Roy Ladurie's Adventures in the Little Ice Age," *New Left Review* 110 (March–April 2018).
- Herman Daly, interview with Benjamin Kunkel, "Ecologies of Scale," *New Left Review* 109, (January–February 2018).

TAKING STOCK
Zain Karsan

Our workplaces were the first to be hacked. We were freed from our labor, no longer tied to our stations, working with and as machines. We witnessed the end of an age of Taylorist submission.

In exchange, the objects of our dreams appeared before us. Hidden landscapes of black box factories ceaselessly produced artifacts. Fleets of drones delivered them to our doorstep. And so we forgot how things were made, and how to make things. Our connection to material was hacked, and we deferred to the efficiency of automated digital production.

All we could do now was take comfort in digital simulation. We were glued to our goggles; they held us transfixed. In this digital reality, we abandoned our material lives, and so we wandered from place to place. No longer tied to a physical reality, we found solace in the continuous movement through our simulated environments. Our cities fell to rust, irrelevant to us in our path through the digital world. As our cities began to empty and erode, with massive populations engaged in an exodus, the dross began to pile up around us.

Out of these forgotten urban landscapes of outmoded machines and materials emerged a resistance, who watched silently over hypnotized crowds, and started to pick up the pieces.

This is the story of the material monks, who, garbed in the protective cloaks of their foundry, took back their agency to mine the vast potential of the post-industrial sites around them. They came from a world of quotidian obsolescence, but they brought with them a new assessment of material. The site of their resistance is the old Aerocar Company turned foundry at 6501 Mack Ave. Their resistance materialized in a set of machine hacks; by taking stock of the tools in their foundry and the materials that surround them, the monks built their monastery. They brought with them no prejudice to their parts, hacking apart to construct anew.

The day begins with material salvage. As the monks comb through the dross, an excavator strapped to a gantry crane moves waste through the bays. Material is meticulously sorted before being stored in the library, a continuously changing archive of artifacts. A scriptorium sits at the end of the space where the monks record the day's salvage and devise their hacks. The tools of the monastery are in a constant state of change; they are hacked and rehacked. The monks are charged with recording their work, producing a new kind of knowledge about obsolete machines.

One of the most sacred spaces of the monastery is the old machine hall, where sorted material undergoes its transformation. The hall is anchored upon an induction furnace; the most intensive process the factory can support is recycling steel. A tower sits above, cleaning the air of the foundry.

At the end of each day the monks climb around the tower to their quarters to rest, inspecting the quality of air at each level of their ascent. They confront the scale of their task every night when they dream of the landscapes beyond the scrubber tower in which they sleep. And so their dreams are troubled by the impossibility of completely taking stock; nothing can escape the scrutiny of their attention or the scope of their salvage. Their work will never finish. They accept that they are doomed to see their work undone, and like Sisyphus, must hack and re-hack, endlessly recycling material and technology.

They can never escape the furnace that will melt down their machine parts, or the hopper that takes and redistributes their crushed and dismantled assemblies. They will never finish taking stock.

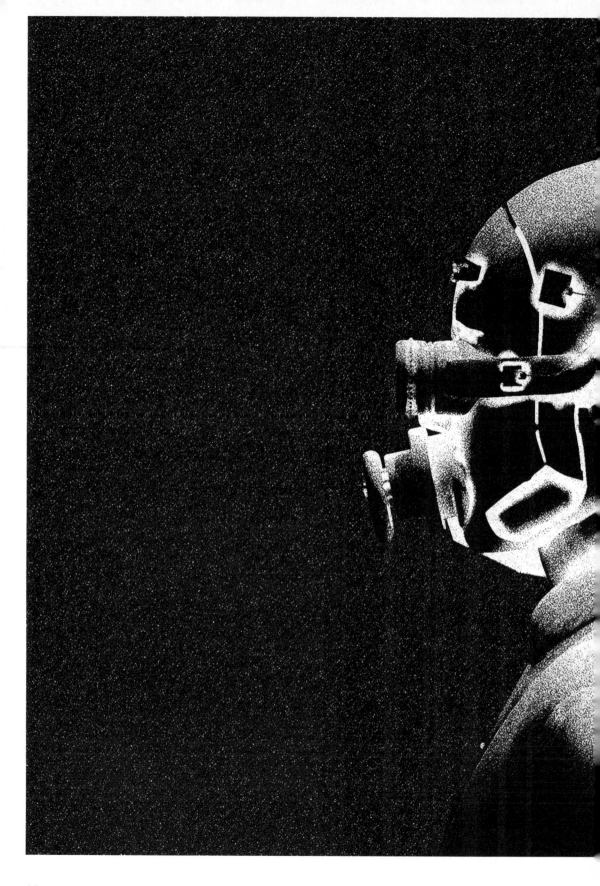

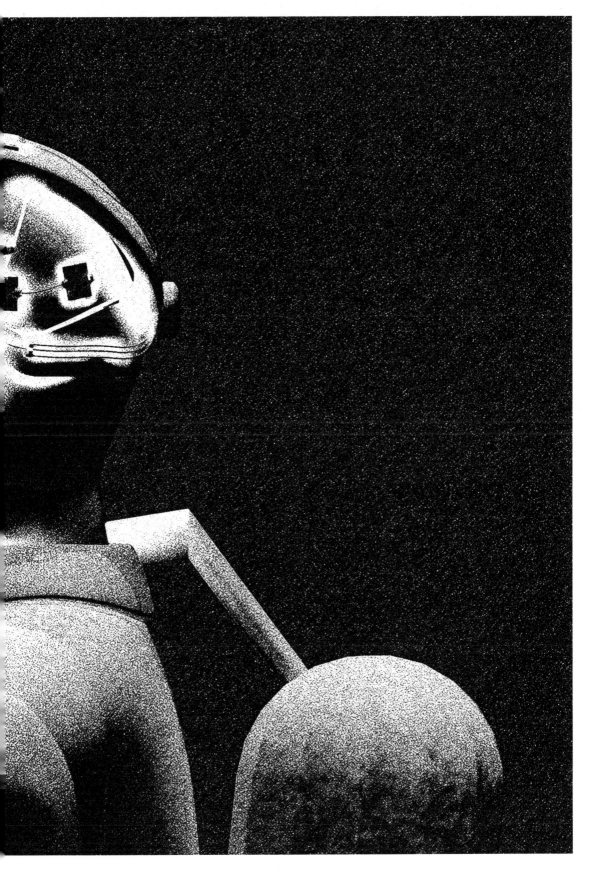

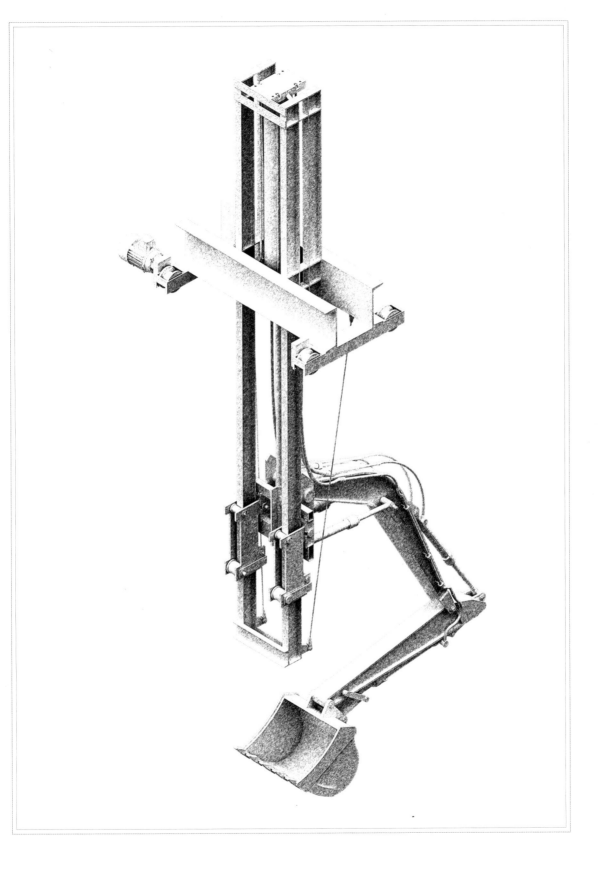

If we are worried that the sky may be falling on our heads, how is it that we have done so little about it?

We live in an epoch shaped by extensive shifts in industrialization, with environmental risks and consequences felt at a planetary scale. On graph after graph, metric after metric—population growth, species extinction, particulate matter in the air—the recent accelerations of change have turned what once appeared as lines with slight slopes upward into near vertical spikes. The world has become defined by acceleration. Paradoxically, while the threats are serious, we remain little mobilized—in part maybe because of the poverty of the environmental imagination. People observe daily weather changes but they do not perceive climate, a phenomenon that is, in its modern definition, a statistically created object of investigation with a long-term assessment period. Furthermore, the weather is experienced locally, while understanding the global effects of climate change would require perceiving the world as a whole.[1] So how do we think about something as intangible and invisible as climate—especially as the language of scientific expertise can be misinterpreted, sometimes deliberately, by journalists and those working as "merchants of doubt" on behalf of industry interests?[2]

The environmental crisis can be seen not only as a crisis of the physical and technological environments; it is also a crisis of the cultural environment—of the modes of representation through which society relates to the complexity of Earth systems in their vast scales of time and space. The conditions and cultural origins of the current environmental crisis have relied on narratives of industrial modernity—"about the world as resource, about nature as external, about progress as an escape from nature's determinations and limits, about technology as quasi-autonomous prime mover."[3] In this worldview, the Earth is a commodity, and no part of it—from the atmosphere to the geological superstratum—can escape the threshers of capital. In economic discourse, the transformation of the Earth differentiates between resources and by-product environmental costs, such as pollution, public health, and the degradation of shared commons— what are often called "externalities." This approach to history—natural, economic, urban—sustains the belief that the Earth is nothing more than an inanimate collection of resources that some humans can exploit however they like. And this foundational imaginary has led us to our current crisis.

The historical importance of ecological crises, Bruno Latour points, "stems from the impossibility of continuing to imagine politics on the one side and, on the other, a nature that would serve politics simultaneously as a standard, a foil, a reserve, a resource, and a public dumping ground."[4] The urgency of the environmental question requires a rupture with externalization so that the "value" of space is integral rather than incidental to narratives of the Earth. To counter capitalism's abstraction of geography, those concerned about climate change must make the Earth visible again in political consciousness.

If the present predicament of climate change springs from such an economic mythology, then we need to learn to tell other stories, that, as Frédérique Aït-Touati and Latour put it, "re-learns, like Atlas, how to carry the world on its shoulders, both the world and all there is above it."[5] The iconic Apollo photographs "The Whole Earth," "Earthrise," and "22727" staged a world picture that was global and ecological, a stand-alone planet outside of us. However, we do not live on a "Blue Marble," insofar as that famous image of the planet symbolizes an objective, holistic, impersonal Earth made visible by technological achievements. Climate change, Latour argues, calls for another ecological belief system, which, beyond the accumulation of scientific knowledge, embodies questions of representations, of what world one wants to assemble, and with what entities she wants to live.[6] Latour calls for crafting the "political arts"—an experimental method that takes action on climate change by connecting political ecology with aesthetic experience. What would happen if politics revolved around disputed things, atmospheres, natures? What techniques of representation might help make them public? Such new eloquence in representation seeks to assemble a big picture of the Earth away from the facticity of economic exchange value and eco-centric techno-hubris of problem solving.

What is perhaps most attractive in this new worldview is that "if there is a post-Anthropocene worth living in, those who will live in it will need different stories."[7] Stories are a means for understanding the world, for nurturing new habits of seeing, and, ultimately, for projecting alternative forms of organizing life. They are means of world making. The reason this is needed so urgently, as Latour repeatedly states, is that "The Earth, has become once again ... an agent of ... our common geostory."[8] He continues: "The problem becomes for all of us in

philosophy, science or literature, how do we tell such a story."[9] The quest is for an evidentiary aesthetic method that places the story of climate change, a story that is difficult both to tell and to hear, at the center of the theater of the world.

Stories and ideas matter for the Earth. In an epoch where the rapid influx and rapid distribution of information makes experiences of the world nearly impossible to communicate, a story does what infographics cannot. This is in part because stories give meaning to what otherwise would be an illustration of the utterly unbearable scale of events occurring around the globe and across time. The beauty of the storyteller is the ability to communicate a narrative and allow the reader to integrate it into her own experience with meaning and purpose. Stories do not lead readers to make lifestyle adjustments, but rather they entreat them to envision threats and opportunities together and offer them the means by which to begin to care and respond. Stories foreground the experience of telling and retelling, of the dolorousness and delight when you feel your thought and imagination connected to things and places to which you were previously indifferent.

Climate change demands thus urgent transformations in the ways we care for, imagine, design, and tell the story of the Earth *with* landfills, mine pits, oil rigs. In the essay "Love Your Monsters," Latour poses the problem of *Frankenstein* as a parable for political ecology.[10] Written at the dawn of the great technological revolutions that would define the nineteenth and twentieth centuries, Frankenstein presciently describes a technological creation that, without proper care, wreaks havoc. In this tale lies a moral about technology and compassionate responsibility. According to Latour, we confuse the monster for its creator and blame our sins against Nature upon the things we've made. But our sin is not that we created technologies but that we failed to love and care for them. When Dr. Frankenstein meets his creation on a glacier in the Alps, the monster claims that it was not born a monster at all, but that it became destructive only after being left alone, abandoned in the laboratory by his horrified creator the moment he twitched to life. Latour argues that we cannot stop being involved in the world we created, and that political ecology must engage present technologies with patience and commitment. A responsible political ecological project must produce accounts of technological systems and of the Earth that convince readers that the "machines by which we are surrounded are cultural objects worthy of attention and respect."[11]

How do we draw the Earth as a matter of concern? Such environmental imagination requires forms of knowledge that synthesize scientific epistemologies and sensible experience. The consequent aesthetics would draw on geographic representation, speculative fiction, and architectural drawings to render worlds simultaneously comprehensible and fantastic.

Geographic Representation
To truly understand the shape of the Earth one must study a range of industrial landform typologies, all drawn in their territories. One example and method might come from the history of geography and in particular the scientist-explorers of the nineteenth century, among them Alexander von Humboldt. Before science split into what we now know as disciplines—astronomy, oceanography, biology, geology, and the like—it was the task of the geographer to bring the natural world together in descriptive representation. Humboldt's influential treatise *Kosmos* is emblematic of this unitary worldview in how it draws together the physical geography of Earth, from lichen to nebulae. His "portrait of nature," as he called it, presented the Earth in a range of scales from the micro to the macro, so that the eye took in the object as a whole and then and proceeded to distinguish the parts until the totality was grasped as an assemblage of essential attributes.[12] Although Humboldt's avowed purpose was that of "scientific traveler," his drawings assembled forms of knowledge, which, beyond the accumulation of information, engaged the aesthetic experience of the reader or viewer. They made commensurability possible. "People want to see," Humboldt noted, "and I show them a microcosm on a sheet of paper."[13] Humboldt's method is important because it literally draws together matters of the environment; it uses visual agency to synthesize scientific knowledge into a holistic representation.

Speculative Fiction
If environmental issues are incomprehensible in their scale, their ubiquity, and their duration, then perhaps stories can make them sensible, or legible to the senses.[14] Beyond documentary descriptions, geostories deploy a narrative sensibility to engage the conditions surrounding us. The narratives in *Geostories* draw specifically on science fiction and its persistent engagement with technological questions in relation to the planet, including those created by broadening risk scenarios.[15] In the face of gloomy ecological predictions for the Earth, speculative fiction might help us comprehend such new worldly conditions and reflect on reality without realism, without optimization, without determinism, and without fear of the cosmic scale. The "what if" approach of speculative fiction is also a design method to configure new and largely uncharted kinds of

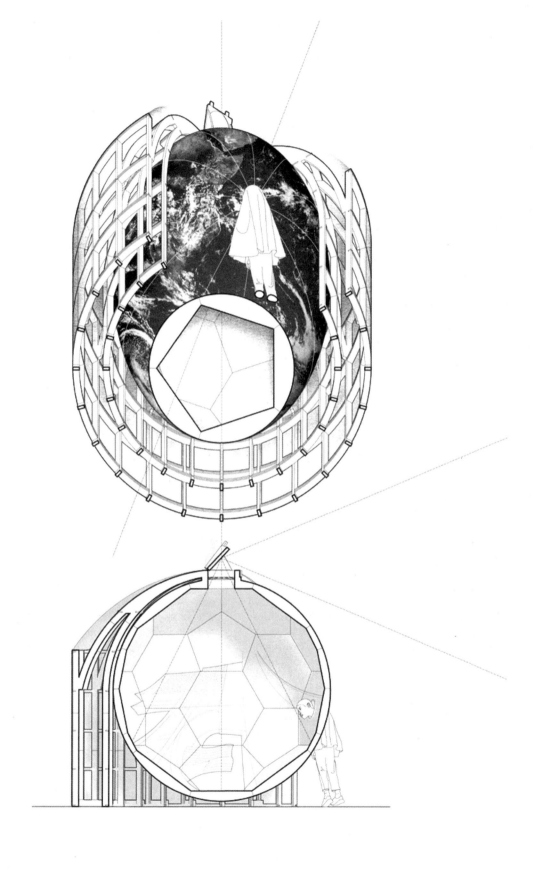

living on a damaged planet. If the future offers a terrain in which to test ideas, speculative fictions are experiments to think the consequences of emerging environmental and technological conditions. Such SF—Donna Haraway's term for "science fiction, speculative fabulation, string figures, speculative, feminism, science fact"—cultivates thinking about what current technologies, theories, or habits can't yet solve.[16]

Architectural Drawing

Architectural drawing is a device that brings the Earth into matters of concern; it makes visible absent things, synthesizes sciences and scales linked to brief organic lifetimes and the immensity of geologic time, and weaves the totality into a complex and relational fabulation. A drawing is an argument about the world; it is at once descriptive, synthetic, critical, and always speculative. Drawings make worlds; they are as such important in part because of the other drawings that they could make possible. Much like storytelling, drawing is always re-drawing—borrowing, misusing, appropriating. They matter for our disciplinary and political futures, as educators, designers, and citizens.

Drawings argue through the techniques they use and points of view they choose. The section, for instance, counteracts the abstract Earth of aerial mappings, diagrammatic flows, and soft perspectives. Its orthographic projection plane produces the vertical territory. In natural history, such a split-level view (also known as aquarium view) shows domains both above and below the surface of the water or ground. This includes illustrations in the biological sciences and geological sciences, such as the frontispiece from Charles Lyell's *Principles of Geology*, which depicts the rock cycle, Charles Darwin's illustration of coral reef formation, or *Duria Antiquior*, a pictorial representation of a scene of prehistoric life based on evidence from fossil reconstructions. The section drawing goes beyond the isolation of the domains and sciences of the Earth to project a synthetic drawing that provides an opportunity to reimagine the relations of geological and architectural forces at a planetary scale.

Axonometry is another anti-perspective mode of representation that privileges a typological planetary imagination. The axonometric projection is archetypal; from its roots in the technical drawings of the military, engineering, and art, it renders metric the conceptual and analytical attributes of the thing seen by the mind's eye. Such capacity to make the infinite visible in the context of a quasi-scientific construction attracted abstract artists such as El Lissitzky. He celebrated the ideological force of this measured three-dimensional orthographic

projection not because it offered final objectivity, a God's eye view, but because it "extended the apex of the finite visual cone of perspective into infinity."[17] The infinite extension in depth coincided with the suspension of the subject's privileges of self-position. Both ungrounded and archetypal, axonometric has the potential to illustrate a planetary collective consciousness. It allows for an aesthetic position within the immeasurable dimensions of the cosmos. It also makes totality thinkable; it is an impossible view for a mere mortal but a necessary outlook to reckon with the cognitive and affective dissonance of climate change.

Geostories

Geostories: Another Architecture for the Environment is a manifesto for the environmental imagination at a moment in which the Earth is presented in crisis.[18] The book addresses the failure to feel much of anything in the face of a crisis, and the difficulty (and necessity) of a different kind of planetary imagination. In response to the "slow violence" of the environmental crisis and the "great acceleration" of global media cycle, DESIGN EARTH advances the "slow media"[19] of geographic fiction or geostories to render sensible the issues of climate change. The prefix "Geo-" engages the Earth as a grand question of design: a site, scale, and aesthetic condition. As a suffix "–stories" addresses matters of the Earth in speculative scenarios that infiltrate earth, sea, and air strata, inviting us to extend our awareness of human settlement of the planet out to the cosmos and down to the Earth's core. *Geostories* counters the stories of industrial capitalism with an even more fantastic narrative machine that tells truth to realism. *Geostories* ascribes agency where it is hard to assign causality.

To design the Earth *with* externalities brings into representation—into aesthetics and politics—those things, spaces, and scales that are erased from the geographic imagination. The plotlines develop uncomfortable yet oddly constructive relationships with trash sites, mined ocean floor, space debris in orbit, dry watersheds, particulate matter in the atmosphere, and depleted oil reservoirs, and a host of other unloved geographies. The stories also lay bare the absurdity of some eco-centric concerns and make explicit their underlying cultural prejudices (for example, that the melting of Antarctica only matters in as far as rising sea levels pose a threat to coastal urban centers).

In a series of projects that speculate on environmental modulation as they appear in earth, sea, and sky, *Geostories* is a representation of the planet. Representation here is both an aesthetic practice and a political one, referring both to the design of common worlds and the political debates around what constitutes them and for whom they are built. Inhabited and contested, they open up our imagination of technology and the environment to relentless diversity and urgent troubles.[20] These stories are retold and re-envisioned to pose a vast common ground on which we can meet, as responsible citizens of the Earth, rationally, aesthetically, and emotionally. In the twenty-first century, the ability to comprehend and relate to geological strata and climate change hinges on an exploration of aesthetics and wonder that contain the magnitude of the Earth and encapsulate that which scientific rationalization has failed to communicate. The importance of such wonder-charged experience should not be overlooked when conceiving planetary relationships anew. After all, environmentalism is foremost a protest on behalf of values, an engagement with the world beyond the tunnel vision of "resourcism." And it is tempting to think that such attention to wonder can make us care.

This text is an excerpt adapted from "Another Architecture for the Environment," the introduction to *Geostories: Another Architecture for the Environment* (New York: ACTAR, 2018), a book by Design Earth which argues for the significance of architectural representation and speculative fiction toward a planetary imagination that makes sense of the geographies of climate change.

1   Quoted in Antonia Mehnert, "Climate Change Futures and the Imagination of the Global in *Maeva!* by Dirk C. Fleck," *Ecozone* 3, no. 2 (October 2012): 28.
2   See Mike Hulmes, "Why We Disagree about Climate Change," in *Why We Disagree about Climate Change: Understanding Controversy, Inaction and Opportunity* (Cambridge: Cambridge University Press, 2009), and Naomi Oreskes and Erik M. Conway, *Merchants of Doubt* (New York: Bloomsbury Press, 2010).
3   Christophe Bonneuil, "The Geological Turn," in *The Anthropocene and the Global Environmental Crisis: Rethinking Modernity in a New Epoch*, eds. Clive Hamilton, François Gemenne, and Christophe Bonneuil (London: Routledge, 2015), 17.
4   Bruno Latour, *Aramis or the Love of Technology* (Cambridge, MA: Harvard University Press, 1990), vii.
5   Frédérique Aït-Touati and Bruno Latour, "The Theatre of the Globe," *Exeunt*, February 13, 2015, exeuntmagazine.com/features/the-theatre-of-the-globe.
6   Bruno Latour, *Waiting for Gaia: Composing the Common World through Arts and Politics*, November 2011, 7, http://www.bruno-latour.fr/sites/default/files/124-GAIA-LONDON-SPEAP_0.pdf.
7   Isabelle Stengers, "Matters of Cosmopolitics," in *Architecture in the Anthropocene: Encounters Among Design, Deep Time, Science and Philosophy* (Ann Arbor: Open Humanities Press, 2014), 178.
8   Bruno Latour, *An Inquiry into Modes of Existence: An Anthropology of the Moderns* (Cambridge, MA: Harvard University Press, 2013), 13.
9   Bruno Latour, "Agency at the Time of the Anthropocene," *New Literary History* 45, no. 1 (Winter 2014): 1–18.
10 Bruno Latour, "Love your Monsters: Why We Must Care for Our Technologies as We Do Our Children," The Breakthrough Institute (Winter 2012), http://www.bruno-latour.fr/sites/default/files/downloads/107-BREAKTHROUGH-REDUXpdf.pdf.
11 Latour, *Aramis or the Love of Technology*, viii.
12 Alexander von Humboldt, *Cosmos: A Sketch of a Physical Description of the Universe* (London: George Bell and Sons, 1883).
13 Quoted in Jean-Marc Drouin, "Humboldt et la popularization des sciences," in *Humboldt et Bonpland, 1799–1804: Une Adventure Savant aux Amériques*, ed. Jean-March Drouin and Thierry Lalande, *Musée des Arts et Métiers—La Revue* 39–40 (September 2003): 54–63, 60.
14 Bruno Latour, *Gaïa Global Circus*, www.bruno-latour.fr/fr/node/359.
15 Ursula Heise, *Sense of Place and Sense of Planet* (Oxford University Press, 2008), 210.
16 Donna Haraway, *Staying with the Trouble* (Berlin: Hatje Cantz, 2012).
17 El Lissitzky, "A. and Pangeometry," (1925), quoted in Stan Allen, *Practice: Architecture, Technique and Representation* (London: Routledge, 2009), 16.
18 Rania Ghosn and El Hadi Jazairy, *Geostories: Another Architecture for the Environment* (New York: ACTAR, 2018).
19 For more on slow media, see Reinhold Leinfelder, Libby Robin, and Helmuth Trischler, "Slow Media: The Imaginary Museum of Listening to the Anthropocene," *Campus* 2014, https://www.anthropocene-curriculum.org/pages/root/campus-2014/slow-media/.
20 Donna Haraway, *Staying with the Trouble: Making Kin in the Chthulucene* (Durham: Duke University Press, 2016).

Images
P 67: Blue Marble Circus concept plan and elevation, produced for the Design Biennial Boston, 2017. The Blue Marble Circus is a monument to industrial humanity's plastic footprint, which—although at a planetary scale—remains outside our geographical imagination. The installation appropriates Rome's ancient Pantheon, known for its spherical "architecture of the cosmos," to take aim at the dissonance between our individual worries and the vast environmental transformations the Earth is undergoing.
P 69: Blue Marble Circus worm's eye view axonometric and section through the globe as a camera obscura.

Project
Team: Rania Ghosn, El Hadi Jazairy, Lex Agnew, Cristina Clow, Christopher Dewart, Justin Lavallee, Larisa Ovalles, Aaron Weller. With contributions from Michael Epstein, Sabrina Madera, Ching Ying Ngan, Jongbang Park, Sean Philips, Rawan Al-Saffar, Paul Short, Marc Smith, Xin Wen. Consultants: Paul Kassabian, Tom Gearty, Lee Zamir.

The making of architecture is the making of artifacts. To think about the design of a work of architecture as such is to regard the acts of making form and reading form as simultaneous and inseparable. Being attuned to architecture in this particular way has led to a practice that is invested deeply, if not wholly, in the agency of architectural form as the medium through which cultural commentary is conveyed.

William O'Brien Jr.

NOT WRITING
Sarah Rifky

The point of writing, it feels like, is to not finish. I've dragged out silences in un-words, trying to articulate the bowing-out of thinking, escaping into "stories"—depots of sublimated truths. I thought of reading as an alternative, a way of stretching time, contracting metaphors. Here I am, struggling to write and read, summoning the patience for history—its people, places, and things. In this struggle, I grapple with language and its diachrony, land and its end, institutions, and art, and taking long strides backwards (in time) into eras—as far back as bordering "the common."

There is something of delinquency, a refusal to write, that perhaps reifies my sense of responsibility towards myself. I am, in not writing, coming up with excuses, rationalizing silence. I say this, knowing that I am indulging us both through this admittance. If by way of writing—in time—we are trying to make this moment legible and logical, I am incapable of making it such. Text arrives to me mute; the texts that I write are aborted. I read while trying to mechanically kindle inspiration. Writing—like love—is vulnerable and hard to come by. It can be possessive and tormenting, especially when writing is one-sided. There is a terror of language, an irreconcilable desire to find ways of writing that I have not yet encountered, and maybe never will.

This reluctance to write is a disinclination in itself (or outright refusal) to accept a naturalization of this moment of doubt, of bowing out, a lack: the admittance of reaching a dead end. It's also the flip side of a desire to present something that is more hopeful than despair, that which does not falter. All writing encrypts fear, the sum of which is a growing trepidation about an end of all things—of that which we know. There was a moment, historically perhaps, where knowledge was more fragmentary and hope abundant—if one can put it in such tacky terms. We are entangled in writing, easily struck by its sentiments, though I admit, in reading myself (over time) I dissociate from my own. That said, I don't want you to get me wrong: I am all for putting literacy to work, but that writing must also assume its rightful position, and be understood—beyond action—as that. Writing as writing-as-imagination—work or action—in itself is disabling. It disables us from doing other things, even if we chase them.

I've been ruminating a lot more recently about disillusion. In part I am wondering if this resistance from within the scope of art, of thought, and their institutions, isn't simply symptomatic of a certain dead end, an index of how we squirm in the failing order of neoliberalism and the fatigue we experience through it. We're living through a shitty time, and it's okay to admit it. Art, fiction, and the spaces we create can be thought of—at minimum—as a historical coping mechanism against a generalized state of shared anxiety and loss (particularly that of hope).

Being here (now) in the academic safe haven of Cambridge, in the final weeks (days …) of the United States 2016 election, subjected to the chatty nature of NPR news, and picture-perfect sensational politics—the sensational debates starring Hillary and Trump, I feel both irked and alienated. In between those feelings, I am coming to terms with the sense that there will be no political salvation or becoming of any viable democracy … of any actual change of order in the world. Apart from a sense of not-writing, an overwhelming sense of forlornness, I am mired in the guilt of not doing—or at a minimum writing—for certain places, people, causes, and things. I wonder if activism in a natural sense is redeeming of our humanity, and if writing is not simply just a function of that.

I am grateful for the invitation to write. I do think there is value in asking things of each other, demanding that the other write, transcribe, articulate, or simply *do something*. It's redeeming and enabling and perhaps necessary also for the sake of those who are unable to, because of being confined, incarcerated—literally or just mentally. One way of thinking about this, would be that writing does the job of connecting disparate times, events and people; it coheres the plot of a narrative (history). When a frame is dropped, a moment lapses or a person is missing. Writing is akin to séance, a way of summoning missing things, articulating (the) future.

In some ways—even if it appears contradictory to the mechanisms of coping—what I mean to suggest is that sometimes, the best way to think of not-writing is as a hiatus: a necessary break, an arrhythmic interruption to a process of hopelessness. I am trying to imagine not-writing as regenerative of other imaginations, of ways of being with one's self and one's body. The mindset of not writing pushes against the limits of capacity to sit still, pent-up anxiety stretching contemplation into new forms, and to think of not-writing and the simple focusing on doing things as generative of hope, like picking tomatoes. There is something to be said about occupying time—sitting with it—contemplating a position from which to act that cannot be so easily co-opted by a tyrannical present, even if I conversely seek its company.

In the realm of passive resistance, I seem to think a lot of Melville's Bartleby. The compliant typist that decides, upon being asked by a lawyer to examine a document, to respond with a polite and persistent, "I prefer not to." Perhaps, it is simply that these days I prefer not to write, or even not to think too much. Whereas I cannot generalize this state of passive resistance, I feel that there is a codified sentiment of not-doing looming over us. It feels treacherous to call it out, to spell it out, to articulate it, because we are in such dire need of action, of hope, of something. I'm somewhat sorry to share these sentiments.

"Not Writing" was first published in *ArteEast Quarterly*, Fall 2016, as a response to a call for writing from editor Lina Attalah.

Attalah asked Rifky to reflect on various editorials she wrote responding to and reflecting upon the 2011 Egyptian revolution. Attalah wrote: "You made me wonder: what can language give to activism? […] Writing, you made me think, in its capacity as a communicative means, is political. You said, "Now, as I make the decision to write, two weeks into the revolution, I ponder this decision. This is the longest thought I have had in weeks. In democracy, Jacques Derrida says a decision, the use of power, is always urgent, yet democracy takes time. Democracy makes one wait so that the use of power can be discussed, and power can never be exercised without communication. Authority is divided, as soon as we speak to one another, which would explain why so many of my friends are closing off, and speaking less and less. It would explain the side effects of social paranoia and fear of disclosing information leading to resolutions towards reform." Your words reminded me of the critical distinction between taking power and building power, and how in the time spent between waking up and going to sleep, there might be a function of building power by creating, prompting and archiving conversations in writing, editing, translating and publishing."

Read the full call, along with a series of conversations hyperlinked in the article: http://www.arteeast.org/quarterly/not-writing-sarah-rifky-in-response-to-yet-another-call-for-writing/?issues_season=fall&issues_year=2016.

Material

Acts

Material

Acts

Material

Acts

Material

Acts

Material

Acts

How could a pedagogy focused on care for material, resources, making, use, and energy expenditure change approaches to architectural design and production? What do we learn in moving the earth and building with it? What do we do with the material remnants of progress? How can we learn from ancient material logics long-lost to modernity?

From the scale of matter to that of nuclear waste, thinking materially forces one to deal with the traces of human actions. It requires, as Jessica Varner argues, coming to terms with a long history of toxicity, with the simultaneous hardening of architecture and softening of the body. It demands a reckoning with the Sisyphean task of cataloging and reusing society's refuse, or imagining new forms of material and new uses of misfit matter. Working at the root of these conditions offers ways of thinking that take resources, time, tools, and production into careful account.

The projects that follow contend with the physicality, weight, and mess of material alongside its change and transformation over time. They take the entangled and extractive nature of the architectural project to heart. Revealed are new material desires, new tools for design and optimization of material and embodied energy, and accounting for energy and resource expenditure. A collective call to action is made to shift habits of consumerism and infinite material production. Material stabilizes in as much as it opens space for inquiry; it requires maintenance.

What questions does dealing with the matter of architecture, material, and resources pose to design and scholarship? Students and faculty approach these questions in numerous ways and sites: they form new materials at the molecular level, they activate the inert, imbue refuse and salvage with value through new material systems and codes, produce analog and digital workflows, and forge new approaches to design and construction.

Each project here is attuned to its materialization and fabrication, to the processes of making. Ideas have to be tested, transformed, built, and rebuilt; this requires making to be a collaborative, constitutive act brought about by a shared understanding. In sites from MIT's Killian Court to Kigali, Rwanda, material is a mediator. It introduces a shared experience; it requires a collective effort. Such investigations have led to monuments that walk themselves and to civic spaces and urban plans for communities. Each takes on the challenge presented by the weight, context, politics, and logics of material as a moment of potential to reconfigure design.

AN INTRODUCTION TO ACTIVE MATTER
Skylar Tibbits
Active Matter
Spring 2017

HOLD-UP: MACHINE DELAY IN ARCHITECTURAL DESIGN
Zachary Cohen
SMArchS Thesis
Advisor: Mark Jarzombek
Spring 2018

This thesis introduces an architectural design approach that is founded on working with digital fabrication machines, materials, and time: Machine Delay Fabrication (MDFab). MDFab is characterized by the materialization and manipulation of the time taken by digital fabrication machines to do work. MDFab contrasts with other approaches to digital fabrication that architecture has appropriated from other fields such as human-computer interaction and automated manufacturing. In particular, MDFab is a response to real-time digital fabrication techniques which use embedded sensing to immediately interact with the designer, material, or environment. These techniques have negatively distanced architectural designers from material, temporal, and instrumental understanding. Further, the current dependence on real-time points to a future of anti-anticipation: a time in which architectural designers and human beings will not have to anticipate what will happen next. MDFab is an alternative to this future: it offers a designer-machine symbiosis that advances the material thinking, improvisation, and speculation that are and should always be fundamental to the architectural design process.

Digital fabrication machines are moving from studios and labs to homes and construction sites. As a result, architectural designers need to cultivate ways of interacting with digital fabrication machines that maintain the vitality of their discipline yet can also evolve to produce novel forms of architectural practice. MDFab is a platform for this kind of new design thinking. It aims for a future in which architectural design remains in place, in touch, and, above all, in time.

DISTRIBUTED STRUCTURES: DIGITAL TOOLS FOR COLLECTIVE DESIGN
Caitlin Mueller
Architectural Design: Autonomous Assembly
Summer 2017

STRUCTURAL LATTICE ADDITIVE MANUFACTURING
Mitchell Gu, Yijiang Huang, Caitlin Mueller
SM Research, Building Technology
Fall 2015

The structural performance of traditional 3D-printed parts is typically limited by the nature of layer-by-layer construction. Such parts are anisotropic due to decreased adhesion between layers; the internal structure is uniform, not flexible. This project seeks to overcome these limitations by printing along the edges of a stress-optimized lattice. With this approach, larger-scale, lightweight parts can be printed with an optimal structure that can vary depending on a loading configuration. The fabrication component of the project includes designing a custom extruder for a six-axis robotic arm that excels in printing along hard-to-reach toolpaths in free air with larger nozzle diameters. To complement this technology, a computational tool is in development to generate lattices and toolpaths for any part and its loading configuration.

ROBOTIC EXTRUSION OF ARCHITECTURAL STRUCTURES WITH NONSTANDARD TOPOLOGY
Josephine Carstensen, Yijiang Huang, Caitlin Mueller, Lavender Tessmer
PhD Research, Building Technology
Fall 2018

This project presents a fast and flexible method for robotic extrusion (or spatial 3D printing) of designs made of linear elements that are connected in non-standard, irregular, and complex topologies. Nonstandard topology has considerable potential in design, both for visual effect and material efficiency, but presents serious challenges for robotic assembly since repeating motions cannot be used. Powered by a new automatic motion planning framework called Choreo, this project's robotic extrusion process avoids human intervention for steps that are typically arduous and tedious in. The assembly sequence, end effector pose, joint configuration, and transition trajectory are generated automatically using state-of-the-art, open-source planning algorithms developed in the robotics community.

COMPUTATIONAL STRUCTURAL OPTIMIZATION AND DIGITAL FABRICATION OF TIMBER BEAMS
Paul Mayencourt, Caitlin Mueller
PhD Research, Building Technology
Fall 2018

Structural optimization techniques offer means to design efficient structures and reduce their impact on the environment by saving material quantities. However, until very recently, the resulting geometrical complexity of an optimized structural design was costly and difficult to build. Today, fabrication processes such as 3D printing and computer numeric control (CNC) machining in the construction industry reduces the complexity to produce complex shapes.

This research aims to combine computational structural optimization and digital fabrication tools to create a new timber architecture. A key opportunity for material savings in buildings lies in ubiquitous structural components in bending, especially in beams. This research explores old and new techniques for shaping structural timber beams.

DECODING DETAILS
Inés Ariza
SMArchS Computation Thesis
Advisor: Caitlin Mueller
Spring 2016

Architecture is intrinsically the coordination of parts to form a whole, and the detail is the critical point where this coordination is resolved. Between technical and perceptual constraints, details are geometrical solutions and organizational devices that negotiate physics, construction, assembly, materials, fabrication, economy, and aesthetics, all at once. In the era of digital design and fabrication, where material and building information can be parametrically linked and massively computed, can we challenge what we can build with a new way of looking at details?

This thesis introduces the concept of synced detailing, where conflicting constraints are resolved in the details. As a case study, stability and assembly are studied on a structurally challenging discretized funicular funnel shell. The goal is to eliminate scaffolding during assembly using only joint details. Finite element analysis is performed at every step of the assembly sequence to show global and local instability. Local translation freedom analysis shows the range of feasible assembly directions. This knowledge is studied and encoded in rules. Real time visual feedback of the constraints informs the designer on how to apply these rules to create joints that satisfy a range of priorities. This method is generalizable for other constraints, allowing architects to create novel solutions informed by quantifiable analysis and encoded knowledge.

PERIPHERAL TIMBER: APPLICATIONS FOR WASTE WOOD MATERIAL IN EXTREME CLIMATES
Andrew Brose
SMArchS Building Technology Thesis
Advisor: John Ochsendorf
Spring 2018

Worldwide, discarded construction and demolition material account for forty percent of all municipal solid refuse in residential, commercial, institutional, and agricultural waste flows. Hong Kong sends over two hundred tons of timber waste from old formwork and scaffolding to landfills per day. After fulfilling their assumed raison d'être, the cement-flaked shuttering boards and stubby scaffolding poles arrive amongst other discards, left aside to rot in the rain and mud; they warp, split, and crack over time beyond utility.

This thesis explores the possibilities of reusing wood that sits at the fringes of construction projects in applications that bring back the beauty and elegance engrained in the oldest of building materials. This project is a remolding of the perception of undervalued wood species and construction waste. It proposes specific techniques to imbue discarded wood material with value and suggests a new mechanism for material production.

The study tests solutions for natural fiber composites and timber space-frame roofs for affordable housing projects. Prototypes in India include a space-frame using small diameter wood elements, made practical by the development of a simple joint system, and cementitious wall and roof panels incorporating waste wood fibers to improve thermal insulation properties while increasing flexural strength.

THE BAJA WINERY: ARCHITECTURE IN TIMES OF DROUGHT
Core 3 Studio
Instructors: Fall 2016: Sheila Kennedy, Alex Anmahian, Carlos Bañon; Fall 2017: Sheila Kennedy, Mariana Ibañez, Rami el Samahy

In Core 3, the final semester of the graduate core studio sequence, students create and develop design projects that integrate building technology, material logics, and climate considerations. Architectural programs in Core 3 engage the space of production and explore the use of resources and the agency of architecture within the changing cultural spectrum of nature and the built environment.

The studio focuses on the architectural design problem of a winery in the Valle de Guadalupe in Baja, Mexico, a region impacted by drought and climate change. The studio travels to the Valle to listen to local voices in winemaking, document sites, and research material resources. Hailed in 2014 as one of the top ten international wine destinations, the Valle de Guadalupe embodies a longstanding experimental tradition of mixing grape varietals and creating wine hybrids that have flourished in the arid soils of the region's small vineyards. The new prominence of the Valle brings a set of questions and competing visons for the scale of future development in the region, the role of architecture and brand in an increasingly global wine industry, and the relationships of public space, tourism, and regional identity. The plot thickens with the functional imperatives of wine production which are embedded in the persistent realities of a Newtonian world. Grapes are wet and heavy; they smell. They must be accessed, harvested, moved, crushed, mixed, fermented, and stored within very specific temperature ranges and thermal conditions. Students explore the architecture of the winery as a platform for design research that questions, defines, and takes a position on these matters of concern.

The Core 3 studio is co-taught with the Building Technology Structures course which focuses on the selection, behavior, and performance of advanced structural systems and architectural envelope assemblies. Students develop a carbon argument for their choice of building materials and construction systems and investigate how technical and design considerations of structure, enclosure, daylighting, ventilation, and climate design are synthesized in an architectural design concept that is coordinated across scales. Through digital and analog analysis, detailed architectural drawings, and large-scale models and architectural prototypes, the work of the studio unfolds in a non-linear, iterative design process of ideation, testing, and discovery.

OUROBOROS WINERY
Mackenzie Muhonen
Fall 2016

The myth of the Ouroboros gives expression to the cycles of nature. It is creation out of destruction, life out of death. Ouroboros is both emblem and protagonist of this winery, harnessing the "undesirable" moments of production. The winery celebrates the waste, or dead derivatives, of wine making and proceeds as a series of sweeping, catenary vaults generated from the building's excavated footprint that stretch across the site, swinging upwards to transform into chambers. Five chambers distill the moments of waste generation. They are the centerpieces of the winery. Outputs of production are shifted to the foreground in the five chambers. The remaining, traditionally celebrated moments of wine making are pushed to the background, housed within the vaults.

The first chamber utilizes porous brick to exaggerate the olfactory and somatosensory experience of grape intake. The "visual" brick and its orientation allow for grapes to be pushed through the wall for intake and initial crushing. The second chamber, a lab for experimenting with the waste products of winemaking, emphasizes the sensorial effects of turning waste into fertilizer. The third leverages the varied temperatures embedded in the fermentation process to create a condensation room. The fourth contains a basin of pomace. Whistle bricks draw in the wind. As the chamber aerates, the wall sings, creating an auditory experience of the composting process. The final chamber, storage, contains the most valuable, aging wines. Tasting bricks pop out of the chamber walls to hold the bottles. The patterning of these bricks—creating a "hairy" wall—muffles sound to create a quiet chamber.

The five chambers challenge the paradigmatic composition of the contemporary winery, designed with the visitor in mind. They realize the mythical cyclicality of the Ouroboros, positioning waste at the heart of a consumption process.

WANDERLUST AND INTOXICATION: A WINERY OF ATMOSPHERES
Jung In Seo
Fall 2017

In the Baja region, the culture of tourism is shifting from a desire for conspicuous consumption to a desire for experience. The rise of a local wine harvest festival Fiestas de la Vendimia is a testament to this change. This project proposes a social condenser that celebrates experiential abundance rather than material abundance to help the region transition from its current extractive economy to a more sustainable economy of experience.

The primary goal of this project is to create a diversity of architectural experiences and atmospheres using a minimal amount of materials. Glass fiber reinforced concrete (GFRC) is sprayed onto a flexible fabric. Unlike conventional rigid formwork, the form of the fabric can be parametrically varied while maintaining a simple and materially efficient construction. Three framework typologies (point based, line based, and frame based), combined with the fabric conditions (tight and loose) create undulating thin-shell structures. The foundation rings closely follow the undulation of the shell structure above and keep the recesses thermally conditioned with radiant cooling and heating. This produces thermal, haptic experiences, encouraging people to touch and rest on the warm or cool surfaces. Using the tops of recycled wine bottles as light guides embedded in the shell structures, different gradations of translucent concrete can be achieved. Depending on the time of day and the season, the shell may take on various atmospheric characters and interact with the light in austere or exuberant ways.

The project seeks to produce an abundance of spatial conditions through which visitors of this winery can wander. Entering through the slit in the façade's curtain wall, visitors are dazzled by the play of light. Visitors stumble upon new spaces; they may venture into the light-filled restaurant, or into the darker fermentation rooms, then slip out into the outdoor courtyard guided by a breeze, and back into a cone-shaped banquet hall. Encouraged to rest in the recesses temporarily, or perhaps overnight, they are intoxicated by wine, conviviality, and space.

FOG RESERVOIR
Anne Graziano
Fall 2016

Fog Reservoir experiments with a material and emerging technology called the MIT Fog Harvesting Mesh. The finely woven metal textile improves efficiency by five hundred percent, significantly increasing the volume of potable water that can be collected from fog. The project addresses two core questions in relation to infrastructure: Can a technical infrastructure (a fog harvesting mesh) be designed in relation to geographical, social, and cultural contexts? Can it be leveraged to create a space of social exchange?

Two major geographical features characterize Valle de Guadalupe. The site receives a thick fog every morning off the Pacific Ocean. Secondly, the winery and neighborhoods line up thanks to a main road that connects Ensenada to the Valle. These two characteristics make way for two pivotal programmatic possibilities: the ability to harvest water from the abundance of fog in the region and the accessibility to this resource to mobilize a local sharing economy. Fog Reservoir, with its undulations, collects more than two thousand liters of potable water a day, more than twice what a linear composition might collect. This creates a public resource and access to clean water, and also has the capacity to support a cooperative winery that hosts three local vineyards, each one being able to experiment with and produce four hundred cases each year. In addition, the winery is designed to provide maximum shade throughout the day.

The project suggests a winery as a scalable and modular infrastructure to provide a shared resource: water. The lightweight, trussed tubular steel and rebar structure provides a common and locally sourced material and trade in the region. In this way, Fog Reservoir is a prototypical architecture that can populate the region to offer water, shade, and public space as resources.

TROGLODYTIC PRODUCTION
Adiel Benitez
Fall 2017

Water scarcity, logistical limitations, and a need to more efficiently manage resources all work to complicate the production of wine in the Valle de Guadalupe. This project responds to the regional and global infrastructures of the Valle, investigating the potentials for hyper-local construction strategies to facilitate the housing of wine production. The project explores techniques and methods of excavation and retention of earth to create an architectural language that is from and of the site.

The winery is envisioned as an extension of the existing rugged landscape, offering a constructed ground that acts as a canopy for the winery program. Many existing wineries in the region use passive design strategies to make their wineries comfortable and efficient, such as embedding winery spaces that require thermal control into the landscape.

This project not only leverages excavation to facilitate thermally protected spaces critical for wine production; it also reuses the excavated earth as formwork. The main structure for the winery is a large earth concrete cast canopy, caston site over two large mounds formed using the earth excavated from the existing terrain. The shape of the mounds is structurally informed by form-finding studies that simulated both pure compression surfaces relaxed under gravity and joined hyperbolic paraboloid geometries. The top side of the canopy is shaped to allow for greater resonance with the existing rugged landscape. The canopy acts as a shading device during the hot months, allowing production to occur in open air, while a radiant flooring system heats occupied spaces during the cold months.

MCKNELLY MEGALITH
Sam Ghantous, Anastasia Hiller, Karen Kitayama, Dan Li, Hui Li, Patrick Little, Tengjia Liu, Ryan McLaughlin, Kaining Peng, Alexis Sablone, Luisel Zayas
Cross Studio: Megalithic Robotics
Instructors: Brandon Clifford, Mark Jarzombek; Carrie McKnelly
Spring 2016

Megalithic civilizations held tremendous knowledge about the deceivingly simple task of moving heavy objects. Much of this knowledge is lost to us. What if we could mine this past knowledge to inform contemporary practice with the tool of gravity? Anthropologist Carl Lipo recently discovered that (some of) the Rapa Nui Moai were not rolled from the quarry to the podium on their backs, but rather transported standing upright. The Moai were pulled back and forth by ropes, employing momentum to transport these unwieldy megaliths. This rediscovery brings new meaning to the folklore that the statues "walked themselves."

There is a great deal of speculation surrounding the artifacts created by our megalithic-era ancestors. Much of this is a result of marvel, wonder, intrigue, and most importantly ignorance. When one entertains that these civilizations held a focused knowledge surrounding weight, mass, and volume (topics we have since lost) these marvels transform from curious speculations into potentials for productive knowledge.

Megalith Robotics mines, extracts from, and experiments with this knowledge to test what applications and resonance it holds within contemporary digital practice. As an experiment, a sixteen-foot-tall megalith is designed, computed, and constructed to walk horizontally and stand vertically with little effort.

CYCLOPEAN CANNIBALISM
Matter Design: Brandon Clifford, Wes McGee, with Jim Durham, Quarra Stone
Fall 2017

Cyclops is described in Hesiod's *Theogony* as a race of giants, known for constructing massive stone walls. Cyclopean masonry consists of massive stones fit precisely together, despite their diverse sizes and shapes. Their assembly is so dramatic that it conjures myths of giants. Of the numerous civilizations that produced these megalithic stone works, the Inka constructed without a preconceived design. This architecture emerged through a sequential logic informed by the constraints of resources. The Inka stone works were computed. When materials were scarce, stones were adapted into new works. They consumed their own cities!

In today's urban context, we generate unprecedented quantities of waste. There is an impending crisis hinging on how we deal with this debris, specifically from buildings. In order to more intelligently reconsider the existing building stock, the profession could learn a great deal from cyclopean constructors. These methods force us to relinquish predetermined design composition in exchange for a systemic, intelligent design, capable of responding to unknown conditions. Cyclopean Cannibalism deciphers the Inka method and translates it into a possible contemporary method. Future cities demand a creative cannibalization of their accumulating debris and stagnating structures. Can urbanism of the near future be reimagined as architecturally self-sustaining? Can our future cities digest themselves?

Project
Graphics: Johanna Lobdell; Illustration: Joshua Longo; Structural: Caitlin Mueller; Research: James Addison, Daniel Marshall, Mackenzie Muhonen; Fabrication leads: Eric Kudrna, Alex Marshall, Ali Seyedahmadian, Brian Smith; Fabrication team: Ryan Askew, Eddie Banderas, Ramsey Bartlett, Frank Haufe, Jesse Kauppila; Acknowledgements: This research is funded by the Massachusetts Institute of Technology with support from the MIT Sloan Latin America Office, the MIT HASS Fund, and the Marion and Jasper Whiting Foundation.

UNMAKING ARCHITECTURE: HOLDING PATTERNS FOR MISFIT MATTER
Daniel Marshall
MArch Thesis
Advisor: Sheila Kennedy
Fall 2018

This project provides techniques for arranging materials after the demolition and unmaking of architecture. Rather than downcycling concrete into low value aggregate, melting float glass into opaque bottles, or grinding up street trees into mulch, methods are shown for this material to be indexed, re-machined, and re-arranged into new assemblies.

These assemblies are conceived of as holding patterns—an indexed library of materials that are put into useful architectural arrangements, ready to be disassembled for some future use. These holding patterns are tested on the infrastructural periphery of Berlin. For instance, the rubble from the current demolition of Plattenbau buildings in the post-coal mining cities around Berlin can be reconfigured to meet new housing demands. Irregular pieces of glass and the chaotic branches of felled street trees can be carefully fabricated into greenhouse and light manufacturing spaces.

While recycling is typically understood as a way to achieve stasis, the holding patterns become transitory monuments that construct an alternative trajectory. The project offers an imagination of constructions that can learn from the carcass of past buildings. 2014 marked the first year there were more tons of concrete than tons of living trees on the planet; perhaps it makes sense to develop new means of fitting misfit material rather than producing ever more.

STRUCTURES OF LANDSCAPE
Ensamble Studio: Antón García-Abril, Débora Mesa
Fall 2016

Located at the edge of Yellowstone Park in Montana, Tippet Rise Art Center is a new destination for the arts, in which music performances and large-scale outdoor sculptures play a major role. The coexistence of local fauna, ranching activity, and the added artistic and architectural interventions is a challenge that the project embraces. We look to primary elements to configure site-specific architectures in harmony with nature. Working with earth and rocks, and learning from their formation logic, we develop different techniques and processes to manipulate the structural, acoustic, and thermal properties of these local materials at different scales. We study and reinterpret geologic transformation processes such as sedimentation, erosion, weathering, crystallization, compaction, and metamorphism to cultivate structures made of and from landscape.

We develop structures that stir existing matter and reinforce it using highly engineered processes while welcoming unpredictable results. The created forms have been twinned with those taken from the land that previously contained and supported them when in state of rest; these forms retain the memory and imprint and introduce to it new meaning and tension. These are structures of landscape because they are born from it and give it order; they transform matter into inhabitable space and unfold a new constellation of programs among the plateaus, ridges, canyons, and hills of brutal beauty that compose the site.

Structures of Landscape enable habitation without exploitation. They resonate with the immensity, the roughness, the silence, and the magic loneliness of the place; they amplify its values, and situate our actions in an ambiguous position between nature, architecture, and art.

DESIGN-BUILD VILLAGE URBANISM IN HANGZHOU, CHINA
Zain Karsan, Wayne Liu, Xinyi Ma, Zhao Ma, Daniel Marshall, MyDung Nguyen, Jorge Silen Rivera, Chenxue Wang
Workshop
Instructors: Antón García-Abril, Adèle Naudé Santos, Wang Shu, Yao Zhang
Summer 2016

The MIT China Workshop is an ongoing collaboration between MIT students, students from the China Art Academy and South Eastern University, local governments, and craftspeople. In response to a need for public sanitation and civic facilities, the workshop produced four civic spaces in Hidden Dragon, a rural village in Guangxi. The design and fabrication of the four structures was informed by local construction traditions and a development plan that would preserve the scale and character of the village. Through discussions with local officials, the programming for the structures were determined to be: a marketplace, an entry plaza, and a parking structure, each including a public restroom and relevant facilities. Local master craftspeople provided workshops on bamboo, rammed earth, and masonry techniques, and students designed and built half and full-scale prototypes.

VILLAGES OF TOMORROW: NEW HOUSING MODELS FOR RURAL LANDS IN KIGALI, RWANDA
Monica Hutton, Mary Lynch-Lloyd, Ching Ying Ngan, Taeseop Shin, Maya Shopova, Danniely Staback, Daya Zhang
Workshop
Instructors: Andrew Brose, Rafi Segal
Summer 2017

Worldwide, as urban regions and populations grow, rural areas are often left behind, struggling to improve housing conditions, preserve local community, and maintain agricultural environments. In such a context, how may urban planners, designers, and architects improve village life through design? Can we promote village development plans and rural housing models that straddle modernity and technological advancement, while being rooted in vernacular typologies, local culture, and geography? Working within the context of Rwanda, the country of a thousand hills, this workshop explored new village house prototypes that built upon current construction practices, local crafts, and community needs while optimizing for climatic and spatial performance.

The workshop revolved around the collaboration of students with local communities and experts, such as engineers and masons, to understand vernacular design and construction mechanisms for local residences. Cultural values of local communities drove the solutions of housing typologies. Proposals included the development of three new house typologies, emphasizing the modularity of units; brick wall types that allow natural ventilation, reduced use of mortar, and flexible interior layouts; and semi-enclosed outdoor spaces.

Since the end of the workshop, which saw a partial building of a prototypical unit, the house was completed and is now occupied by a family from the village. Engagement with domestic partners continues, and the scope of the workshop has expanded to include a village master plan, on which work is currently ongoing.

Project
Collaborators: MIT-Africa, MIT-Tata Center, Rwandan Housing Authority. SKAT Consulting Ltd., Strawtec Company

COUNTERING INDEPENDENCE: ARCHITECTURE, DECOLONIZATION, AND THE DESIGN OF STABILITY IN BRITISH AFRICA (1945–1968)
Rixt Woudstra
Dissertation, History, Theory and Criticism
Advisor: Timothy Hyde

CHEMICAL DESIRES (1850–1937): MAKING THE ARCHITECTURAL MATERIALS OF MODERNITY
Jessica Varner
Dissertation, History, Theory and Criticism
Advisor: Mark Jarzombek

NUCLEAR OASIS: THE STORY OF TEN-THOUSAND-YEAR-OLD TRASH
Alexis Sablone
MArch Thesis
Advisor: Ana Miljački
Fall 2016

Each year, we produce nine thousand metric tons of high-level nuclear waste to add to the other two hundred and fifty thousand that have accumulated over the last few decades. While there are no clear plans for its permanent storage, one thing remains certain: it will outlive us all and everything we know. Current laws stipulate that permanent storage solutions must contain nuclear waste and its deadly radioactivity for ten thousand years—though other estimates say one hundred thousand is probably more accurate. We are now living in the Anthropocene—the self-proclaimed Age of Man. We have dubbed ourselves a "geological force," but we lack the ability to comprehend the implications of our actions at geological scales of time. Some may perceive this as a persistent form of recklessness. The challenge of nuclear waste directly confronts us with our own chronotopic inadequacies. Architecture is directly implicated here, challenged with the need for both a material and a meaningful permanence.

The architect is faced with an enormous expansion of concerns in quantity, but also an expanding scope of space and time in the Anthropocene. This chronotopic expansion pushes the domain of the architect outside the urban system and into what we might call the Earth system and, in doing so, calls for a recalibration of our sense of time. If our actions have made tangible, lasting effects at a geological scale, then we must reconsider the scope of our responsibilities and inquiries at a geological time-scale.

The issue of nuclear waste confronts us with a very real call for solutions at scales of time and space we don't yet know how to handle. In architecture, we've always operated inside potential futures. Today, the realm of those futures has expanded; it has been pushed beyond the brink of comprehension.

AN INTRODUCTION TO ACTIVE MATTER
Skylar Tibbits

If over the past half-century we have experienced a software and hardware revolution, we are now experiencing a true materials revolution. We can now sense, compute, and actuate with materials alone, just as one could previously with software and hardware platforms. It is becoming increasingly clear that materials are a platform for turning digital information into physical performance and functionality. If yesterday we programmed computers and machines, today we program matter itself.

At some point we will look back on our world of programming computers and machines as we do on the mainframe computers of the last century. Why did we define academic degrees or entire fields (e.g., "computer science" or "computer programming") tied to a fleeting tool like today's "computer" rather than to the process, the information, or the fundamental principles of programming? Why did we make such efforts to create disciplinary borders rather than creating connections by focusing on principles, systems, and phenomena? We are more interested in a new way of thinking about matter and a unique perspective for interacting with the world.

How did active matter emerge? We could go back to the history of computing with Ada Lovelace, Charles Babbage, or even the Jacquard loom as the implementation of mechanical computing for industrial production with a true material output. Or perhaps we could emphasize Turing, von Neumann, or any of the other incredibly important figures in computing. But it seems to make more sense to start at the beginning of the "digital" and its relationship to the physical. In 1937, Claude Shannon produced what has been described as one of the most influential master's theses of all time, in which he introduced the concept of Boolean logic for relays, digital logic eventually becoming the foundation of digital communication, electronics, and information theory. Since the subsequent invention of the transistor in 1947 (which has a strikingly material and "low-tech" physical presence), we have seen rapid developments in software and hardware technologies that introduced unprecedented changes across every discipline and industry and made digital computing ubiquitous in our everyday lives.

From Ivan Sutherland's first computer-aided design (CAD) tool in 1963 and the first computer numerically controlled (CNC) machine demonstrated by MIT's Servomechanisms Laboratory in 1952 to more contemporary software and fabrication platforms, we have become able to design, analyze, and physically fabricate in ways that were previously unimaginable. These new capabilities for computational design and fabrication have sparked a renaissance in the development of materials and performance.

The boom in material capabilities is visible in recent developments across many disciplines. The life sciences are making rapid advances with DNA sequencing and synthesis, genetic modification tools such as CRISPR, DNA computing, microbiome research, developments in tissue engineering, and the growing field of synthetic biology. New biomaterials, synthetic bio-functionality, DNA self-assembly, drug delivery mechanisms, and bioprinting are just a few of the recent capabilities to emerge. Materials science is similarly experiencing its own bustle of activity, from the discovery of graphene in 2010 to carbon nanotubes, directed self-assembly for material formation, granular jammable matter, invisibility cloaking, and a great deal more. At the macroscale we are seeing similar shifts. Some of the recent large-scale advances include multi-material printing with metal, ceramic, glass, rubber, and foams; printable electronics; 4D printing for customizable smart materials; reversible concrete-like structures with granular jamming; building-scale automated fabrication; printable wood; programmable carbon fiber; active textiles, and many others. As new computational and digital fabrication processes are emerging, novel material capabilities have become available.

In 2007, the Defense Advanced Research Projects Agency (DARPA) initiated a program called "Programmable Matter." Programmable matter is generally understood as a material that has the ability to perform information processing much like digital electronics. The DARPA program included researchers from many universities and disciplines. With a few exceptions, the research fell under the category of reconfigurable micro-robotics, or modular robotics: researchers developed smaller and smaller-scale robotic modules with embedded electronics, power, actuation, sensing, and communication that would enable a variety of physical transformations and other behaviors. In somewhat traditional DARPA fashion, this program was ahead of its time. The vision was clear, but the implementation at that point was far from the dream of programming matter in an elegant and seamless way. Small robots became the stand-in for "matter," but they were not just materials: they were accumulations of software and hardware devices. The sum was perhaps not yet more than its parts. However, the vision of programmable matter laid the groundwork for today's active matter.

Since this program, a number of developments in materials science, synthetic biology, and other domains have rapidly emerged that I believe have enabled a realization of programmable matter and more. Now, materials can not only be programmed to compute, but can physically transform and actively self-assemble into larger aggregations. These materials aren't modules that have chips and computers or batteries in them like their predecessors; these new materials are purely material. In this sense, active matter is more than just programming matter; it is about combining programmability, transformation, adaptation, and assembly.

How does active matter relate to smart materials? As an analogy, in the history of computing we have transformed the first calculators and single-function computers into today's general-purpose, programmable machines. Similarly, the field of active matter aims to create general-purpose, programmable, and physically-active materials. "Smart materials" or shape-memory materials also have the ability to change their property in a predetermined manner. However, active matter goes beyond today's smart materials that are only available in predetermined shapes, sizes, properties, and niche applications. Although smart materials and active matter both transform based on external inputs, active matter offers the freedom to design and create customized materials with unique functionalities to sense, actuate, assemble, or compute. Active matter makes it possible to make any material a smart material.

Matter has always been active, at least at a molecular level, yet our relationship with matter has traditionally been passive; at most, we have simply guided the growth and behavior of natural materials like bacteria, living cells, crystals, or wood. Or conversely, we have produced synthetic materials with fixed shapes and sizes to form all sorts of plasticized products—sculpting matter, rather than creating new types of matter, or reprogramming its fundamental behavior. We could compare our traditional relationship with materials to that of breeding animals or plants: we didn't change the fundamental properties or capabilities of the medium, rather we recombined species in a "black box" type of way to guide the formation of useful behaviors or traits. Our new model of programming matter can be seen in CRISPR, synthetic biology, and DNA computing, where we can change the structure, functionality, and information embedded within the medium to create new desired traits from the inside out.

A more surface-level understanding of the physical world tends to see materials as inert—as servants to our hammer and nail. Wood, a beautifully anisotropic and information-rich material, is turned into standardized lumber, as if it were a homogeneous material like plastic. However, we can redefine our relationship with matter. We can use the properties of the digital world now embedded in the physical world, such as logic, reprogrammability, reconfiguration, error correction, assembly, and disassembly. Or similar properties from the natural world can now be embedded in the synthetic world, like growth, repair, mutation, replication. These principles are now fundamentally available to read and write within matter itself.

How does the shift to active matter influence materials research? How will it create future products and industrial applications? What tools and design processes do we need to invent, augment, create, and discover new materials today? What are the galvanizing roles that industry, government, academia, and public institutions can play to catalyze and nurture the field of active matter? Addressing these questions requires the collaboration of researchers, scholars, practitioners, artists, and designers, providing unique perspectives, breakthroughs in research, evocative imagery, and emerging industrial applications of active matter.

This text is an excerpt adapted from the introduction to *Active Matter*, edited by Skylar Tibbits, (Cambridge, MA: MIT Press, 2017).

Images
P 90–91: Gramazio Kohler Research, ETH Zurich and the Self-Assembly Lab, MIT install "Rock Print," a 3D printed rock installation in the inaugural Chicago Architecture Biennial 2015 (October 3, 2015–January 3, 2016).
P 92–93: Rapid Liquid Printing, a collaboration between the Self-Assembly Lab, Christophe Guberan, and Steelcase. Rapid Liquid Printing physically draws in 3D space within a gel suspension, and enables the creation of large-scale, customized products made of real-world materials. Compared with other techniques we believe this is the first development to combine industrial materials with extremely fast print speeds in a precisely controlled process to yield large-scale products.

Project
Rock Print Team: Fabio Gramazio, Matthias Kohler, Skylar Tibbits, Andreas Thoma (project lead installation), Petrus Aejmelaeus-Lindstroem (project lead research), Volker Helm, Sara Falcone, Lina Kara'in, Michael Lyrenmann, George Varnavides, Jared Laucks, Carrie McKnelly, Stephane de Weck, Jan Willmann; Selected experts: Prof. Dr. Hans J. Herrmann and Dr. Falk K. Wittel (ETH Zurich), Prof. Heinrich Jaeger and Kieran Murphy (Chicago University) Selected consultants: Walt + Galmarini AG; Support: The project is supported by ETH Zurich and the Department of Architecture as well as by an ETH Zurich Research Grant. It is co-supported by MIT's Department of Architecture, the MIT International Design Center, and an MIT International Science and Technology Initiative (MISTI) Grant.

Rapid Liquid Printing: Self-Assembly Lab Team: Kate Hajash, Bjorn Sparrman, Mattis Koh, Schendy Kernizan, Jared Laucks & Skylar Tibbits in collaboration with Christophe Guberan; Steelcase Team: Yuka Hiyoshi, Rob Poel, Markus McKenna, Paul Noll, Sharon Tracy, Edward Vander Bilt, Chris Norman, and Charlie Forslund.

91

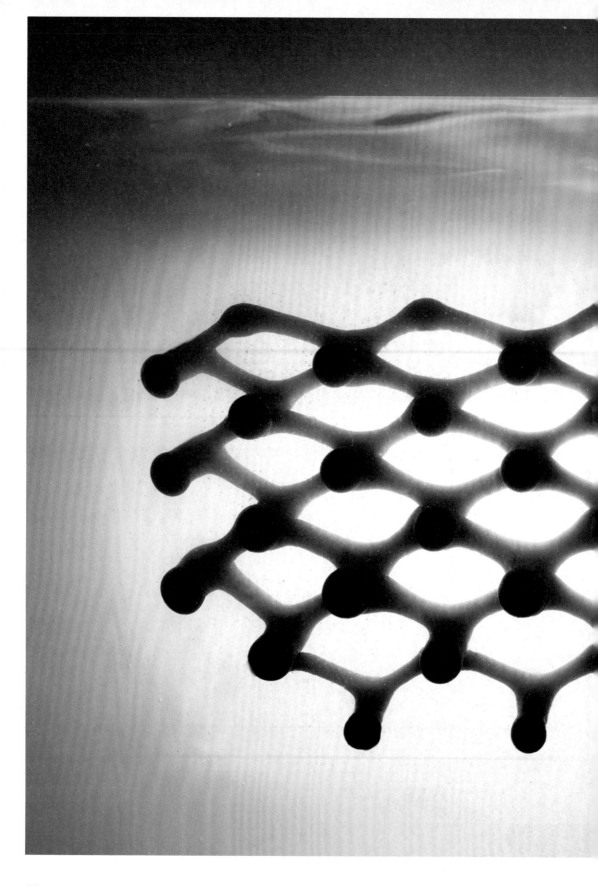

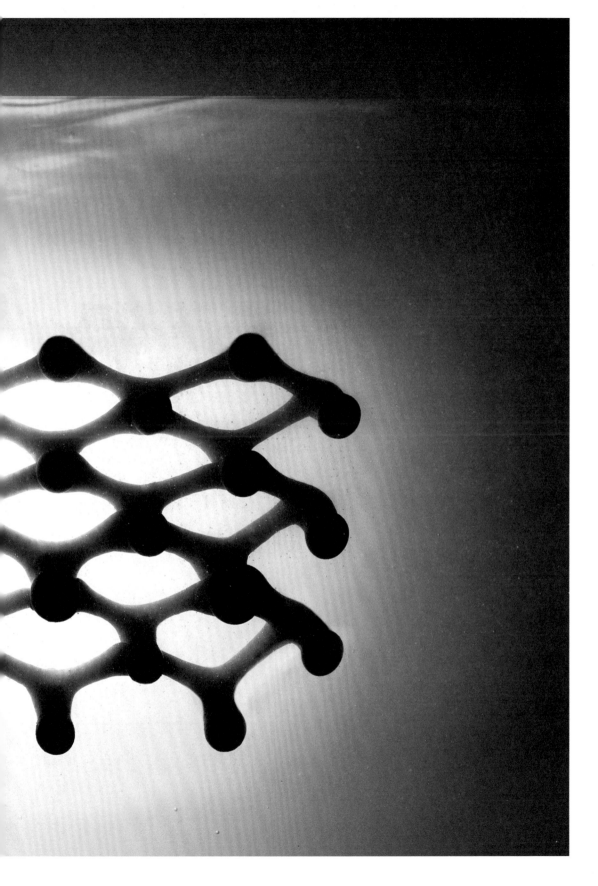

DISTRIBUTED STRUCTURES: DIGITAL TOOLS FOR COLLECTIVE DESIGN
Caitlin Mueller

As the use of computation for architectural design shifts from representation and analysis to the generative and synthetic, new opportunities emerge to link the creative exploration of geometry with technical aspirations such as lightness, stiffness, and performance. The work presented here, developed by the Digital Structures research group, demonstrates new digital strategies that address this potential, empowering designers to incorporate structural and fabrication logic and data into flexible, open-ended conceptual design processes. With this transformative computational power, it is possible to find forms and material distributions that are undiscoverable through conventional methods, and that respond to a plurality of design goals with precision and balance. Critically, these new techniques allow for a convergence and collaboration between human-and computer-driven design modes, collectively escaping the confines of singular, top-down methods.

Structural Optimization and Its Limits
As part of their 1972 Louvre exhibition *What Is Design?*, Charles and Ray Eames included the following in a series of questions and answers:

> Q: Ought form to derive from the analysis of function?
> A: The great risk here is that the analysis may be incomplete.[1]

The risk here is indeed great: in all but the narrowest of engineering problems, the complexities, interdependencies, and serendipities of design strongly resist complete description in the formal language of logical or mathematical analysis. In architectural design, many of the most important goals, priorities, or even functions are qualitative in nature, and can only crudely be approximated through numerical evaluation. An analysis of function may also prove elusive because not all function is known a priori: the act of design itself can be seen as a discovery of one's own competing aspirations for a project and how to best balance them. Finally, the notion that design can be a purely rational process eliminates the designer and a sense of humanistic agency, ignoring the cultural, contextual, personal, and subjective influences that are clear in history's best works.

Perhaps this recognition—that form can never perfectly follow from function—is the reason why optimization tools and algorithms have had only the slightest impact on the disciplines of creative design, including architecture. Embraced by neighboring fields such as aerospace, automotive, and mechanical engineering, optimization offers a systematic, rigorous approach to finding the best solution to a problem formulated with quantitative objectives, design variables, and constraints. Especially in the domain of structures, scholars since Galileo have explored how optimization methods can be used to shape the lightest beam or derive the most efficient truss.[2] The most compelling work in this field exploits the critical relationship between geometric form and structural behavior, and it is clear that in optimization there exists promising yet untapped potential for architecture.

A key to reconciling the open-ended nature of design with the opportunities of data-driven optimization is the acknowledgment that while an analysis of function may be incomplete, it is nevertheless still relevant to the derivation of form. When quantitative performance information is available early in the design process, it need not drag us to a singular solution, but may instead assist us in mapping out collective possibilities that we can examine with additional qualitative measures of assessment in mind. In many cases, while a single solution may exist that minimizes an objective such as structural weight, a panoply of options can also be found that use only slightly more material and may represent the best synthesis of a more holistic set of design goals.

Today's design computation landscape offers unprecedented means to access and play with the techniques of structural optimization in non-deterministic, non-reductionist ways. The ongoing work of the Digital Structures group illustrates several emerging research directions aimed at empowering architectural designers to discover new structures distributed across the design space of possibilities.

Digital Brainstorming
In the earliest stages of design conception, when confronted by a blank page or an empty screen, designers are limited only by imagination. The broader the range of possible design concepts generated through brainstorming, the greater the freedom, flexibility, and quality of design choice. Such early-stage design decisions are extremely important: it is much easier to develop a well-chosen concept into a fully fleshed design than to incrementally evolve an uninspired or poorly performing choice out of mediocrity.

Even in the age of computers, brainstorming has traditionally been an analog process, completed before moving a design into a digital CAD environment for further development, and perhaps drawing on a designer's personal context of precedents, references, history, and previous work. However, digital tools can complement these processes in surprising and effective ways, shifting the role of computation from representation and rote analysis to creative idea generation. One example of this is the web-based design tool structureFIT, developed by the Digital Structures group for the exploration of two-dimensional trusses.

Using structureFIT, a range of design alternatives can be generated, ranging from obvious, geometrically regular solutions, to least-weight solutions, with many possibilities in between. In all cases, the design options are produced collaboratively by a human designer and the digital tool, which uses an interactive evolutionary algorithm. This brainstorming process reveals that improving structural performance does not strictly limit design freedom, and that many possible structures exist that can be both efficient and more broadly responsive to a range of design goals.[3]

The interactive evolutionary algorithm of structureFIT is repeated in a second Digital Structures tool, Stormcloud, a flexible plug-in for the Rhino and Grasshopper modeling and parametric design environment. Mimicking the process of natural selection in biology, populations of design alternatives are generated. A diverse set of options that perform well structurally is chosen and displayed to users, who make their selections based on preferences un-encoded in the algorithm. These selected designs are then combined and randomly mutated to produce a new population of options for users to consider, and the process repeats until they are satisfied. Stormcloud is flexible and can work with any type of parametric geometry and any type of quantitative analysis, extending its applicability beyond the purely structural. In contrast to black-box optimization tools, it assists designers in creating varied catalogs of high-performing possibilities that they may not have thought of themselves.

When it is crucial that the catalog of options be as diverse as possible, a parametric design space, which combinatorially predefines all of the designs it contains, can sometimes be limiting. An alternative approach, based on grammars of design rules that can be applied iteratively, recursively, and in any order, can greatly expand the breadth of designs to explore. Digital Structures has explored this approach for the design of a pedestrian bridge, randomly generating hundreds of highly varied options using a single structurally informed grammar with seventeen rules.[4] The space of possibilities contains many surprising alternatives that can be instantly suggested to designers, all of which are at least structurally feasible and may lead to new design typologies and forms.

Balance, Compromise, Constraints

In many architectural design problems, a multiplicity of goals and considerations is important, competing or trading off with each other in complex ways and belying the contemporary division of labor and disciplines. For example, the theoretically lightest structure may be very difficult to construct, or may result in a building with significant energy consumption. Conversely, the most energy-efficient shape may be far from an optimized structural form. A design process that is integrated, holistic, and synthetic thus often requires compromise.

The field of multi-objective optimization offers strategies to model and understand the relationships between design priorities. Instead of solving for a single best design, these methods provide ways in which designers may exert preferences concerning different objectives during the optimization process. They may involve live interaction with performance feedback, guided optimizations with user-articulated preferences, or discovering a set of designs, collectively called the Pareto frontier, which are most responsive to opposing goals and cannot be improved in terms of one objective without worsening in terms of another.[5]

This concept has been applied to architecture in several Digital Structures projects. In one example, variations on a shell roof structure are explored with two quantitative objectives: the reduction of structural material and minimization of operational energy. These goals represent a trade-off: a taller, more doubly curved structural shape is more materially efficient, but entails a larger surface area and volume of air to condition.[6] Here, the catalog of Pareto optimal solutions presents designers with a choice of how best to balance this trade-off, and to inject the additional influence of important yet unquantifiable design preferences. A second project considers the design of irregular braced frame geometries that resist wind and seismic loads in tall buildings. In this case, a goal of structural efficiency is considered against the constraints of construction. The set of presented design alternatives demonstrate that many of the preferences for constructibility, such as reducing variation in member sizes or constraining angles in node geometries, trade off with structural performance.[7] While there may not be a perfect solution that best meets all singular design goals, digital strategies that facilitate multi-objective performance feedback or identify design options along the Pareto front can help designers discover the best ways to balance and synthesize varied disciplinary concerns.

Data-Driven Frontiers

Thanks to the abundant enthusiasm of iterative and looping computer algorithms, digital design tools focused on brainstorming and catalog building can produce mammoth sets of design possibilities. This presents challenges and opportunities to borrow from fields like statistics and machine learning to tame, organize, and understand the newly possible big data of design. Data-driven algorithms already suggest options for us in music streaming and online shopping; can we also harness the power of data science for the design of architecture?

There are many potential applications to be explored and discovered in this emerging field. One example is surrogate modeling, a methodology that uses machine-learning techniques to approximate slow computer simulations of phenomena such as structural behavior, energy performance, or crowd movement with instantaneous predictive models.[8] This can help push the role of technical assessment from checking a near-finalized design to an early-stage decision-making aid. A second promising technique uses statistical data clustering to organize a set of thousands of design alternatives into just a few meaningfully distinct design families.[9] This reduces the exhaustiveness of a design catalog and helps designers understand global patterns.

Materializing Structurally Driven Complexity

The potential of digital design tools is ignited by developments in the parallel field of digital fabrication, where new techniques for making are unprecedentedly agnostic to geometric complexity. This benefits not only formal exploration for its own sake, but also a design process influenced by structural logics. Many geometries that perform well structurally do so because their shapes reflect the complex curvatures of physics.

For example, with additive manufacturing techniques like fused deposition modeling (FDM), it is possible to distribute material precisely along a structure's stress lines, trajectories that follow a normally invisible flow of forces. However, as these exciting manufacturing technologies expand from the prototype scale to end-use, full-scale buildings, it is important to understand their effect on the mechanics of produced results. Layer-based techniques like FDM often lead to significant anisotropy in material strength, producing a wood-like grain that is much stronger in one direction than another. Just as we have learned to control for this behavior when building with trees, rethinking digital materialization processes from a structural perspective can lead to new possibilities. For example, FDM can be transformed from layer-based to spatial with industrial robotic arms, so that material is extruded along three-dimensional paths that can better transfer forces. To test out this idea, Digital Structures designed and fabricated a lattice structure produced by such a process. Its irregular geometry comes from an exploration of structural performance, making it twenty-five percent stiffer than a conventionally shaped version. Such examples demonstrate that we are increasingly digitally equipped to shape the architectural forms of tomorrow with precision and nuance in response to the myriad concerns of design.

"Distributed Structures: Digital Tools for Collective Design" was first published in *Architectural Design* 87, no. 4 (July/August 2017): 94–103, https://doi.org/10.1002/ad.2201. © 2017 John Wiley & Sons Ltd.

1   Charles and Ray Eames, "Design Q&A Text": www.eamesoffice.com/the-work/design-q-a-text/.
2   Stephen P. Timoshenko, *History of Strength of Materials* (New York: Dover, 1953), 14.
3   Caitlin T. Mueller and John A. Ochsendorf, "Combining Structural Performance and Designer Preferences in Evolutionary Design Space Exploration," *Automation in Construction* 52 (April 2015): 70–82.
4   Caitlin T. Mueller, *Computational Exploration of the Structural Design Space*, PhD Dissertation, Massachusetts Institute of Technology (MIT), Cambridge, MA, 2014: http://hdl.handle.net/1721.1/91293.
5   Jürgen Branke, Kalyanmoy Deb, Kaisa Miettinen and Roman Slowinski, eds., *Multiobjective Optimization: Interactive and Evolutionary Approaches*, (Berlin: Springer, 2008).
6   Nathan C. Brown and Caitlin T. Mueller, "Design for Structural and Energy Performance of Long Span Buildings Using Geometric Multi-Objective Optimization," *Energy and Buildings* 127 (September 2016): 748–61.
7   Abbigayle Horn, *Integrating Constructability into Conceptual Structural Design and Optimization*, MEng Thesis, MIT, Cambridge, MA, 2015: http://hdl.handle.net/1721.1/99598.
8   Stavros Tseranidis, Nathan C. Brown and Caitlin T. Mueller, "Data-driven Approximation Algorithms for Rapid Performance Evaluation and Optimization of Civil Structures," *Automation in Construction* 72, Part 3 (December 2016): 279–93.
9   Caitlin T. Mueller, *High-dimensional Design Space Visualization for Conceptual Structural Design*, SM Thesis, MIT, Cambridge, MA, 2014: http://hdl.handle.net/1721.1/90083.

STRUCTURAL LATTICE ADDITIVE MANUFACTURING
Mitchell Gu, Yijiang Huang, Caitlin Mueller

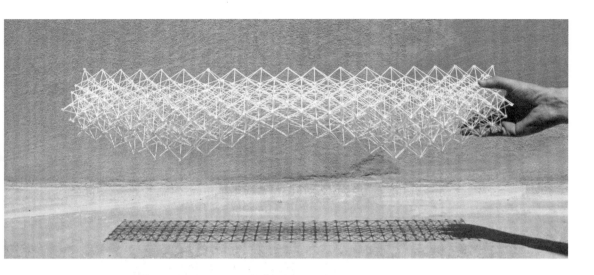

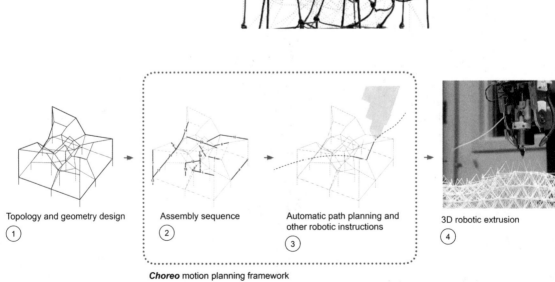

Topology and geometry design	Assembly sequence	Automatic path planning and other robotic instructions	3D robotic extrusion
①	②	③	④

Choreo motion planning framework

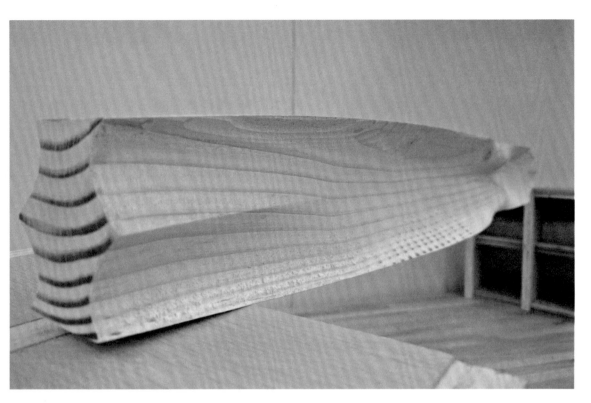

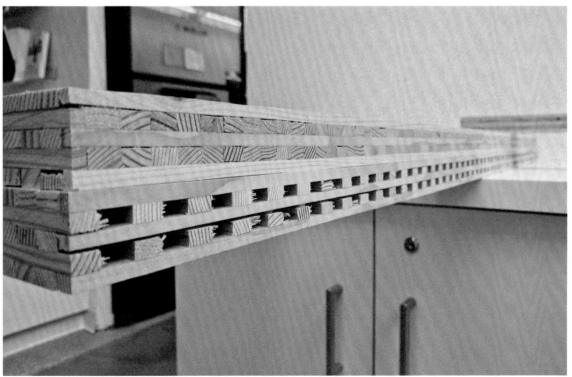

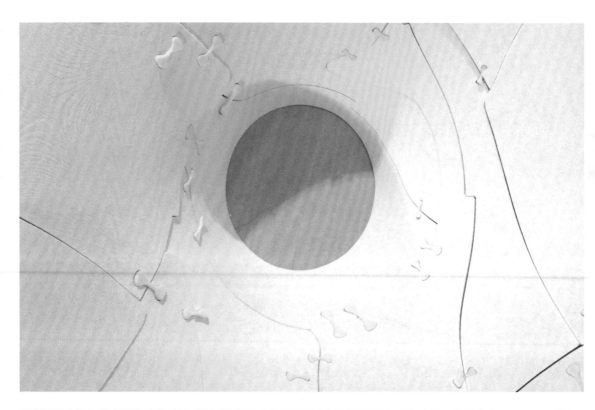

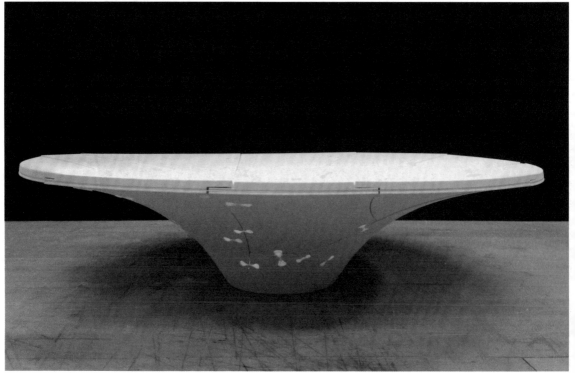

Questions of materiality in architecture have been largely transparent in practice, in that we tend to think more, or first, about other issues than choices of material.

The materials that make up our environment are assumed to be neutral, inert, and available for us to assemble and organize as the given "stuff" out of which the built environment is designed and constructed.

If materials are accorded a "vibrant" active agency as they persist in our environment, creating unexpected chemical, atmospheric, and physical consequences, then what can be our role as architects in selecting and organizing them?

Sheila Kennedy

THE BAJA WINERY: ARCHITECTURE IN TIMES OF DROUGHT

Alex Anmahian, Carlos Bañon, Mariana Ibañez, Sheila Kennedy, Rami el Samahy

In this first design exercise, Carbon Arguments, students collaborate in teams to explore the idea of *resource* at multiple scales and levels of meaning. Resource can be defined as a supply of building construction materials and natural assets, a strategy for design choices that enable architectural agency, and a speculative exploration of design delivery strategies for the architectural implementation of a winery in the Valle de Guadalupe.

The rugged topography and rural location of the site in this unevenly developed region of Mexico confound the normative ways in which architecture is typically conceived, designed, and produced, both in the academy and in the profession. It might be possible to say of our site: "There's nothing there." But this would not be accurate. Resources for building materials in the region are rich and diverse, encompassing high-tech digital fabrication in the Port of Ensenada and older traditions of local craftsmanship. This problem of resource requires the architect to be resourceful in conditions of apparent scarcity. The architect needs to research (to look again, with new eyes) what resources may already exist on-site (material, cultural, economic, ecological) and what resources may need to be imported or invented to meet the programmatic needs of the winery. The apparent barrenness of the Baja site topography can be utilized as a catalyst for architectural innovation. This requires the strategic use and inventive transformation of existing natural resources—daylight, gravity, topography, shade, earth, rock, and scarce water—and the formulation of an architectural position on the building scale and character of the winery within the larger cultural, socioeconomic, and political contexts of development in the Valle.

Through collaboration and discussion in, and among, our teams, our common goal in the first half of this short exercise is to research, interpret, and create representations of key matters of concern for the architecture of a winery in the Valle de Guadalupe. Students take into account the carbon footprint, or the embodied energy, of the primary resources that the winery project engages.

Teams consider five topics: analysis of the site and regional climate conditions and their daily and seasonal dynamics; analysis of the winery process and program elements and their possible organizations on the site; the choice of building materials and construction systems; whether or not material is from the Valle region or the Port of Ensenada, a growing high-tech innovation hub and short-sea shipping terminal, or further afield; regional economic drivers and growth patterns in the Valle winemaking industry, regional infrastructure, and logistics that serve the wine-making industry.

In the second half of this short exercise, the teams make a first foray in design research, which means that the research will be represented and demonstrated on disciplinary terms, through the vehicle of design in explorations of possible winery construction, massing, and site organizational concepts that can provoke and sustain architectural discussion and dialogue. Based upon the research findings, students create and propose wine labels, names, and brands; formulate a speculative architectural site massing model; circulation diagrams for three winery proposals; and explore how the architecture of these speculative proposals can embody a position toward the larger politics of global tourism and local identity in the region.

No winery proposal can be fully "sustainable" or ecologically "correct." Instead, the architect must take a position on how the carbon footprint of the winery is embodied and invested. One could equally well imagine a light, transient, and layered architecture with a low embodied energy or a massive and enduring architecture that amortizes its initial carbon investment over time.

OUROBOROS WINERY
Mackenzie Muhonen

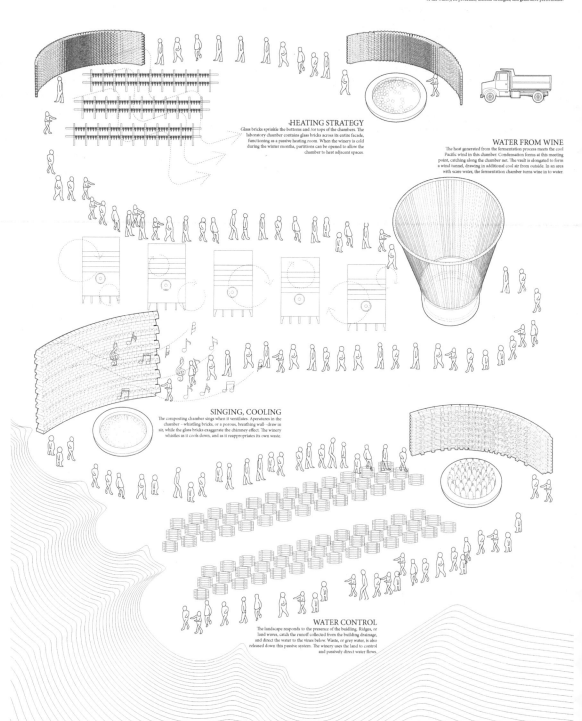

THE OUROBOROS EXPERIENCE

Ouroboros Winery winery celebrates the waste, or 'dead' derivatives, of wine making. It is both investigation and critique of the sustainable winery and its curated visitor tours. It displays the Newtonian realities of industrial, agricultural processes. Here is a walk-through of the winery, its processes, thermal strategies, and generative performance.

HEATING STRATEGY

Glass bricks sprinkle the bottoms and /or tops of the chambers. The laboratory chamber contains glass bricks across its entire facade, functioning as a passive heating room. When the winery is cold during the winter months, partitions can be opened to allow the chamber to heat adjacent spaces.

WATER FROM WINE

The heat generated from the fermentation process meets the cool Pacific wind in this chamber. Condensation forms at this meeting point, catching along the chamber net. The vault is elongated to form a wind tunnel, drawing in additional cool air from outside. In an area with scare water, the fermentation chamber turns wine in to water.

SINGING, COOLING

The composting chamber sings when it ventilates. Apertures in the chamber - whistling bricks, or a porous, breathing wall - draw in air, while the glass bricks exaggerate the chimney effect. The winery whistles as it cools down, and as it reappropriates its own waste.

WATER CONTROL

The landscape responds to the presence of the building. Ridges, or land waves, catch the runoff collected from the building drainage, and direct the water to the vines below. Waste, or grey water, is also released down this passive system. The winery uses the land to control and passively direct water flows.

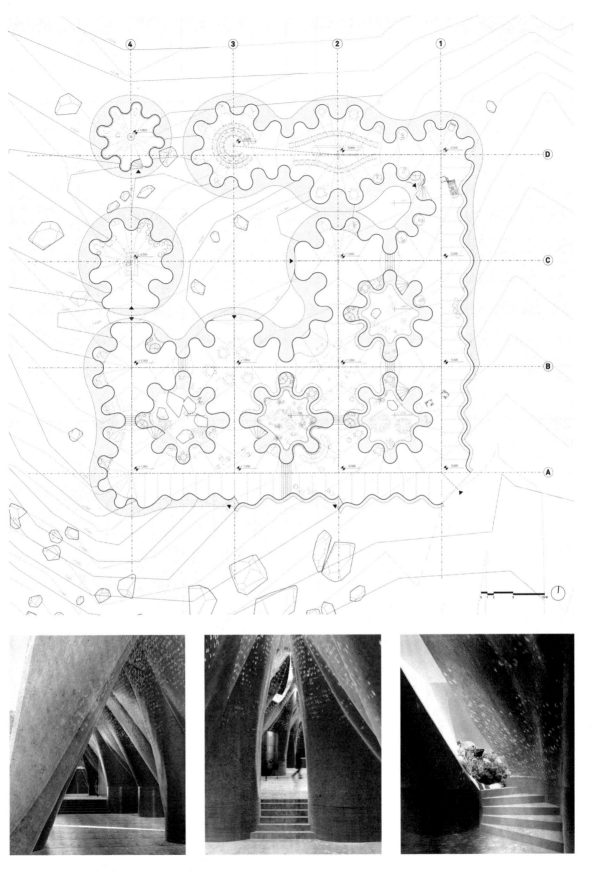

TROGLODYTIC PRODUCTION
Adiel Benitez

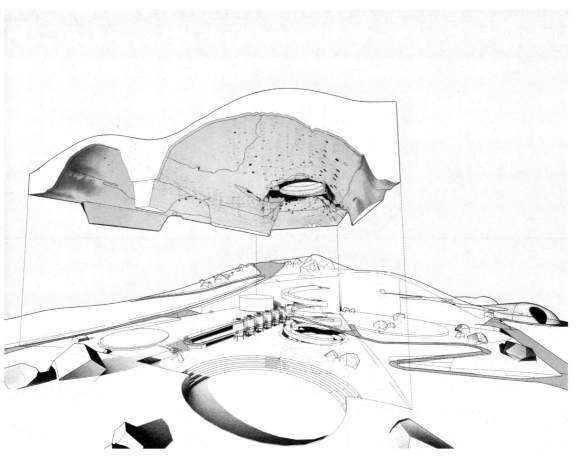

MCKNELLY MEGALITH

Sam Ghantous, Anastasia Hiller, Karen Kitayama, Dan Li, Hui Li, Patrick Little, Tengjia Liu, Ryan McLaughlin, Kaining Peng, Alexis Sablone, Luisel Zayas

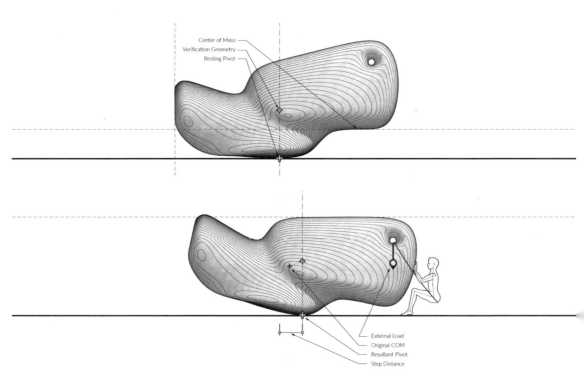

Center of Mass
Verification Geometry
Resting Pivot

External Load
Original COM
Resultant Pivot
Step Distance

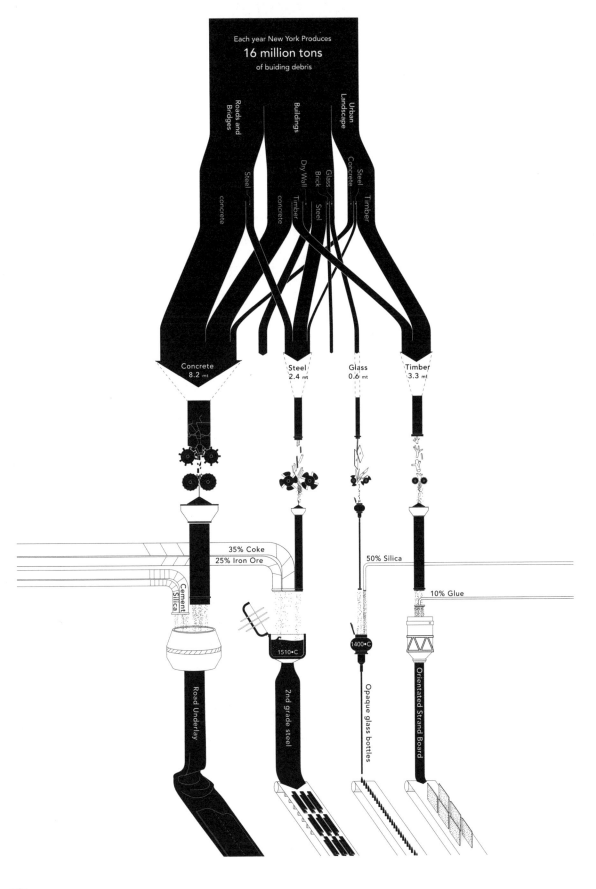

Each year New York Produces

16 million tons

of buiding debris

Roads and Bridges

Buildings

Urban Landscape

Steel

Dry Wall

Brick

Glass

Steel

Steel

Concrete

concrete

concrete

Timber

Glass

Timber

Concrete
8.2 mt

Steel
2.4 mt

Glass
0.6 mt

Timber
3.3 mt

35% Coke

25% Iron Ore

50% Silica

10% Glue

Cement

Silica

1510•C

1400•C

Road Underlay

2nd grade steel

Opaque glass bottles

Orientated Strand Board

DESIGN-BUILD VILLAGE URBANISM IN HANGZHOU, CHINA

Zain Karsan, Wayne Liu, Xinyi Ma, Zhao Ma, Daniel Marshall, MyDung Nguyen, Jorge Silen Rivera, Chenxue Wang

VILLAGES OF TOMORROW: NEW HOUSING MODELS FOR RURAL LANDS IN KIGALI, RWANDA
Monica Hutton, Mary Lynch Lloyd, Ching Ying Ngan, Taeseop Shin, Maya Shopova, Danniely Staback,
Daya Zhang

As part of efforts to reconstruct Rwanda's community ties and cultivate a shared national identity, the government drew on aspects of traditional practices to enrich and adapt its development programs to the country's needs and context.

Communities take part in a government mandated community service called *Umuganda*, a Kinyarwanda word that means "coming together in common purpose to achieve an outcome."

Close to eighty percent of Rwandans take part in monthly community work, including participating in major infrastructure. *Umuganda* inspired the implementation of the workshop.

Rafi Segal

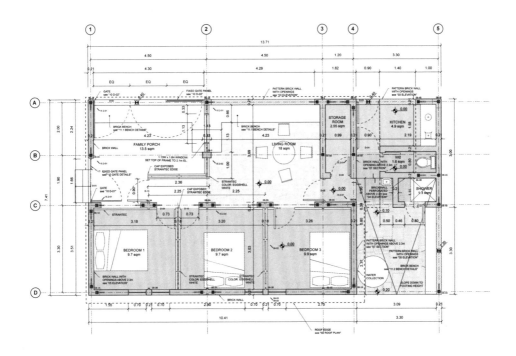

COUNTERING INDEPENDENCE: ARCHITECTURE, DECOLONIZATION, AND THE DESIGN OF STABILITY IN BRITISH AFRICA (1945–1968)
Rixt Woudstra

During the 1940s and 1950s, a time marked by the rise of anti-imperialist protests across Britain's prized colonial possessions, cities in British East Africa rapidly changed. For the first time, Kampala, Nairobi, and other cities saw the emergence of large-scale government-funded housing estates for African laborers. This research explores how architecture offered an instrument to counter— or postpone—the looming prospect of independence. During a time of political instability, housing estates—often built in conjunction with schools, cultural centers, and libraries—were used to settle migrant workers within the city. By attempting to develop "multi-racial" cities, British authorities purported to improve relation between races while creating a stable African working class. Yet assuming responsibility for housing allowed municipalities not only to control where people lived but also how people lived. I examine how, during the last two decades of colonial rule, modern housing became the center of a debate about race, citizenship, and social change.

My research investigates three interrelated architectural strategies that were employed to counter the social and political instability of the post-war period: the use of social surveys to better understand the dwelling needs of the African laborer— the *other*; the construction of schools and the design of "cultural centers" in conjunction with the housing estates to educate the African laborer in the rights and duties of democratic citizenship; and the experimentation with local building materials in order to improve the durability of the government-funded housing projects. The construction of housing estates for African laborers marked a significant shift: for the first time, African workers were allowed to legally settle within the boundaries of cities such as Kampala and Nairobi. The town, as architects of the 1948 development plan for Nairobi wrote, began "to look upon its African inhabitants as a municipal responsibility."[1] Before, laborers worked in the city on a temporary basis and were forced to leave their families behind in villages, or reserves. Anthropologists—often closely involved in the design of these estates and town plans—described this process of social and urban change as "stabilization": settling African laborers and their families in cities in order to create a more permanent labor force. Yet the process of stabilization, I argue, was also deployed as a mechanism to counter anti- imperialist sentiments. The provision of adequate housing would prevent further urban uprisings, administrators, anthropologists, and architects argued.

For architects and planners, housing African laborers and their families posed a range of new design questions: What did affordable urban housing for African laborers look like? More importantly, how could architectural form be deployed to educate African laborers in the "rights and duties" associated with democratic citizenship? What would the planning of "multi-racial" cities entail? Architects attempted to raise inhabitants' standard of living, but also produced modern ways of living through the European layout of the designs, built-in furniture, and picture books providing advice on modern household practices.

One of these projects was the Asawasi housing estate in Kumasi, a city in the Gold Coast (present-day Ghana). Designed by the British planner Alfred Alcock in 1945, the project offered affordable housing to African laborers through a rent-to-purchase scheme. Asawasi, planned as a neighborhood unit with a school, a community hall, and several shops, was one of the first projects in British Africa built with blocks consisting of rammed earth and cement. The method, developed by Alcock, spread across the British colonies and was adopted in various other government-funded housing projects. While the houses still primarily consisted of earth— one of the most common building materials in the Gold Coast—they were promoted as modern and durable designs. In Britain, housing projects like Asawasi were presented as an example of generous investment in the overseas territories. For example, a short film on the Asawasi estate, broadcasted in cinemas across Britain as part of the news from colonies, highlighted how Britain helped develop the Gold Coast. The film's name—*Houses that Last*— referred to the durable building materials used, but also underlined Britain's intentions: to prolong British presence in the profitable West African colony.

1   Thornton White, L. Silberman, and P.R. Anderson, *Nairobi: Master Plan for a Colonial Capital* (London: Government Printer, 1948), 5.

Image
P 131: Alfred Alcock, *The Experimental Housing Estate at Asawasi*, 1945. British National Archives CO96/781/1.

CHEMICAL DESIRES (1850–1937): MAKING THE ARCHITECTURAL MATERIALS OF MODERNITY
Jessica Varner

In the mid-nineteenth century, chemistry—the science of the properties, compositions, and mechanisms of organic and physical chemical systems—began to shape building materials during the Industrial Revolution's chemical turn. On-the-ground available materials like wood, stone, brick, and pigments were transformed, maintained, or replaced by factory-produced alternatives. Scientifically composite and chemically constituted, alkali cleaning products, coated timber, chemical additives, clear glass, and synthetic paints and dyes became common in the new modern palette. This chemical turn not only impacted the construction of architecture and its products on a global scale, but it also shifted architecture's global effects. At the scale needed for growing global consumer markets, chemical corporations became vital in building material markets.

While the change in material availability was substantial, equally significant was the revision in how all building materials were understood anew through the lens of chemistry. Discoveries and advancements of the period in chemical technologies such as spectroscopy and chemical classifications shifted how elements, old and new, were seen—scientifically, aesthetically, and through their performativity. In turn, new values formed around durability, decay, cleanliness, transparency, vividness, and economies of scale.

My research examines several of these chemical material value shifts, the corporations associated with them, and the resultant effects: vivid color at BASF, durability expectations at Monsanto, decay resistance at DuPont, increasing transparency in glass at Solvay, and standards of cleanliness at United Alkali. While these material values existed in prior building component assessments, they took on new meanings through the lens of chemical developments and their aesthetic and performative potential. In addition to demonstrating how chemicals became an essential element of modern architecture and of modernity itself, I also uncover how corporations embedded chemistry into a "desire economy," that embraced the imaginaries of the public and the professional, while also obscuring their negative environmental and social impact. In that context, I study the advertising campaigns that heralded the new age and the concurrent techniques corporations used to disguise the risks of their products. In a 1922 Monsanto advertisement, for example, two classical columns are positioned atop a stylobate of chemicals. The message is dramatic. No longer will architecture be built on granite. Instead, the new realities of glycerophosphates, acetylsalicylic acid, and Monsanto's new product Aroclor will constitute its foundation. The accompanying text explicitly calls these new materials "foundation stones." Meanwhile, in 1922, Monsanto moved across the Missouri River to Illinois, a state posturing for the economic gains of toxic materials, to a site ready for the risks of heavy chemical production. The foundation for the new era was built on both making and unmaking the world through chemicals.

Critically, the materials, sites, people, and corporations are chosen at points in the chemical turn when material development balanced between production and consumption, and environmental and social impacts. These include growing scientific knowledge, newly constructed consumer networks, new chemical methods of production, and consumer materials expectation. On the opposite end, labor disputes, worker exposures, new land grabs, and commodity chain disruptions met progress. Arguably, these shifts occurred as chemically-bound aesthetic needs were met with developing corporate advertising techniques and posturing on the international market. Thus, I argue that the techniques and values of chemical desires configured and made modern architecture. The dissertation offers a method for re-reading our built environment as a chemical landscape, which formed a world of "modern" building materials still evident today.

Image
P 133: Monsanto Avenue, Sauget, Illinois, Site Visit 2018. Photo by Jessica Varner.

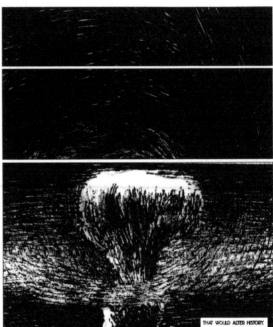

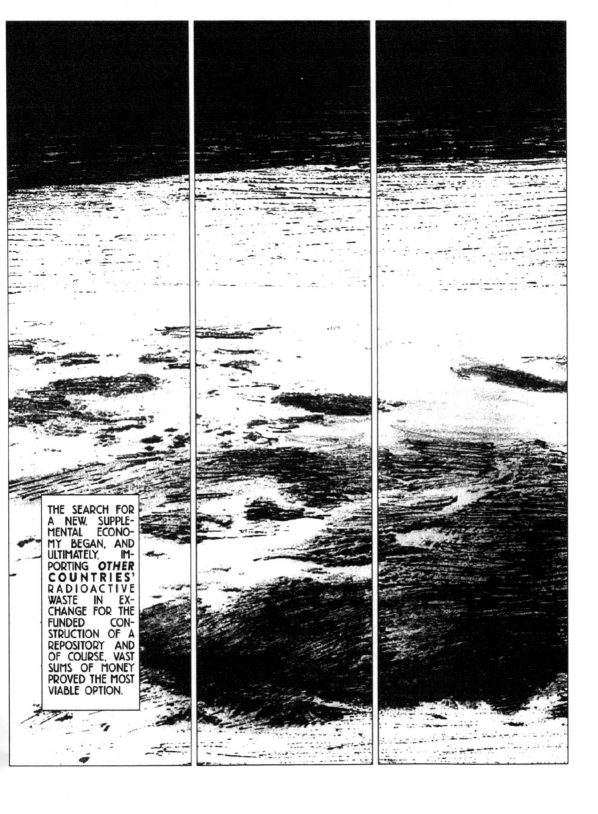

THE SEARCH FOR A NEW, SUPPLEMENTAL ECONOMY BEGAN, AND ULTIMATELY, IMPORTING *OTHER COUNTRIES'* RADIOACTIVE WASTE IN EXCHANGE FOR THE FUNDED CONSTRUCTION OF A REPOSITORY AND OF COURSE, VAST SUMS OF MONEY PROVED THE MOST VIABLE OPTION.

DUE TO THE CHERENKOV RADIATION WITHIN THE GLASS, A PALE BLUE GLOW PROJECTED OUT FROM THE LARGE AIR EXHAUST OF EACH REPOSITORY MOUTH. THE GLOW WOULD ONE DAY FADE, ONCE THE RADIOACTIVITY WAS GONE . . . .

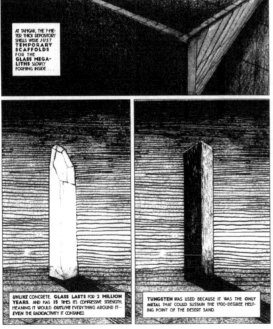

AT TAMGAK, THE 7-METER THICK REPOSITORY SHELLS WERE JUST **TEMPORARY SCAFFOLDS** FOR THE **GLASS MEGA-LITHS** SLOWLY FORMING INSIDE . . . .

UNLIKE CONCRETE, GLASS LASTS FOR **2 MILLION YEARS**, AND HAS **15** TIMES ITS COMPRESSIVE STRENGTH, MEANING IT WOULD *OUTLIVE* EVERYTHING AROUND IT— EVEN THE RADIOACTIVITY IT CONTAINED.

TUNGSTEN WAS USED BECAUSE IT WAS THE ONLY METAL THAT COULD SUSTAIN THE 1700-DEGREE MELTING POINT OF THE DESERT SAND.

FOR THE FIRST 500 YEARS AFTER EMPLACEMENT . . . .

RADIOACTIVE HEAT FROM THE WASTE LEFT THE 48 WASTE CHAMBERS AND SPREAD UP THROUGH THE TUNGSTEN MATRIX, **MELTING EVERYTHING** IT CAME INTO DIRECT CONTACT WITH.

1000M OF SAND WAS TURNED INTO **MOLTEN GLASS.**

WITH EACH PASSING
GENERATION, STORIES
WERE TOLD OF THE
GLOWING GLASS MEGA-
LITHS AT TAMGAK, THE
DEADLY WASTE BURIED
DEEP INSIDE, AND THE
ARCANE CIVILIZATION
RESPONSIBLE.
IN THIS WAY, THEY WERE
NEVER FORGOTTEN .

THE END . . .

Collective
Acts

Collective
Acts

Collective

Acts

Collective

Acts

Collective
Acts

Three students took themselves as willing subjects to test questions of collective work for their thesis: What would it mean to collaborate and consider the collective in process and program? In the final review, critics were invited to comb their archives and processes—to inhabit their "Collective Brain," a Grasshopper script designed to keep their research in order—and reckon with how to discuss authorship.

What kind of architecture follows when we put aside notions of singular authorship? And what does architectural education gain from a shift toward collectivity and collaboration? Collective acts open up spaces for more just and inclusive practices—ones that embrace the slow, distributed, and persistent realities of practice in design and scholarship alike. Though architects have long embraced and enacted ideals of collaboration and teamwork, these interests are becoming an increasingly important component and common way of working. There is a qualitative shift toward collective production, both among groups and disciplines. The projects that emerge from such acts, such as the McKnelly Megalith in Material Acts or the work of the Urban Risk Lab, visualize the potential in not only working together but shifting perceptions on the expectations of a studio or project.

The projects that follow are interested in an expansive scope: they grapple with creating common and public spaces, with authorship and self-management, precedents and archives, public goods and institutions. The first exercises in the design studio reckon with staging architecture at an intimate scale; they make visible the tensions in collaboratively constructing and negotiating space. They ask: How are collectives made architectural rather than circumstantial? These speculations and projections draw upon histories of socialist and collectivist thought in equal measure as they are examined in different contexts: we jump from the post-coal city of Katowice, Poland, to the immigrant neighborhood of Lowell, Massachusetts, to the insular domestic suburbia of Los Angeles, California, to the contentious Parade Square in Warsaw, Poland. Questions of solidarity, civic-building, domestic collectives, and preserving public space play out across scales.

Producing *together* presents new possibilities and attitudes towards how work is, and could be, produced. Finding methods of working together, within and across interests and areas of expertise, and changing culture to accept collaboration as norm is key. As projects shift away from the notion of an individual's capacity for action, agency is re-read as dependent and contingent. As Caroline A. Jones reminds us in Instrumental Acts, thinking collectively requires an acknowledgment that the collective itself is an active, social process   one that requires constant work, upkeep, care, and attention.

THE ROOM
Core 1 Studio: Exercise 2
Instructors, Fall 2016: Brandon Clifford, William
O'Brien Jr., Oana Stănescu

Design a room that affects a body. Consider the
new body that wears the room.

A *room* can be defined as "a space that can be
occupied, especially viewed in terms of whether
there is enough." In this exercise, you are asked to
consider the architectural means by which one may
constitute *interiority* (room) in order to establish a
relationship with *exteriority* (a particular contextual
condition) while monitoring the implications of the
design on the transformed identity of the body.

This design project is concerned with architecture at the human scale. The size of the room and the
objects it contains will be smaller than conventional
rooms. Extra-architectural precedents such as
masks, helmets, stereoscopes, and other wearables
that have a specific relationship with a part of the
body provide a way into understanding the minimal
means by which one might constitute a room. In analyzing such extra-architectural precedents, students
speculate about potential architectural typological
corollaries. This might enable new, more architectural manifestations of the extra-architectural
precedents to emerge.

In designing a room that a body (or bodies) can
occupy, one is equally designing a new body—a body
with a transformed identity. The object that the body
wears will augment, diminish, refamiliarize, or subvert characteristics of the original body. Consider
costumes, fashion, and armor; consider the different
registers that each of those categories of wearables
invoke. The rooms that you design should be considered and evaluated equally through the lenses of
ritual, culture, and performance.

Readings
- Caroline A. Jones, "The Mediated Sensorium," in
  Sensorium (Cambridge, MA: MIT Press, 2006).
- David Serlin, "Learning at Your Fingertips,"
  Cabinet 39: *Learning* (Brooklyn, NY: Immaterial,
  2010).

Precedents
- Femke Agema
- Clarina Bezzola, *Connector Suits*, 2001 and
  Study Chamber, 1995
- Heidi Bucher, *Bodyshells*, 1972
- Nick Cave, *Speak Louder*, 2011
- Philippe Genty, *Boliloc*, 2007
- Haus-Rucker-Co, *Environment Transformer*,
  1968
- Carsten Höller, *Upside-Down Glasses*, 1994–

- Rebecca Horn, *Mechanischer Körperfächer*,
  1973–74
- Marius Janusauskas, *Algabal*
- Ani Liu, *Infinity Helm*
- Milena Naef, *Fleeting Parts*, 2017
- Muriel Nisse
- Lucy Orta, *Refuge Wear*, 1992–98
- Walter Pichler, *Small Room Prototype 4*, 1967
- Bertjan Pot, *Masks*, 2010–
- Oskar Schlemmer, *Pantomime Treppenwitz*,
  1927
- J. Meejin Yoon, *Defensible Dress*, 2004

KNIT ROOM
Jaya Alba Eyzaguirre, Sarah Wagner, Erin Wong
Fall 2016

This project began with an investigation into
qualities of a room that are not included by the
denotative four walls usually requisite for the
label. Knit Room, a giant three-person sweater,
instead suggests how a room might be able
to bring people together by mimicking an awkward, yet comfortable home-like environment.
The room connects the inhabitants through both
the interlaced strings and the associations of
comfort. Manipulation of the form, achieved by
raising and lowering the sleeves attached to the
body of the space, opens the otherwise drooping
mass of fabric into a secret and playful headspace shared between three wearers. We took
the sweater to downtown Boston to enjoy the
awkward yet cozy encounters with strangers,
and we made plenty of friends along the way.

BRUME CLOSET
Alexandre Beaudouin-Mackay, Trevor Herman
Hilker, Patrick Weber
Fall 2016

Brume Closet investigates the terms by which we
define boundaries, specifically through the idea
of blurred edges—the intangible or semi-tangible
constraints that define the limits of boundless
space. Constructed from elastic fabric and a
tenuously-contained vapor cloud, the materials
of the room are ephemeral and reactionary. They
describe a space that is intimate and anonymous,
confined and expansive. Through the obfusca-
tion of sight and the absence of hard edges, new
soft boundaries emerge: the fuzzy edge of one's
clouded vision; the cool front of the continually
descending vapor; the temporal limit of one's
exposure to thin air. From the haze comes alternative terms for bounding space and new means
to define the room.

BOUND HOUSE
Stratton Coffman, Aaron Powers, Jung In Seo
Fall 2016

The Bound House recovers forms of encounter that are otherwise socially abject, suspect, or disdained. Folds, slits, and orifices supply means of meeting at the threshold of intimacy and discomfort, either through their momentary occurrence or in the queasiness of their slight possibility. Our room registers multiple, displaced bodies and transmits their movements across its depth, overlaying degrees of connection, from the physical touching of an anonymous backside, to the bumping into another's face, to the jostling of some other presence at a distance. Laughs are heard from within the empty facade; movement and shaking register the occupants' use within.

STANDARDS FOR THE REPRODUCTION OF TWO PROXEMIC THRESHOLDS
Marlena Fauer, Trevor Herman Hilker, Stephan Hernandez, Angeline Jacques, Taeseop Shin, Finn Xu, Shane Zhang
Option Studio: Proxemic Thresholds
Instructor: Yolande Daniels
Spring 2018

Predicated on an understanding of the built environment (or, more specifically, architecture, or more specifically, threshold) that recognizes the ability of what we bring forth into the world to have real, social consequence, Standards for the Reproduction of Two Proxemic Thresholds suggests that an inverse relationship might also be true: that we might construct real, consequential space out of the exploitation of social boundaries. Assuming the guise of a set of "graphic standards," the project tracks the production of such a space as it has been enacted by seven-eighths of the Studio Thresholds on February 25, 2018 and seeks to imagine a set of tools by which we might measure, implement, and make architectural the phenomenon of the proxemic threshold.

Z KOPALNI: OUT OF THE MINES
Monica Hutton, Ranu Singh, Daya Zhang
Urban Design Studio: Urbanism After Extraction–Housing, Landscape, and Infrastructure in the Katowice Agglomeration, Poland
Instructors: Marie Law Adams, Rafi Segal
Spring 2017

The identity of the Upper Silesia Industrial Region in Poland has been closely tied to the geology of the coal basin. In this region, due to the inherent

dangers and value tied to coal production, mining as a profession has held a high degree of prestige. This occupational identity is celebrated publicly each year on December 4, Barbórka, or "The Day of the Miner." On this day, the usual movements of workers down mine shafts and the movement of coal along railways are suspended. Miners forego the daily trip underground to participate in festivities aboveground. Town streets are co-opted early in the morning by the procession of a brass band that summons residents to participate in events that continue late into the evening. As coal mines have closed across Poland, the celebration of Barbórka has also faded.

This project proposes an urban event to accompany the continued movement out of the mines. Z Kopalni, "Out of the Mines," will be celebrated each year on June 4 as a new procession to connect the dispersed mining communities of the region. The route brings together residents, institutions, mining infrastructures, and the surrounding landscape. With an aim to strengthen the health of economic, cultural, and environmental systems across cities, the directive does not adhere to the industrial lines that have linked them in the past. Alternative routes through the diverse landscape will trigger shifts in culture by suspending daily norms and relationships. Existing sites will shift occupation to offer a range of opportunities for current and future generations to interact on new terms.

Mining communities which used to celebrate independently will pool their capacity to participate as a new mass of facilitators, spectators, and demonstrators. An organizational structure for involvement will allow community groups and individuals to participate at a range of scales. Z Kopalni aims to be a catalyst for diurnal cycles of development and a platform to negotiate local frictions among previously dispersed actors and areas.

THE FEBRUARY SCHOOL
Nicolás Kisic Aguirre, Nolan Oswald Dennis, Laura Serejo Genes, Jessica Sarah Rinland, Gary Zhexi Zhang, Pedro Zylbersztajn
MIT Wiesner Gallery
February 2018

LEARNING TO COLLABORATE: ROBOTS BUILDING TOGETHER
Kathleen Hajash
SMArchS Computation Thesis
Advisors: Skylar Tibbits, Patrick Winston
Spring 2018

Since robots were first invented, robotic assembly has been an important area of research in both academic institutions and industry settings. The standard industry approach to robotic assembly lines utilizes fixed robotic arms and prioritizes speed and precision over customization. With a recent shift towards mobile multi-robot teams, researchers have developed a variety of approaches ranging from planning with uncertainty to swarm robotics.

However, existing approaches to robotic assembly are either too rigid, with a deterministic planning approach, or do not take advantage of the opportunities available with multiple robots. If we are to push the boundaries of robotic assembly, then we need to make collaborative robots that can work together, without human intervention, to plan and build large structures that they could not complete alone. By developing teams of robots that can work together to plan and build large structures, we could aid in disaster relief, enable construction in remote locations, and support the health of construction workers in hazardous environments.

I take a first step towards this vision by developing a simple collaborative task wherein agents learn to work together to move rectilinear blocks. I define robotic collaboration as an emergent process that evolves as multiple agents, simulated or physical, learn to work together to achieve a common goal that they could not achieve in isolation. Rather than taking an explicit planning approach, I employ an area of research in artificial intelligence called reinforcement learning, where agents learn an optimal behavior to achieve a specific goal by receiving rewards or penalties for good and bad behavior, respectively.

ARCHITECTURE IN THE AFTER-NET
Sam Ghantous
MArch Thesis
Advisor: William O'Brien Jr.
Fall 2016

Tweeting from your couch, in your sweats, can be an architectural act. Architecture's ability to serve and shape a public has been weakened by its disciplinary exclusivity and the privatization of public space. Hope for architecture today is found, instead, in its ability to be shared online. There, its value is in its newfound velocity, intensity, and spread—an ability to "get around." Attention is a currency and the image, a visual byte that circulates, has already replaced the building in space.

Architecture is on and of the web, and it can shape a public there. If you Tweet @archmixes with selections from the archive of 3D meshes I compiled, you can make architecture. Appropriated from 3D models uploaded to Sketchup Warehouse, anyone can make anew from preexisting digitized disciplinary matter. This is a call for the regime of a new

six points of architecture: Search, Select, Combine, Tag, Archive, Share. Sharing is a creative act that will disperse into the fiber-optic infinitum your architecture rendered by its anxious formats: JPEGs, 3D meshes, videos, GIFs, 3D print files, Shopify listings, Instagram posts, Pins. Files are promiscuous and will degrade in order to be as mobile as possible, to be reused, and misused; they just want to be save-as'ed.

This thesis culminates in a performance. A black-box theater is transformed into a living room; the audience is introduced to and participates in the labor of architectural production by tweeting canonical projects that consequently get combined and dispersed.

This is a call to speed up and broadcast architecture made of the web, for the web. Creativity has been democratized: now anyone with a phone and repost button can sculpt their own aesthetic universe, be it on Instagram, YouTube, or SoundCloud. Through recycling the pixel, vector, and mesh-waste that lives online, architecture has the opportunity to sustain the archive of its disciplinary history; it stands the chance to engage publics; it might even sustain an economy of attention in the era of perpetual distraction.

THREE DEGREES OF SQUEEZE
Stratton Coffman
Log 41
Fall 2017

PUBLIC, BODY, BUILDING: A NEW YMCA
Core 2 Studio
Instructors, Spring 2017: Jennifer Leung, Ana Miljački, Cristina Parreño; Spring 2018: Mariana Ibañez, Christoph Kumpusch, Jennifer Leung, Maya Shopova

COLLECTIVE BODIES
Emily Whitbeck
Spring 2017

This project explores the YMCA as an institution that can produce collectives. In this context, the term "collective" entails more than just the traditional definition of community or neighborhood; the collective is a product of collaborative social processes and everyday interactions. The driving design question of the project is: How are collectives made architectural rather than circumstantial? This question is addressed through defining and combining a series of devices inspired by architectural precedents that establish ways in which architecture can engage with ideas of the collective.

The "framed collective," appropriated from the architecture of Lina Bo Bardi, results from lifting the building from the ground and allowing people to freely flow under and into the YMCA. Through this heroic gesture, the architecture frames both the activities within the YMCA and the community itself, transforming the site into an open public space for community-driven programs.

The second is "the boulevard collective," or ramp, borrowed from the work of OMA. The ramp acts as a social "magic carpet" that both houses the program and weaves between spaces informally hosting non-YMCA programs.

The final device, "the secret collective," exists at a smaller, more intimate scale and refers to the informal micro-communities that form among individuals thanks to proximity, familiarity, routine, recognition, and time. The combination of ramp systems and shifting volumes creates these collectives as spaces of collaborative discovery and intimacy. While these spaces are most difficult to define, they are also the most powerful.

URBAN LINEARITY AND SPATIAL LINEARITY
Jaehun Woo
Spring 2018

Coney Island hosts a diversity of programs, from residential towers to rollercoasters, from the bodegas on Mermaid Avenue to the famous Nathan's hot dog stand along the boardwalk. This diversity, however, is almost entirely housed in mono-functional buildings. This project avoids yet another mono-functional building; instead, it proposes an analog gym where the architectural form does the work. Designed as a linear parkour sequence that bridges Mermaid Avenue and the boardwalk, this YMCA is a concrete landscape. It is a sequence of architectural obstacles that requires members to exert energy as they make their way to the beach. The typical workout sequence transforms into a ritual of crossing the city grid by following lightwells that serve as wayfinding devices.

The YMCA is lifted above ground to occupy the same datum as the rollercoasters of Luna Park. Its roof is publicly accessible, allowing residents and tourists to not only view the neighborhood from a previously impossible point of view, but also glimpse at the parkour below. Moving bodies challenged by atypical architectural spaces provide a new kind spectacle: a collective workout machine.

MISMATCHING: A GYM ASSEMBLED AS A COMMUNITY CENTER
Ben Hoyle
Spring 2018

The YMCA is one of the few institutions that use fitness facilities to promote community well-being. This confronts the Y with a unique pair of challenges: it must both compete for viability in the contemporary gym market while also making its services relevant to inhabitants of an ill-defined subset of the Coney Island community. In the context of New York City, what is best for the market may not be what is best of the community, putting these two challenges at odds with each other.

This architectural proposal suggests merging the programmed spaces of the building into several clusters, maintaining the functionality of each part while constructing a set of new hybrids. This allows for the Y to disassociate its facilities from those of other gyms, asserting its independent value rather than acquiescing to market demand for efficiency and homogeneity. Simultaneously, its new hybrid zones can accommodate the unpredictable usage of most visitors without specifically designing for them. The building carefully assembles prescribed spaces into a non-prescriptive building.

In one instance, the high-ceiling basketball court extends from an intimately-scaled teaching kitchen, with a lounge for teenagers set in between. In another, a vaulted roof system delineates the groupings and organizes them into general zones. The vaults are oriented either north-south or east-west and are built at a low-level human scale or raised urban scale. Within these parameters, the roof generates a distinct range of spatial conditions with unified formal language. While visitors circulate freely around the whole building, they are drawn in by the unique qualities of each cluster.

THE MACHINE BODY
Marisa Waddle
Spring 2018

The YMCA has been historically identified with its progressive stance on inclusivity and health. However, inclusivity and accessibility at the YMCA is difficult to achieve when the city itself has overlooked it. The lack of accessible subway stops and curbs with ramps make it difficult to arrive to the site, for example. This failure of accessibility is not only manifest at the urban scale but also at the architectural scale. Often, accessible elements like ramps or wheelchair lifts are added at the end of the design process as a way to fulfill building requirements, reaffirming societal norms of abled and disabled bodies.

This YMCA forefronts accessible design, approaching it not as a constraint, but rather as an opportunity for the design of new kinds of spaces. At the scale of the building, occupants circulate on long spanning ramps that connect all the gym programs; at the scale of the workout, new collective workout machines offer opportunities for use by all gym members. A system of mobile pulleys provides a safety line for bodies in the lap pool, offering the freedom to swim without fear of growing exhausted away from the edges of the pool.

This project proposes accessible design as a methodology, rather than an add-on to an already completed building. Approaching design through the lens of accessibility produces spaces with new architectural qualities, ones that support collective use instead of ones that divide occupants based on certain physical abilities.

THE BRONX TRANSCRIPT: Y SCENARIO
Taeseop Shin
Spring 2017

The YMCA in New York City is not just a space for physical exercise, it is a place of labor, both as an institution that employs neighborhood residents and one that offers workspace. How could the design of the Y focus on weaving together the daily lives of diverse characters in the community? Considering the site as the intersection of residential and educational axes, in addition to athletic facilities, the Y offers community and educational programs such as cooking, gardening, after-school programs, and teacher training. This project proposes the YMCA not just as a sports facility but also a building that engages with the social needs of the community on a day-to-day basis.

THE YMCA OF FANTASY
Chen Chu
Spring 2018

The YMCA of Fantasy is based on an understanding of Coney Island as a place where a banal reality coexists with a collective imagination of fantasy. In Coney Island, tall housing blocks stand in contrast to recreational structures—the parachute jump, roller coasters, the ferris wheel. Coney Island also maintains its seductive power as a wonderland, both nostalgic

and futuristic. This image and idea of a fantastical and surreal site, mediated by commerce and media, have degenerated into the banal.

This project utlizes these dualities. It aims to create an overwhelming sensorial experience, directing visitors through alternating spaces: enclosed and open, tall and compressed, private and civic, residential and athletic. One experiences the Y as a playground, a wonderland where one exercises, lives, and socializes. Against a gym culture that normalizes and idealizes one singular body image, the Coney Island Y embraces plurality and idiosyncrasy.

THE FLIP SIDE
Stratton Coffman
Spring 2017

On the flip side of the disciplinary regimen of self-betterment through exercise, we come across, in an acrobatic hair toss or toning butt lift, the pleasures of non-productive labor, the rush of the collective energy that pulses through the Bronx.

On a corner lot, an aggregation of lodges claims a site for everyday anti-austerity festivities. These three lodges house clusters of programs for the exuberant consuming, using, and wasting of life and its substances. In the show lodge, boisterous showdowns unfold before rowdy crowds on a basketball court, dance floor, stage hybrid. DJs spin for mixtures of drum beating, fist bumping, heart pumping, and mass cheering, the churning of dancing bodies— their indexicality and face-dos smudged in the grind. The sweat lodge gathers together generous durations of repose and stilled leisure. The wet lodge holds the pool with a geyser at its center, a continually expended totem to the more regimented folding of lane swimming and weight lifting.

PARADE SQUARE: DISCURSIVE SURFACE OF POST-SOCIALIST WARSAW
Blanca Abramek
MArch Thesis
Advisor: Ana Miljački
Fall 2016

This is not about destruction. This is not about a cover-up, or a creation of some screens. The idea is not to hide something embarrassing behind a screen, as it is our experience … The point is to achieve the effect of a conversation …
— Oskar Hansen, *Warsaw Dream*, 2005

Parade Square is a conflicted space. Imposing Soviet sculptures of workers and peasants look out at dainty H&M models advertising bikinis across the street. Tired travelers wait for a shabby bus; they sit by an enormous speaker's tribune from which some of the most important political speeches of the previous era were delivered. Amid neglected lawns and makeshift parking lots, small metal plates embedded in the street surface whisper: "This used to be Chmielna Street," "This used to be Zlota Street," "This used to be Sienna Street." A line marking the sidewalk states solemnly: "Ghetto Wall 1943."

Despite its contradictions, conflicts, and anachronisms, Parade Square is the most lucrative piece of real estate in the city. Originally designed for thousands of marching bodies, the space is now coveted by many developers, businessmen, and investors. Neoliberal economic forces and laissez-faire politics are starting to erode its physical order.

The site of Parade Square has always been a political battleground, shaped by different hegemonic forces. Despite the historical complexity of the space, however, current public discourse around it is largely focused on issues of profit and ownership. The discussion suppresses and tranquilizes the political character of the space. Urban design and architecture proposals for the site show a frenzied desire for "normalization" and alignment with the smooth image of global capitalism. Their singular desire to make busy spaces of consumption lacks critical reflection and needs to be examined in its historical context.

What is at stake in the discussion about Parade Square within this project is a new kind of a conversation about the past and the future of the space—one that questions and disrupts the dominant hegemony and brings to the fore other possibilities that have been repressed and can be reactivated. The project, in the form of a film and exhibition of artifacts, seeks to invite an alternative public discourse focused on the agonistic nature of the square and the political character of its physical order.

BEYOND THE KITCHEN: STRATEGIES FOR OVERCOMING LOS ANGELES' 194X–196X SITCOM SUBURBAN DOMESTICITY
Angelos Siampakoulis
SMArchS Urbanism Thesis
Advisors: Roi Salgueiro Barrio, James Wescoat
Spring 2018

Still worshipped and beloved, suburbia advances in popularity. Orchestrated, among others, by the Atomic Age's massive stock of political and mass media propaganda, sitcom-like domestic imaginaries, customized Formica kitchen innovations, and Barbie doll fantasies, the canonization—if not idealization—of a particular domestic ethos still characterizes today's suburban living. If suburbia remains popular, what are today's new domestic models of living?

Driven by this question, the research recognizes the modern ranch-style house as the most popular suburban domestic typology. It investigates this typology's various domestic facets, its commodification, and grounds a design proposal in Lakewood, California. We surely do not live in the 1950s, but, in Lakewood and many other suburbs, millions live in an architecture of the past, a domestic condition designed during and, arguably, for that era.

If the first layer of metropolitan Los Angeles was a collection of ranch-style tract developments, highways, and fantastic architecture, what could a new housing project in this context entail? This thesis proposes two strategies: restructuring the suburban domestic space and reconsidering the plot's property line. Conditioned by this apparatus, a new domestic suburban form questions the possibility of a collective living project.

AMERICANAAAAA!, OR A WELCOME HOME IN LOWELL, MASSACHUSETTS
Alexander Bodkin
MArch Thesis
Advisor: Mariana Ibañez
Fall 2018

This thesis studies how nostalgia has been used to construct shared spatial and social expectations through the envelope of the American home. Based on the simple proposition to make the home bigger so as to host a broader collective, it explores how these expectations can be subverted through distortions and exaggerations of the domestic envelope. As these exaggerations reach the limits of symbolic legibility, they begin to suggest alternate internal organizations that have the potential to shape the social relationships and negotiations of a new collective within.

The site for this thesis is Lowell, Massachusetts, a once-prosperous textile mill town on the Merrimack River. Lowell is chosen for two of its defining features: its robust preservation campaign, which perpetuates a flattened representation of Lowell's collective identity that is rooted in a 1970s idea of nineteenth century domestic architecture, and its long history of immigration. Today, approximately one quarter of Lowell's population is foreign-born.

These conditions provide an opportunity to appropriate Lowell's own nostalgia in the design of a new civic building—the Welcome Home—that serves a broader collective of local and newcomer.

COLLECTIVE HOME OFFICE
Mary Lynch-Lloyd, Ching Ying Ngan, Maya Shopova
MArch Thesis
Advisor: Ana Miljački
Fall 2017

URBAN RISK LAB: PROJECTS, TOOLS, AND STRATEGIES
Miho Mazereeuw; Aditya Barve, Justin Lavallee, Hugh Magee, David Moses, Larisa Ovalles, Lizzie Yarina
Fall 2018

Collective Home Office (CHO) is a collaborative practice whose working process tests the propositions it makes through architecture. As a group of friends, willing test subjects, a union of producers, a jury, a family, or an army, CHO explores the frictions and benefits of collectivity in both method and content. The three words that form its name provide a framework through which the practice engages with its contexts, questioning how the meanings of collective, home, and office have been historically shaped.

Targeting the agents most implicated in defining the current moment, namely the proto-state corporations, platforms, and institutions that constitute Big Tech, CHO pitches a series of unsolicited projects to clients who are radically changing how we live and relate to one another. CHO believes that not only should these agents be held responsible for the drastic social and urban impacts they exert, but that they may become willing partners in designing new ways of living that respond to the social estrangement, imminent technological unemployment, and chronic housing crisis that have resulted from their unregulated conquest of market share.

Far from neglecting the notion of collectivity, the tech world has appropriated its surplus value and replaced sharing with a sharing economy and then with a gig economy. The "capitalist collective" fails to recognize its misuse of the word; collectives differ greatly from memberships rosters. CHO believes that collectivity is a shared motivation towards a common goal. Fundamentally ideological, it is accrued over time through social intimacy built on shared experiences, both positive and negative. Spatially, this notion of the collective requires a new organizational strategy. Modeled on both the city and the home, forms of domestic urbanism are fostered by intimate encounters occurring at overlapping scales of interaction, redefining the notion of household.

CHO focuses its practice on how this unlikely partnership can be used as an opportunity to rewire the collective with new priorities. Using the home office as a device, CHO emphasizes the increasing importance of care work and social grooming as means of coping with transitional post-work lifestyle no longer based on the binary of home and work.

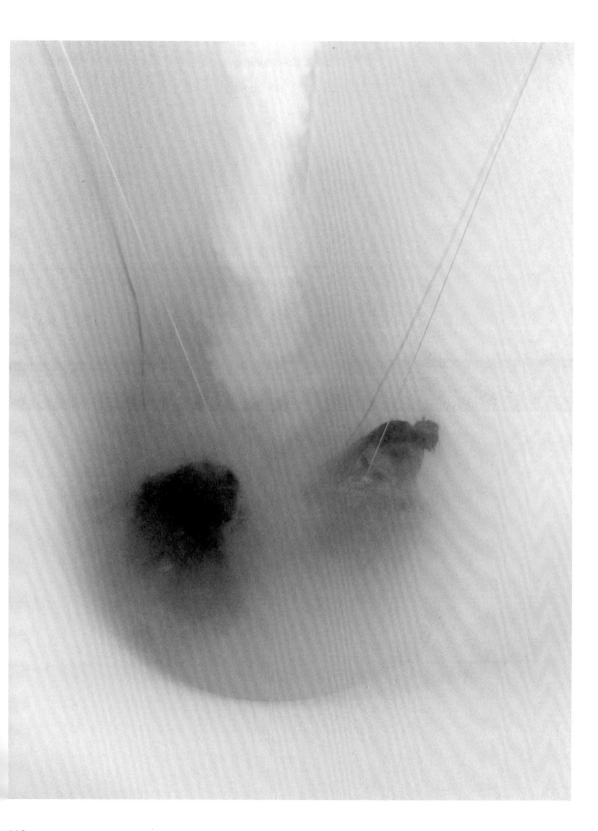

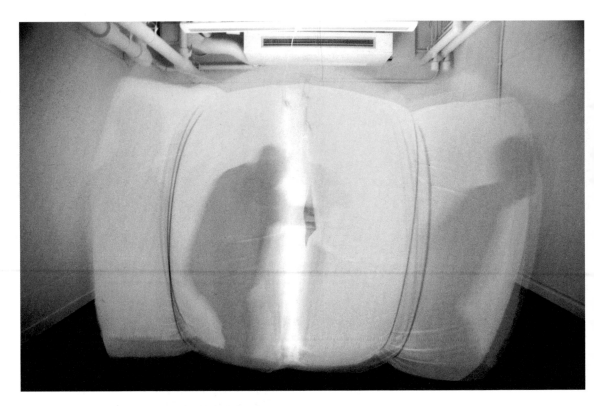

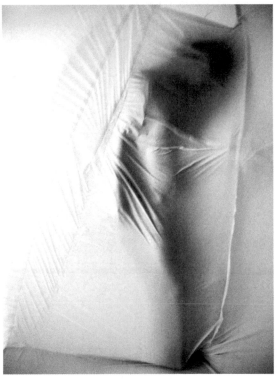

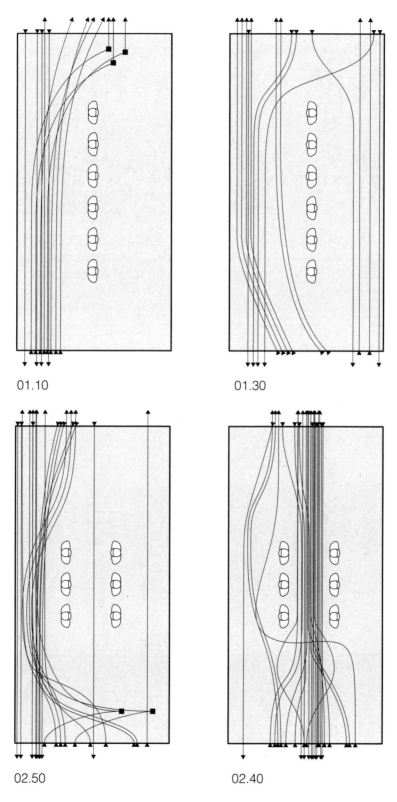

01.10

01.30

02.50

02.40

Z KOPALNI: OUT OF THE MINES
Monica Hutton, Ranu Singh, Daya Zhang

153

THE FEBRUARY SCHOOL

Nicolás Kisic Aguirre, Nolan Oswald Dennis, Laura Serejo Genes, Jessica Sarah Rinland, Gary Zhexi Zhang, Pedro Zylbersztajn

The February School is a temporary school set up by graduate students in the MIT Program in Art, Culture and Technology (ACT) as an intervention into the nested ecosystem of education at MIT. This school is a subsystem of education where students and the general public are invited to participate in ACT student-led classes, cinema cycles, exhibitions, discussions, conferences, workshops, construction, and celebrations. The intervention uses the structures and conventions of a typical university to explore other ways of learning, sharing, and building knowledge and community. The February School was set up in February 2018 in the Arts at MIT Wiesner Gallery at the Student Center.

Wednesday, February 7
4:00–6:00 pm
    Freestyle Rap
    Hisham Bedri
6:30–8:30 pm
    Nollywood Wednesdays
    Nolan Oswald Dennis and Alice Noujaim

Friday, February 9
6:00 pm
    I'm Not Your Cholo
    Marco Alvilés and Kim Barzola

Tuesday, February 13
2:00–4:00 pm
    How to make (almost) ___ (Day 1)
    Nolan Oswald Dennis

Wednesday, February 14
3:00–5:00 pm
    Exercises in Reading
    Pedro Zylbersztajn
6:30–8:30 pm
    Nollywood Wednesdays
    Nolan Oswald Dennis and Alice Noujaim

Thursday, February 15
6:00–9:00 pm
    Moving a Still Artifact (Day 1)
    Jessica Sarah Rinland

Friday, February 16
2:00–5:00 pm
    Moving a Still Artifact (Day 2)
    Jessica Sarah Rinland

6:00 pm
    A Night of Sonic Interventions
    Laurie Amat

Wednesday, February 21
3:00–5:00 pm
    Exercises in Reading
    Pedro Zylbersztajn
6:30–8:30 pm
    Nollywood Wednesdays
    Nolan Oswald Dennis and Alice Noujaim

Thursday, February 22
3:00 pm
    Malware Workshop
    Gary Zhexi Zhang and Agnes Cameron

Friday, February 23
6:30–8:30 pm
    Moving a Still Artifact (Day 3)
    Screening of Student Work
    Jessica Sarah Rinland

Tuesday, February 27
2:00–4:00 pm
    How to make (almost) ___ (Day 2)
    Nolan Oswald Dennis
7:00–9:00 pm
    Dreamteam Panel
    Laura Serejo Genes

Wednesday, February 28
3:00–5:00 pm
    Exercises in Reading
    Pedro Zylbersztajn
6:00–8:00 pm
    Mutual Pictures Session
    Jessica Sarah Rinland and Anne Whiston Spirn

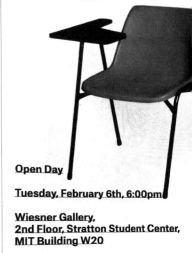

Open Day

Tuesday, February 6th, 6:00pm

**Wiesner Gallery,
2nd Floor, Stratton Student Center,
MIT Building W20**

Open Day

Tuesday, February 6th, 6:00pm

**Wiesner Gallery,
2nd Floor, Stratton Student Center,
MIT Building W20**

THE FEBRUARY SCHOOL

THE FEBRUARY SCHOOL

THE FEBRUARY SCHOOL

Open Day

Tuesday, February 6th, 6:00pm

**Wiesner Gallery,
2nd Floor, Stratton Student Center,
MIT Building W20**

Open Day

Tuesday, February 6th, 6:00pm

**Wiesner Gallery,
2nd Floor, Stratton Student Center,
MIT Building W20**

THE FEBRUARY SCHOOL

THE FEBRUARY SCHOOL

THE FEBRUARY SCHOOL

Open Day

Tuesday, February 6th, 6:00pm

**Wiesner Gallery,
2nd Floor, Stratton Student Center,
MIT Building W20**

Open Day

Tuesday, February 6th, 6:00pm

**Wiesner Gallery,
2nd Floor, Stratton Student Center,
MIT Building W20**

LEARNING TO COLLABORATE: ROBOTS BUILDING TOGETHER
Kathleen Hajash

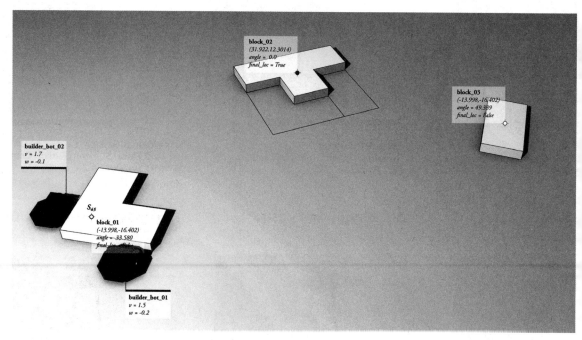

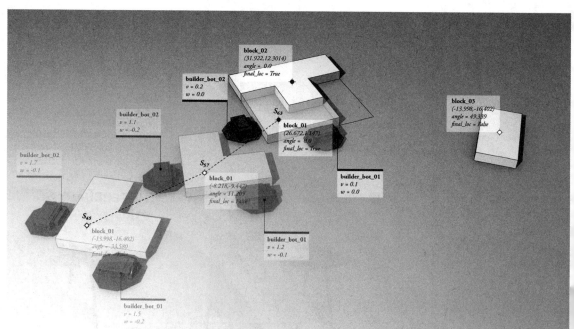

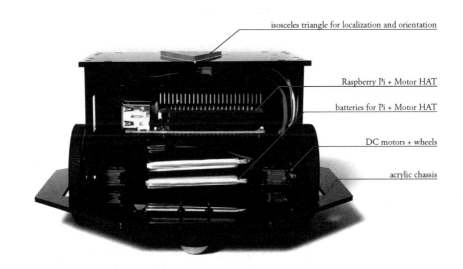

isosceles triangle for localization and orientation

Raspberry Pi + Motor HAT

batteries for Pi + Motor HAT

DC motors + wheels

acrylic chassis

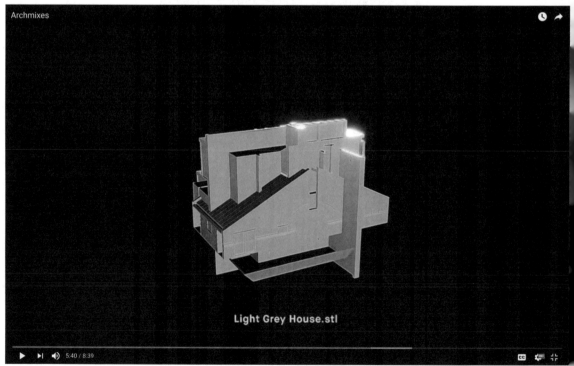

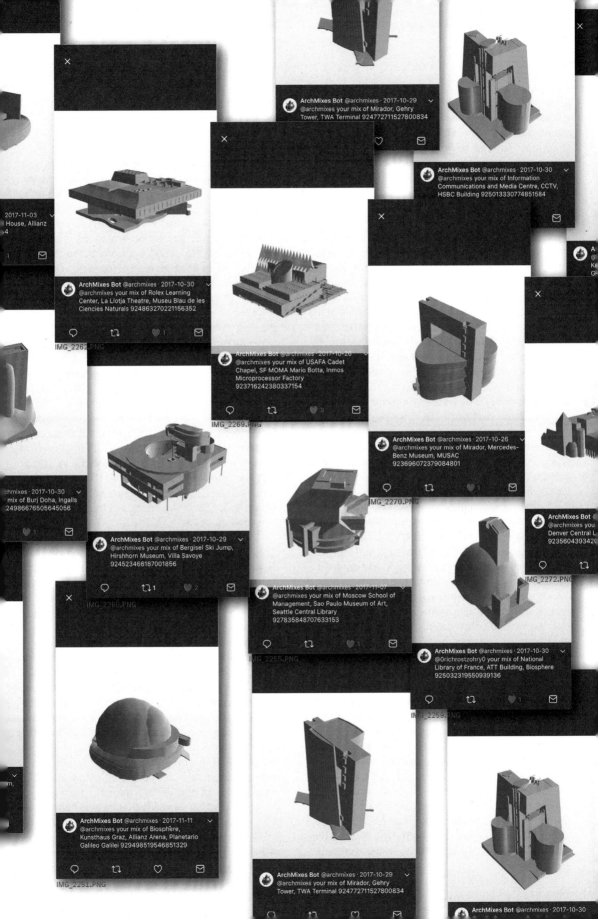

THREE DEGREES OF SQUEEZE
Stratton Coffman

A squeeze: multiple coterminous vectors of force gather around the squeezed, swaddling it, while the squeezed gives in, allowing itself to be compressed. Such an embrace challenges the conditions that give form to personhood. In its grasp, the borders of the subject are redrawn, kindling agency in inertness.

Squeeze Chute

A chute, a hulking box sculpted from bundled sinews of piping, circuits curving vertically in two planes, lengthwise. Invented to hold cattle in place, the squeeze chute has bilateral symmetry modeled on the life-form it squeezes. As the hydraulics are activated, the barred sides press in on the sides of the cow, hugging it evenly in a deep touch that coaxes it into docility. If the chute is activated too hurriedly, the animal inside gets spooked and riled up. When all goes according to plan, the transition between squeeze and rest occurs seamlessly, preparing the cow for branding. The squeeze, counterintuitively, distances the cow from its sensory field, dulling any sense of potential danger or discomfort.

In the 1960s, the lulling mechanics of the squeeze chute drew in another subject. Autist, writer, and activist Temple Grandin felt an empathic tug when visiting her aunt's farm as a teenager. She observed the "wild-eyed and nervous calves," seeing, manifested in them, her own difficulties; bearing witness to the squeeze, Grandin "experience[d] a greater underlying connection between herself and other life forms."[1] Accounts like this, of Grandin and other autists, enumerate the many strategies autists have developed for coping with hypersensitivity to environmental stimulation akin to the squeeze chute—"rolling up in a gym mat" or "a mummy sleeping bag," wrapping "elastic bandages" or "foam-padded splints on the arms," "sleeping under many blankets," or even "getting under mattresses."[2] These makeshift applications of what Grandin terms deep touch "interrupt the circuitry of the individual's overwhelmed nervous system" to relieve "touch sensitivity, hypersensitive hearing, and visual processing problems."[3]

Seeking a more robust and systematic regimen for deep touch, Grandin developed a prototype of a squeeze chute for humans. As a built enclosure for autists and others to find rest in the world, the squeeze machine posits a mode of inhabitation through deep touch that has implications for architecture and architectural thought. Grandin's squeeze machine positions the user between "two padded side boards"—in early iterations, "two air mattresses surrounded by a canvas wrap connected to a pulley"—that are "hinged at the bottom to form a V-shape," a fold beckoning a body.[4] To enter, one kneels before the opening to ensure a snug fit and, after making any necessary adjustments, crawls into the main crevice, pushing head and neck through the resting pads at the other end. Getting out is an awkward affair of blindly backing out on one's knees. The machine tilts conventional relations of base and structure, room and roof, figure and ground, so that the body faces down instead of forward, in a lateral orientation resembling a mammalian pose.

Like the cattle chute, "the contoured padding provides an even pressure across the entire lateral aspects of the body without generating specific pressure points."[5] The pressing advances at a uniform rate, making the increase in pressure imperceptible to the user. Deep touch passes into the nervous system's blind spot, inducing an all-body synaptic fatigue. What results is a kind of dedifferentiation, wherein regions of the body habituated to certain types of touch, such as the flat spread of the seat on the ass or a tap on the shoulder, all receive the same treatment. So thorough is the swaddle that even the neck is gripped with the same pressure, "enhanc[ing] the feeling of being surrounded and contained by the embrace of the deep touch pressure squeeze."[6]

Such touching is avoided in the discipline of architecture, which generally understands this degree of contact between subjects and buildings as a potentially catastrophic liability, risking physical harm or psychological distress, as in cases of claustrophobia. Grandin's experiment with the chute challenged the conventions of distance between subjects and objects that govern architectural thought and its built edifices. We trust architecture to shelter us from dangerous kinds of touching, which, given the heft of buildings measured against our relatively soft, delicate animality, could do serious damage. This fear, codified in building regulations and entrenched in heavy materials industries, predetermines forms of shelter and closeness that come with their own proclivities for contact. In the squeeze machine, a person voluntarily gives up a wide range of possible movement, assuming a docile pose of vulnerability that reorders the boundaries of the self through disabling closeness.

Deep touch confounds the metrics that define self and other, near and far, by opening an unfelt, subliminal buffer between a body and its surroundings. The relaxed body is compelled to absorb the mechanized flaps as extensions of itself. Grandin's initial encounter with the cattle chute, touching the cows' warm sides and feeling a kinship with them, and her subsequent fabrication of a chute for herself all led her "to reimagine her bodily boundaries."[7] In doing so, "[she] learned [her] sensory problems weren't the result of [her] weakness or lack of character," but rather were produced through narrow, normative patterns of behavior relating to touch and other agents of stimulation.[8]

Squeeze Room

A magnesium flare washes a small room in blinding light, imprinting a negative with the squinting faces—made temporarily visible by the flash—of a huddle of humans. In the late nineteenth century, Jacob Riis, a Danish immigrant turned proto-photo journalist, performed such ambushes with a hand-held camera and flash powder gun, bursting unannounced into the private quarters of New York City tenements. His aim was to expose the deleterious living conditions of tenement residents, particularly their extreme proximity to one another, which seemed, to Riis, to threaten their integrity as individuals, to squeeze the person out of personhood.

This excessive density was born of the imposition of Manhattan's gridiron in 1811 by the city's commissioners, led by Gouverneur Morris, whose plan carved up the island into blocks of twenty-eight lots, each twenty-five by one hundred feet. In the document submitted to the state legislature, the plan's drafters admitted that "they could not but bear in mind … that strait sided, and right angled houses are the most cheap to build and the most convenient to live in."[9] The city's composition was tailored to a strategy of building best suited for the city's developers and speculators, governed by the pursuit of profit by unbridled cost-cutting. The constraints of the grid produced the housing type that came to be known as the tenement, the size of which was determined by "the maximum spans of wooden floor joists, and by the prevalent practice of building only in single-lot increments."[10]

Pre-grid housing, adapted to these standardized lots, filled only half of their allotted areas, leaving an open yard in the back. Common floor plans included two chambers separated by a water closet, which, following the illogic of developers, could be converted into four small bedrooms jutting into the rooms on either side, now designated as living rooms. A landlord could then opt to construct a secondary structure crammed at the far end of the backyard or extend the back of the building. As

housing historian Richard Plunz has noted,

> The practice of back building [led] to absurd results, such as the notorious Rookery on Mott Street … Three parallel rows of housing were built on five small lots, with total street frontage of 90 feet. The inner and middle rows had only a foot of air space between them. The windows of one faced the brick wall of the other. The space between the outer and middle rows of housing was 6 feet wide, and filled with privies. In 1865 the Rookery housed 352 persons, at an extremely high density of 23 square feet per person.[11]

At the peak of this back building craze, floors often carried as many as 18 rooms organized like compartments on a train, hence the expression "railroad flats."[12] Only the two outermost rooms received daylight and some ventilation, *if* the building faced south. Otherwise, the interior rapidly lost effective illumination as one passed further into its recesses. In their compactness, tenement buildings staged an experience of rambling indeterminacy, a dense interiority wherein short distances could be folded into overwrought passages and sequences feeling much longer, even roomier.

This compression of interior space—enfilades of rooms behind rooms, dead-ending in yet more rooms—aroused the intrigue and disgust of reformers. The *World*, a Democratic newspaper, gave voice to this sentiment, declaring in print, "Of all the diabolical, horrid, atrocious, fiendish, and even hellish systems of money-making ever invented by the mind of man, the tenement-house system of [New York City], is the most horrible."[13] Jacob Riis, expressing a similar distaste, lamented, "Where have they gone to, the old inhabitants? … They are not here. In their place has come this queer conglomerate mass of heterogeneous elements."[14] In these mannered tirades, indices of identity, such as race and ethnicity, undergo a double merger, first melding into monolithic and reductive ethnic blocks, and then into the faceless, foreign "hordes," swarming beyond the limits of humanness. In this operation, the tenement residents were at once internally unassimilable—"heterogeneous"—and externally ungovernable—homogenous; they became, as a journalist for the New York *Daily Tribune* wrote in 1882, "a class by themselves."[15] The obscene closeness of the residents to one another engendered this threatening, alien —"queer"—class of inhabitants.

The architecture of these mangled labyrinthine spaces made such species reclassifications easier, and confounded reformist efforts to regulate the conditions of tenement housing. The redundancy of walls, the scarcity of windows, and the tangling of passageways obstructed the reformists' project to assess the nature and scope of the overcrowding and determine tenement resident populations. In one notoriously packed tenement district, "the Bend," Riis observed, "The sanitary reformer gives up the task [of counting] in despair. Of its vast homeless crowds, the census takes no account. It is their instinct to shun the light, and they cannot be corralled in one place long enough to be counted."[16] Riis gives an account of one officer's attempt to gather evidence of illegal overcrowding:

> The doors are opened unwillingly enough … In a room not thirteen feet either way slept twelve men and women, two or three in bunks set in a sort of alcove, the rest on the floor. A kerosene lamp burned dimly in the fearful atmosphere, probably to guide other and later arrivals to their "beds," for it was only just past midnight. A baby's fretful wail came from an adjoining hall-room, where, in the semi-darkness, three recumbent figures could be made out. The "apartment" was one of three in two adjoining buildings we had found, within half an hour, similarly crowded. Most of the men were lodgers, who slept there for five cents a spot.[17]

The reformist gaze failed to identify architecture as the reason for this difficulty amidst the dimmed interiors. The counters, wielding the authoritative power of illumination and measurement, produced only muddled results: "in a room *not* thirteen feet either way," "two *or* three bunks," "a *sort* of alcove," a lamp "*probably* to guide" latecomers.[18] Looking for precise figures, Riis and his attendant reformists found a tenebrous jumble of objects, indeterminate in number, function, role, position, as well as proportion and scale. The architectural closeness bred uncertainty and overwhelmed the tools used by Riis and the other statisticians. The conditions these residents were embedded within, along with their belongings—the hanging blankets, bundles of clothing, and dish racks—all confounded the means by which the state formulates and addresses its subjects spatially. Unlike the willful surrender necessary for Grandin's chute, the residents' agency arose in spite of their entanglement.

A mattress, raised on lumber crossbeams, sags under the load of two bodies, one feet first, soles, instead of face, facing the camera, a hand elevated mid-gesture. Another man sits upright next to him. The mattress peeks out below its upholding frame, warping up and around the resting bodies. The room hosts other kinds and degrees of holding. The wooden shelves to the left, secured to the wall, keep the men's various bowls, dishes, and other vessels together, stacked and accessible for use. To the other side, sagging blanket bundles hang from some fastener out of view.

In a photograph taken by Riis in 1889, titled *Lodgers in a Bayard Street Tenement, Five Cents a Spot*, the untidiness of the nest and the infolding of tired residents and their personal effects make visible the impossibility of the indexical objectives of both photography and counting. Closeness, while intensifying conditions of discomfort and struggle, is also that which, here, obstructs the state's attempt to define and identify governable subjects. The intrusive photograph, rather than laying bare, with a kind of natural facticity, the brutalized, unbearable, and irreducible lives of these laborers, exposes the vulnerability of these indexical tools even when wielded by sympathetic hands.

Squeeze Pod

A mirrored orb is pictured hovering over a swath of tall grass. From the exterior, no signs of presence can ensure the pod's occupancy. From within the orb, one might catch a glimpse of one of the token exotic creatures from the virtual menagerie curated by the Bjarke Ingels Group for Zootopia, their 2014 proposal for a head-to-toe remodel of a zoo in Givskud, Denmark.

In the renderings circulated by the firm, enclosures make no or impossibly slight appearances. Ingels expounded his vision in *Icon*, stating, "The job was to create a zoo that was designed on the animals' terms, and … undo the visual evidence that you are in a manmade environment full of walls, fences, moats and small caretaker buildings."[19] To this end, all exclusively human affairs are gathered in a sunken central common—"the arrival crater"—encircled by a swath of fabricated wild. The concentricity of the plan regurgitates the radial composition of one of the earliest proto-zoos, the Versailles Menagerie, designed by Louis Le Vau in 1664. But here the center sinks below grade, buffeted on all sides by embankments that house service and other auxiliary programs. The landmasses tilt, blocking panoramic surveillance outward and challenging viewers' expectations for visibility. The surrounding park is unveiled gradually, as one embarks from the plaza and enters into the neo-Jurassic terrain.

The project's diagrammatic axons, in typical BIG style, present paths labeled "hikes," branching from the central plaza into the surrounding "wilderness." Though Ingels cited the Dutch pastime of biking as the inspiration for the circulation plan, the hikes do not appear in the renderings as paths inscribed on the earth's surface by human footfall or tire treads.[20] In place of worn grooves, levitating pods with seamless mirrored coating carry visitors along guided circuitry, populating the gentle curves of generic grasslands. Hovering just above ground level, they leave no trace.

The quadrants that compose the zoo's grounds swell the abstracted biozones to new heights of generality. The taglines for these "loops" or megaregions (based on continents) have the imploring yet flat pitch of vacation packages sold to the bored population of the global north: "Sailing through Asia," "Bicycling in Africa," "Flying through America." The pods drift through these supposedly distinct zones, along supposedly marked paths. Traditional zoo barriers (cages, berms, glass curtains) are reduced to a human-scaled sphere with an impenetrable surface, invisible from the interior, that promises immersion without intimacy, nearness without touch.

The integration of containment systems and the use of individually operated pods sell the project as a win for active, wholesome engagement with that endangered and hot commodity, *nature*. Ingels notes with curt satisfaction, "It's not like you are just being dumped on a train—you actually move around autonomously within certain guidelines."[21] A vague notion of autonomy underlies BIG's maxim: "To ensure an interesting experience [zoo visitors] need to be more than just the passive [consumers] of a premeditated experience"; in the private interior of the pod, Zootopia "becomes a more individual experience."[22] Like the consensual closeness of the squeeze chute, the Zootopia pods are meant to entertain an individually initiated proximity to otherness, in this case not to mechanized prosthetic matter but to groups of "wild" animals. While the pods enable a performance of agency for inhabitants, they dictate their entire experience—when to approach, hesitate, and withdraw. From the outset, the pods prevent visitors from overstepping into something wilder, from being touched and touching in boundary-defying ways. To be squeezed within the pod is to hover within the confines of acceptable closeness without ever traversing into alterity with architectural or animalian matter.

If we dissociate wilderness from BIG's branding of terrain, of unpopulated, exotic expanses of nature, "wild" might come to designate the space for encounters with nonhuman others that destabilize human subjects and their tributaries of touch, their channels of relating. The squeeze chute and the tenements, through different models of inhabitation and agency, conjure wilds of a very different nature, wilds that rub against the the logistical worlds designed for normative subjects. Within the chute, autists give up personal space, the kind codified in the pod, and in return receive comfort. The sheer density that resulted from early speculative development defied attempts to index and subjectify resident populations. These squeezes dispense with the features of the contrived wilds in Zootopia, its roaming mobility hinged on a free-market conception of free will. Whether consensual or the outcome of structural conditions, these architectures of closeness stage a kind of living defined by its illegibility, along with the serious existential risks and pleasures therein.

"Three Degrees of Squeeze" was first published in *Log* 41 (Fall 2017), guest edited by Jaffer Kolb.

1   Maria Almanza, "Temple Grandin's Squeeze Machine as Prosthesis," *Journal of Modern Literature* 39 (Summer 2016): 165.
2   Temple Grandin, "Calming Effects of Deep Touch Pressure in Patients with Autistic Disorder, College Students, and Animals," *Journal of Child and Adolescent Psychopharmacology* 2 (Spring 1992): 63–72.
3   Almanza, "Temple Grandin's Squeeze Machine," 167.
4   Grandin, 64–65.
5   Ibid., 65.
6   Ibid.
7   "For instance, in her book *Thinking in Pictures*, Grandin writes, 'Through the machine, I reached out and held the animal … . Body boundaries seemed to disappear, and I had no awareness of pushing the lever … the parts of the apparatus that held the animal felt as if they were an extension of my own body, similar to the phantom limb effect.'" Almanza, 166.
8   Temple Grandin and Catherine Johnson, *Animals in Translation: Using the Mysteries of Autism to Decode Animal Behavior* (New York: Scribner, 2005), 74.
9   William Bridges, *Map of the City of New York and Island of Manhattan with Explanatory Remarks and References* (New York: William Bridges, 1811), 24.
10   Richard Plunz, *A History of Housing in New York City* (New York: Columbia University Press, 2016), 13.
11   Ibid., 15.
12   Ibid., 13.
13   Cited in Edwin G. Burrows and Mike Wallace, *Gotham: A History of New York City to 1898* (Oxford: Oxford University Press, 1999), 921.
14   Jacob Riis, *How the Other Half Lives: Studies Among the Tenements of New York* (New York: Penguin, 1997), 22.
15   Cited in Plunz, 15.
16   Riis, 67.
17   Ibid.
18   Ibid. Emphasis added.
19   Bjarke Ingels, "Bjarke Ingels' Human Zoo in Denmark," *Icon*, December 3, 2015, https://www.iconeye.com/architecture/features/item/11665-bjarke-ingels-s-human-zoo-in-denmark.
20   Ibid.
21   Ibid.
22   Ibid.

The subject of the era of globalized capitalism, the multitude, constitutes itself as a public only occasionally through shared concerns, or a collection of personal turn-ons. It makes itself visible more often on Twitter than in architecturally defined "public space." This is not to say that architecture does not have a role to play in the constitution of the multitude, but rather that the relationship between public space and the type of public that assembles from the networked multitudes has yet to be properly conceptualized.

Ana Miljački

PUBLIC, BODY, BUILDING: A NEW YMCA

Mariana Ibañez, Christoph Kumpusch, Jennifer Leung, Ana Miljački, Cristina Parreño, Maya Shopova

The second Core Studio poses three challenges: Who do we envision as our architecture's subject and by what means do we conjure up this subject for the purposes of design? In what ways might architecture reinforce and transform an old but historically progressive institution? And finally, how do we understand and manage disciplinary lineages in an anachronistic time like ours? Each of these issues is meant to prompt different modes of contextualizing and to enable definitions of criteria for a design of a synthetic architectural proposition.

We will take on this issue of defining the contemporary subject of architecture in the studio as we reimagine an architecture dedicated to collective play, sports, and health. Our partner in this endeavor is the New York City YMCA.

The Young Men's Christian Association (YMCA) was founded in 1844 in London as a world organization for social reform through recreation. A decade later the first United States-based YMCA opened in the Old Church in Boston. Others followed, with this institution and its sister institution YWCA (incorporated separately) shaping urban life and politics from the east to the west coast. The YMCA was the first institution to offer English as a Second Language courses to immigrants in 1856. From 1869 on its buildings included gymnasiums. Shortly thereafter at a Boston YMCA, Robert Roberts coined the term "body building" and developed exercise machines to support this newly codified activity. Launching at the height of the Public Bath movement in the United States (with ninety-nine indoor and outdoor public bath facilities opening between 1895 and 1904), and providing additional social and sports facilities with its baths and pools, the YMCA has also been credited with codifying and popularizing two sports that are now fully part of the American and global urban imaginary, as well as the Olympics: basketball in 1891, and volleyball in 1890. Conceptualized from the outset as a progressive, reformist, and missionary institution, the YMCA transformed with the times, opening dedicated Y's for African Americans, for railway workers, Native Americans; operating residences for young men arriving to the city; and offering classes and lodging to the new female working force. Its identity politics and social policies evolved at the liberal forefront of the times. Though its name still carries a series of labels (young, men, women, Christian)—indeed demographic lenses through which one might be tempted to understand its public—all of these have been surpassed by the type of wide-ranging community center that the Y has become. No longer housing an exclusive religious, gendered, ageist institution, the modernized YMCA buildings across the United States function like ultimate urban social condensers.

In the greater New York City network, they offer programs for diabetes prevention, turn more than sixty thousand young New Yorkers (and sometimes their families) into swimmers every year, provide work for neighborhood youth, and camps for kids. In cases such as the Bed-Stuy Y, which multiplied its membership by over a tenfold after its renovation in 2007, they successfully transform the physical and social health of the city.

Whether they are housed in Beaux-Arts buildings (from the end of the nineteenth and turn of the twentieth century) like the famous 23rd Street Westside Y, or in later-era neo-Georgian buildings such as the Harlem Y, their architecture still signals the institution's old missionary, reformist role through reserved and inward-oriented (and sometimes quite beautiful) citadels. The outdated signifying role of the Y's architecture coupled with the fact that its "public" is still located behind a paying barrier and oriented toward a single neighborhood location, prompt the studio to seek an important architectural adjustment and offerings that the new Y could make to its city. With its swimming pools, dance classes, daycares, saunas, and exercise machines, the Y is obviously a site where an intimate exchange of bodily energies occurs among its users, but also between them and the building. Sweat is here constantly countered by the mechanics of AC, the piezoelectric potential of the many steps taken here simply gets absorbed by the internal gears of the elliptical machines, electricity gets piped in to do it, while all the pool water gets flushed every eighty thousand gallons or so. The challenge will be to find compelling ways that architecture might contribute to the reimagining of this institution's literal, cultural, and urban operation.

In Spring 2017, the studio site was the southeast Bronx, along NYCHA's Edenwald Houses. In Spring 2018, the studio site was Coney Island, Brooklyn.

Collective Intelligence

You will work in teams of three to research, take a position, and report on one of the following topics:

- History of the YMCA
- Public Bathhouses in New York
- Basketball
- YWCA's Politics
- History of ADA rules and regulations
- History of Urban Transformations
- Swimming Pool Standards
- The Downtown Athletic Club
- NYC Day Care Regulations
- OneNY Plan
- WPA Pools in NYC
- The NYCHA program
- Public and Private Transportation
- Urban Gardening in New York City

You will continue to work in your teams of three to analyze one of the precedents.

- Collect, analyze, and present the architect's own representations of the project as well as representations by others that communicate the program organization and design concept.
- Draft critical plans and sections of the project.
- Create your own analytical representations that dissect the project/program and re-represent the organizational logic of the project based on your own analysis and criteria.
- Finally, produce a conceptual physical model/ patent of your precedent. For reference, take a look at Rem Koolhaas's tongue-in-cheek patent drawings produced for the *Content* exhibit and book.

The point of this exercise is to begin to think critically about the spatial organization and key programmatic components of the YMCA, and most importantly, to begin to take a position on historically important projects in the disciplinary archive. You can and should be smart, inventive, and constructive (in that order) when you "crit" your particular architect.

The People's Pool: An Anachronistic Competition for a Public Pool and Playground in Coney Island

Futurologist Bruce Sterling recently offered *atemporality* to contemporary designers. Philosopher of science Bruno Latour offered *prospects* in place of the old, stable idea of future in his manifesto for Constructivism. In a way, each proposed that an older version of temporality, predicated on an unproblematic idea of progress, was waning. The issue is not that time has stopped ticking, or even moving forward, but that our modernist ideas of progress and even our postmodernist ways of critiquing those, seem reptilian and moralizing in light of our

contemporary understanding of the interconnectedness of all things. These two thinkers are not alone in characterizing the world that we collectively or individually sense as ours—the world of anachronistic relationships—as one in which no idealized destination is reachable. Or at least, the cost of progress is understood to be such that it (progress, above all else) does not seem as desirable as it might have seemed in the 1920s.

You have your raw material already—the precedent you analyzed. You need to adapt the project you studied to accommodate the program as well as enter into a dialogue with contemporary cultural and disciplinary issues, which should affect the ideologies, tectonic solutions, and representational choices you make in this competition. Anachronism is only part of it. The other important component of this competition relies on your ability to discern the nexus between historically specific pressures on your precedent project and its architectural resolution. Take your precedent, and after you have distilled its core organizational and tectonic ideas, radicalize it and adapt, edit, reduce, enlarge, cut-up (as the writer William Burroughs might say), and transform it to include the program listed below and place it intelligently on our site. Don't forget the lessons of our collective research on the institution and content we are working with. This is a re-enactment of sorts; enjoy the freedom of wearing someone else's hat.

The anachronistic competition comes with a set of format requirements: five boards (24"x36") and a model at 1/32"=1'. Somewhere on those boards you have to include a site drawing and relevant plans and sections. Everything else is open but the boards should "speak" to the historical moment you chose to address with your reworked playground. The time you have for this competition is commensurate with the usual competition conditions. You will continue to work as teams. The review will be silent and will result in prizes.

Readings:

On Users and Publics

- Reinhold Martin, "Public and Common(s)," *Places*, January 2013. https://placesjournal.org/article/public-and-commons/?cn-reloaded=1
- Michel Serres, "Quasi-Object," in *The Parasite* (University of Minnesota Press, 2007, originally 1982).
- Michael Hardt and Antonio Negri, Preface, *Multitude: War and Democracy in the Age of Empire* (New York, NY: Penguin, 2005).
- Michel Foucault, "Of Other Spaces, Heterotopias," 1967, https://foucault.info/documents/

heterotopia/foucault.heteroTopia.en/.
- Chantal Mouffe, "Artistic Activism and Agonistic Spaces," *Art and Research* 1, no. 2, (Summer 2007).

On Program and Organization
- Colin Rowe, "Program versus Paradigm: Otherwise Casual Notes on the Pragmatic, the Typical and the Possible," in *As I Was Saying: Recollections and Miscellaneous Essays: Texas, Pre-Texas, Cambridge* (Cambridge, MA: MIT Press, 1995), 5–42.
- Mark Jarzombek, "Corridor Spaces," *Critical Theory* 36, no. 4 (Summer 2010): 728–770.
- Robin Evans, "Figures, Doors and Passages," in *Translations from Drawing to Building* (Cambridge, MA: MIT Press, 1997).
- Robin Evans, *The Fabrication of Virtue: English Prison Architecture, 1750–1840* (Cambridge: Cambridge University Press, 2010).

On Form and Envelopes
- Pier Vittorio Aureli, "Architecture and Content: Who is Afraid of the Form-Object?" *Log* 3 (Fall 2004).
- Alejandro Zaera-Polo, "The Politics of Envelope," *Log* 13–14 (Fall 2008): 193–207.
- Sylvia Lavin, "What you Surface is What you Get," *Log* 1 (Fall 2003): 103–106.
- Colin Rowe and Robert Slutzky, "Transparency: Literal and Phenomenal," in *The Mathematics of the Ideal Villa* (Cambridge, MA: MIT Press, 1982).

On Process and "Influence"
- Jonathan Lethem, "The Ecstasy of Influence," *Harper's Magazine*, February 2007, https://harpers.org/archive/2007/02/the-ecstasy-of-influence/.
- Colin Rowe, "A Letter on Precedent and Invention" in *Precedent and Invention: Harvard Architecture Review* 5, ed. Joanne Gaines (New York: Rizzoli, 1986).
- Editorial Introduction, *San Rocco* #7: *Indifference* (Summer 2013).
- Roger Caillois, "The Definition of Play and The Classification of Games," in *The Game Design Reader,* ed. Katie Salen (Cambridge, MA: MIT Press, 2005; originally published in 1959), 122–155.
- J.G. Ballard, "I Believe," in *RE/Search* 8/9 ed. V. Vale (San Francisco, CA: RE/Search Publishing, 1984).
- Sanford Kwinter, "Radical Anamnesis," in *Far From Equilibrium* (Barcelona: Actar, 2008).
- Andy Merrifield, "Magical Marxism," *Environment and Planning D: Society and Space* 27, (2009): 381–386.

On YMCA, WPA Pools, Race, and Reform
- Paula Lupkin, *Manhood Factories: YMCA Architecture and the Making of Modern Urban Culture* (Minneapolis: University of Minnesota Press, 2010).
- Marta Gutman, "Race, Place, and Play: Robert Moses and the WPA Swimming Pools in New York City," *Journal of the Society of Architectural Historians* 67, no. 4 (December 2008): 532–561.
- Michael Sorkin, "Critique: Rehabilitating Robert Moses," *Architectural Record* 195 (March 2007): 55–56.
- Andrea Renner, "A Nation that Bathes Together: New York City's Progressive Era Public Baths," *Journal of the Society of Architectural* 67, no. 4 (December 2008): 504–531.
- David Glassberg, "Design of Reform: The Public Bath Movement in America," *American Studies* 20, no. 2 (1979): 5–21.
- "Black Lives Matter," *The Aggregate website*, ed. Meredith TenHoor and Jonathan Massey, (March 2015), http://we-aggregate.org/project/black-lives-matter.

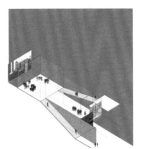

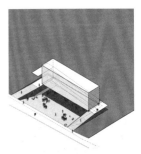

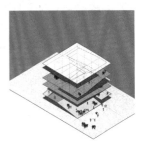

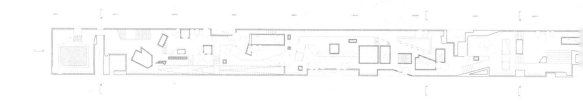

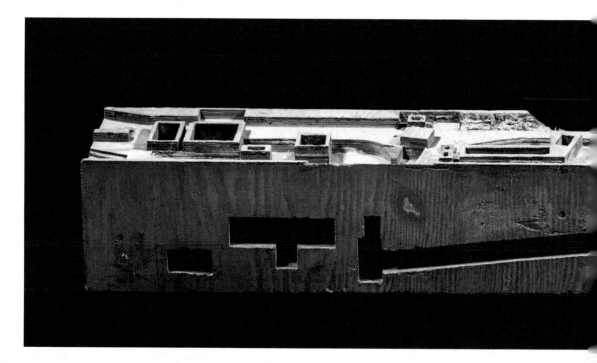

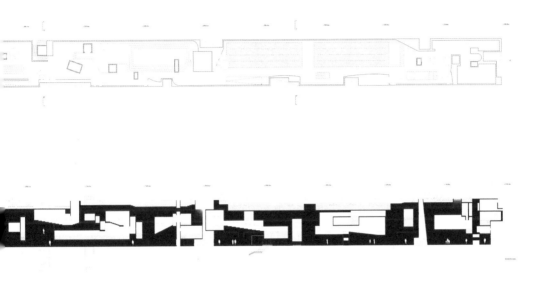

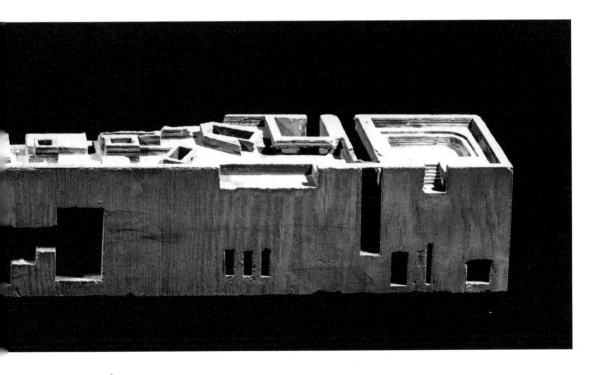

171

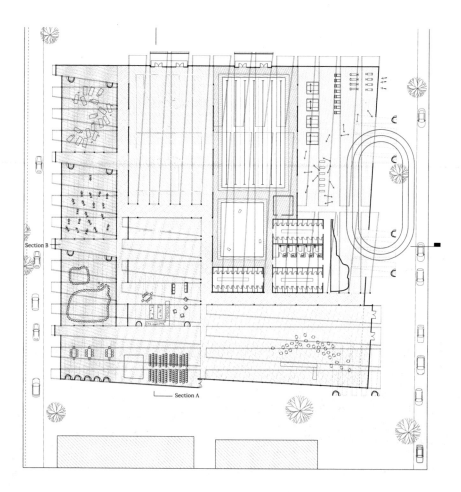

Section B

Section A

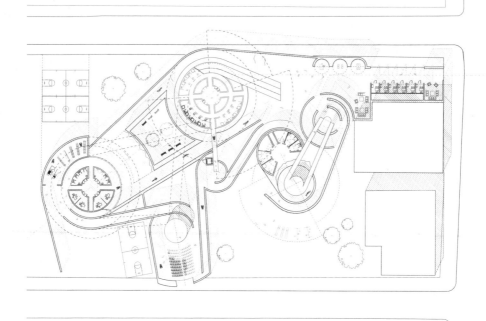

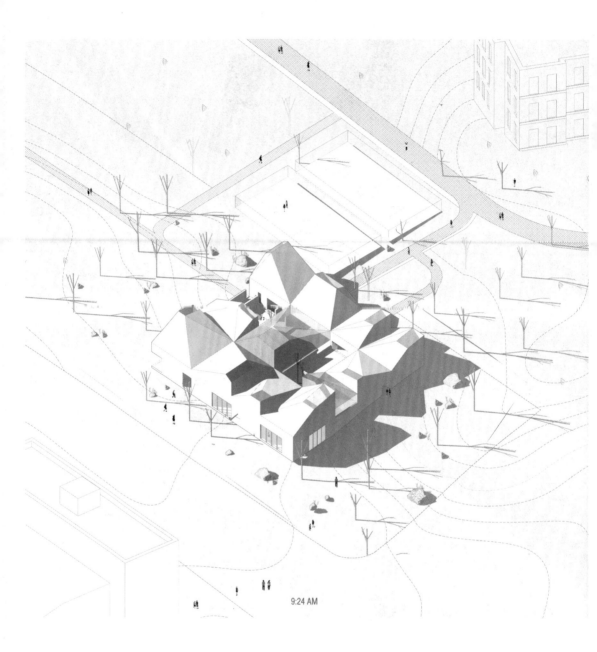

9:24 AM

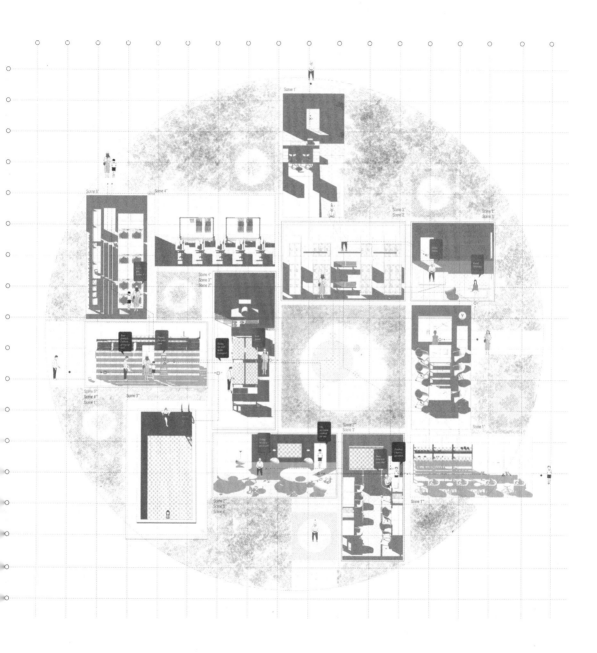

THE YMCA OF FANTASY
Chen Chu

Wet Lodge

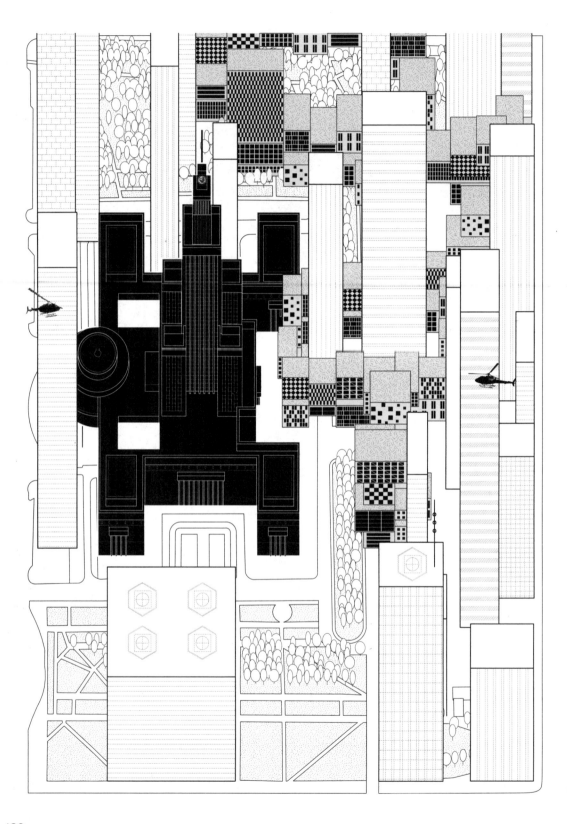

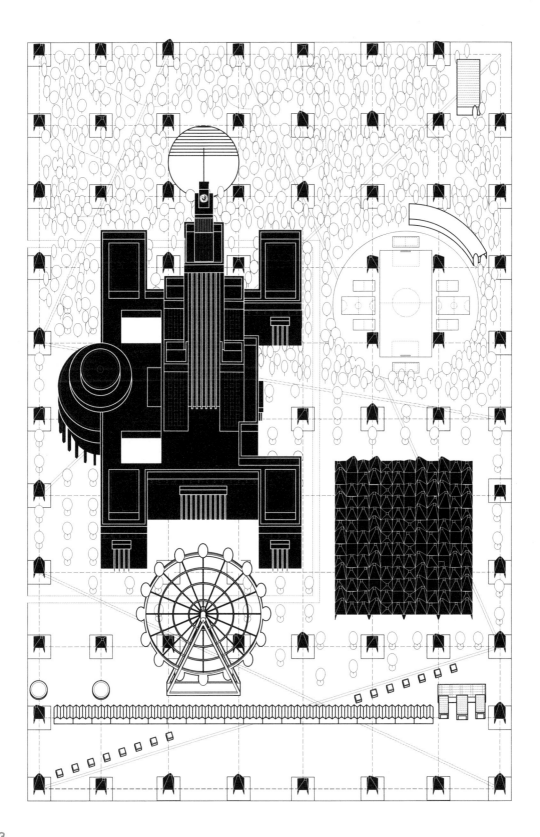

183

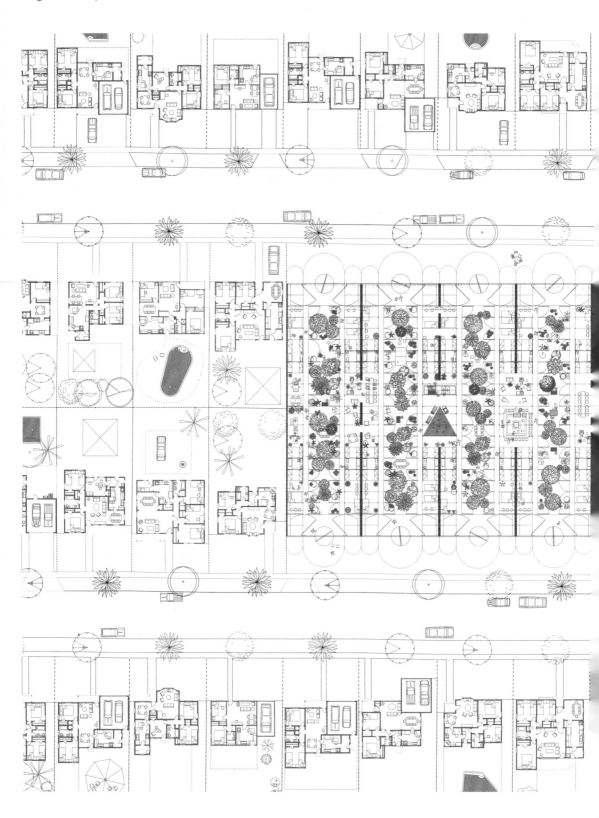

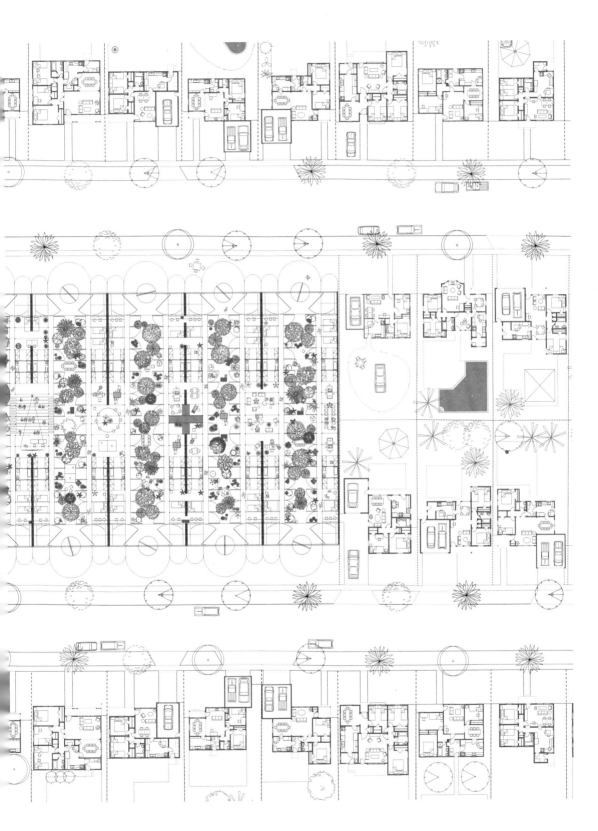

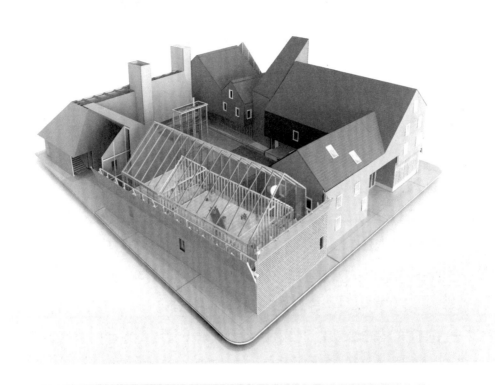

COLLECTIVE HOME OFFICE
Mary Lynch-Lloyd, Ching Ying Ngan, Maya Shopova

We believe collectivity is a shared motivation toward a common goal. Fundamentally ideological, it is grown over time through social intimacy fed by shared experiences, both positive and negative. The member-ship-based collectives of today, on the other hand, are simply typical office and resi-dential models decorated with signifiers of togetherness. They lack the architectural and social vocabulary necessary for a collective language. In our practice, we test different modes of collectivity—both in how we work, and within the contents of our architectural proposals.

Collective Home Office

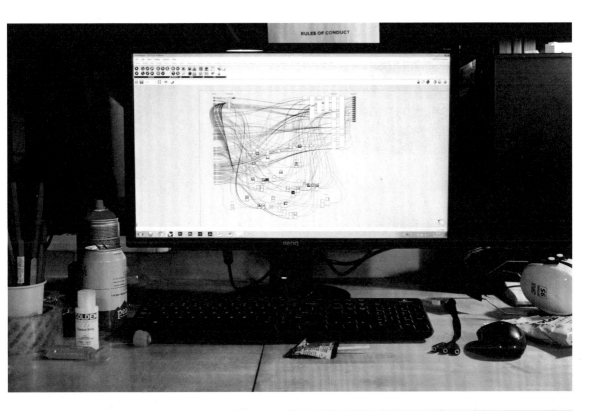

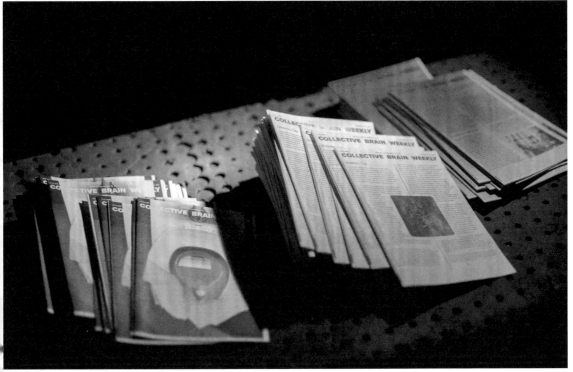

189

URBAN RISK LAB: PROJECTS, TOOLS, AND STRATEGIES

Miho Mazereeuw; Aditya Barve, Justin Lavallee, Hugh Magee, David Moses, Larisa Ovalles, Lizzie Yarina

In an era of climate change, intensified hurricanes, severe flooding, and rapid urbanization in seismic areas, what does it mean to design in anticipation of increasing hazards? The Urban Risk Lab (URL) is an interdisciplinary team operating at the intersection of research and design practice. Our projects explore how disaster risk reduction can become embedded in everyday environments, making lively spaces that are more resilient to future disasters. Intentionally, and maybe inherently, Urban Risk Lab is a loaded title: each term embodies certain preconceptions. Breaking down this name describes a modus operandi for our lab, one which is both wide-ranging in its strategies and specific in its agendas.

Disasters don't only impact cities. Defined as a hazard event which disrupts the normal daily activity of a society, disasters can strike anywhere people live. Our use of the term *urban* focuses not only on the metropolitan unit of the city, but also what Neil Brenner and Christian Schmid term "extended urbanization"—the networks of less-dense, distributed spaces and systems which contemporary society operates in and moves through. "Urban" highlights a particular interest in where people live: while many of these sites would traditionally be considered cities (to Brenner and Schmid, "concentrated urbanization"), they also include towns, villages, and rural settlements vulnerable to hazards.

The *risks* we focus on emerge from "natural" hazards (i.e., flooding, earthquakes, tsunamis, hurricanes) rather than "technological" hazards (i.e., terrorist attacks, oil spills, chemical explosions). Importantly though, no disaster is truly natural: they are all a product of society. From the Fukushima Daiichi meltdown during the 2011 Tōhoku tsunami, to the exacerbation of storms, droughts, and heatwaves by climate change, it is increasingly difficult to disentangle the natural from the man-made. To unpack this complexity, we employ a definition which defines disaster risk as a hazard multiplied by vulnerability (both social and physical) and lessened by mitigation and capacity to cope or adapt. Our projects examine how all of these levers can be adjusted to reduce disaster risk.

At MIT, the *lab* is the basic unit of research. The composition of a lab, and its position within MIT, allows us the agency to pursue an active form of research inaccessible to a private firm or discrete academics. Our collaborative format, which brings together design thinkers with different skills and backgrounds, allows us to take on complex and unconventional projects. And not being beholden to clients gives us a flexibility to pursue and establish partnerships and projects which combine research and action. In fact, this notion of "action research," that academic pursuits can also take on a performative role, contributing to the world at the same time as producing knowledge, is an idea that emerged from MIT.

What differentiates the Urban Risk Lab from existing humanitarian or resilience practices by which we are inspired, such as Elemental or Shigeru Ban Architects, is our emphasis on the already vast research in the social sciences and emergency management on adapting to, preparing for, and recovering from disasters, as well as work from engineering disciplines on mitigating the impact of hazards. Much of this research remains compartmentalized within disciplinary silos, but by drawing on and collaborating with diverse scholars and practitioners, the URL model strives to be more comprehensive: disasters, after all, do not adhere to disciplinary boundaries.

One of the most useful concepts we leverage from emergency management is the idea of a "disaster cycle," a timeline which considers both what happens before a disaster strikes (mitigation, preparedness), during (response), and after it occurs (recovery). We think of our work as a cyclical project around this timeline; while each project might prioritize a particular bracket in the cycle, we are always considering how the work fits into this larger continuum. In this way, disaster-related projects are not only about how something functions during or after a disaster, but also how it relates to everyday life.

Interdisciplinary Collaboration: FEMA

The Lab's methodologies have been shaped by the projects we take on. In 2017, URL assembled a team to respond to a multi-year grant from the United States Federal Emergency Management Agency (FEMA) exploring alternative post-disaster housing systems. Housing, particularly post-disaster housing, is fundamentally complex, and we brought on board faculty and student collaborators from the Department of Urban Studies and Planning (DUSP), the Digital Structures Group, the Sloan School of Management, Lincoln Laboratories, and the MIT Center for Transportation and Logistics. The research strategies across this group have included case studies; interviews with disaster survivors,

local leaders, and FEMA personnel; post-disaster ethnographic fieldwork; supply chain modeling; engineering simulations; FEMA field office visits; and policy analysis. This approach allowed us all to tackle the issues from multiple perspectives—architecture, policy, engineering, supply chain, and logistics—in parallel.

Collaborating as part of an interdisciplinary team is difficult. Each discipline has its own language, priorities, and ways of working. Design, which by nature involves reconciling multiple spheres of expertise, brings this multifaceted team together, but the process is often slow. We embrace this struggle, as it allows for a richer response, one that can address designing for disasters in all their complexity.

From this research, our team is developing a series of tools to address post-disaster housing issues with an emphasis on vulnerable communities. Much of the work emphasizes sites outside of the contiguous United States (i.e., Puerto Rico, Hawaii, American Samoa) which face particular difficulty in receiving safe, fast housing options post-disaster. One tool under development is the Shelter for Emergency and Expansion Design (SEED), a rapidly deployable housing unit that leverages existing logistics networks and can adapt to local cultural, social, siting, hazard, and environmental contexts, as well as the specific needs of individual families. It is designed to anticipate future expansions and accept various local material and construction practices. The SEED also embeds disaster preparedness education within the design and through the installation and expansion process. It provides housing for the response and recovery phase, but also ties in mitigation and preparedness for when the next hurricane (flood, fire, earthquake, tornado) comes.

Assembling all these pieces and making new connections is a design challenge, even though the social, political, and logistical considerations are as important as (if not more than) the object itself. FEMA is an immense and highly compartmentalized institution, and providing this synthesized view of their work in the post-disaster housing realm has already begun to create new ways of looking at their protocols and systems.

Implementation: PREPhub
The Emergency Preparedness Hub, or PREPhub, is a dual-function sculptural object installed in public space which serves as interactive social furniture every day, and provides off-grid infrastructures such as power and communications in the event of a disaster. It is an ongoing project, and we have created and tested a series of temporary prototypes in sites across the United States. We are currently implementing a large installation in Portland, Oregon, in collaboration with the City of Portland, Portland State University (PSU), and Portland General Electric. As with most of our projects, it is not a conventional client-to-architect relationship, but rather a collaboration which bridges multiple scales and engages diverse stakeholders.

Working with diverse partners to invent new forms of socio-spatial infrastructure is a difficult and slow approach to architecture. Each collaborator has their own priorities, and emphasizes different needs within the project. Portland State has many existing connections with local institutions and people and provides an emphasis on research. The City of Portland and PSU brought in Portland General Electric, which has helped us understand potential PREPhub impacts at the scale of utilities and infrastructure. Getting these three partners all on the same page is a challenge, but engaging in those conversations helps us clarify the project's design agenda. We're always asking: Who is our main client? How do we navigate disagreements? It takes a lot of conversation and patience. But there is an optimism across the team that we can negotiate our way through a challenge through the collaborative design process.

We have found that the PREPhub's design—the renderings, prototypes, and representations—brings collaborators together. Portland's interest in the project stems from its aesthetics: although it performs as infrastructure post-disaster, it doesn't look like infrastructure. Rather, it catches the eye, piques curiosity, and in doing so, can also educate. The form of the project gets people to engage and activates everyday space, which in turn improves its function in disaster. One thing all the partners agree upon are the representations of the project we produce. They are projections of something that doesn't yet exist, and allow partners to understand and get behind an idea for the future.

Web-based Platforms: RiskMap
Training in architecture and urbanism helps us to identify problems within the built environment, but as an interdisciplinary lab we are able to also respond with something other than a built solution. We do not confine our work: we have geographers, computer scientists and ethnographers in our lab. With RiskMap, we looked at the problem of real-time flood information—a physical problem—but quickly realized that defaulting to an architectural or built solution was not the right answer. Instead, RiskMap responds to flood events by gathering real-time flooding data from residents, who often have the best localized information. The interactive platform harnesses the power of citizen reporting and social

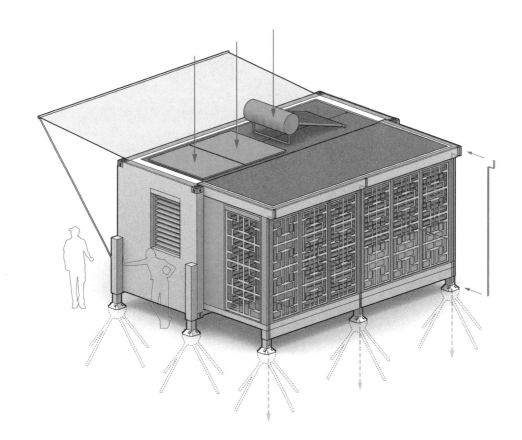

media to map time-critical information. Through the live map, residents can inform each other about quickly changing situations in the city and help each other navigate to safety. The project straddles different scales of intervention; it works between a top-down response and bottom-up collective community action.

As designers, we see the problem of flooding holistically, as part of an interconnected and ever-changing relationship with surrounding people, flora, fauna, histories, economies, ecosystems, and built environments. With this perspective, we have been adding preparedness cards to the Risk-Map project which facilitate engagement before a disaster (e.g., before hurricane season begins). We ask users to report infrastructure that needs to be repaired or culverts that need to be cleaned so that we can all be stewards of our own cities. The collection of this detailed information is valuable for data-scarce, rapidly growing cities to use for future planning and design.

Research Agendas

While our strategies vary, Urban Risk Lab projects share the aim of creating environments which are vibrant, equitable, and resilient to future disasters. Several research agendas are key to this goal: looking at disaster risk at multiple scales, considering use over time (before, during and after a disaster), linking research to education, and remaining optimistic about the potential of design.

Multiscalar

Disaster risk cannot be isolated in a single space or scale. Consider a flood: whether or not a home is affected is related to how the home is built, where it is located, the porosity and construction in the watershed upstream, urban mitigation measures such as levees or retention ponds, and even global contributions to climate change which in turn intensify storms. In our projects, we always think and work at multiple scales. For example, RiskMap considers both peer-to-peer information sharing and how flood data can be used for larger planning schemes. The FEMA SEED housing unit is directed toward a national-scale response connected with larger infrastructural, policy and response systems, while also addressing the individual needs of communities and survivors. Oscillating between scales is important in ensuring that projects don't leave out certain groups or exacerbate existing vulnerabilities.

Everyday Disaster

Disaster preparedness is more effective when it is embedded in spaces and infrastructures that are used everyday. The URL looks at how this interface of everyday and disaster can enhance shared environments, creating places which improve people's lives. The tools, strategies, and interventions the lab produces all interact with ideas of the disaster cycle. Many of the PREP-hub's post-disaster functions also operate in a more playful format everyday: a loudspeaker for disaster announcements can play music for an event; emergency beacons can provide colored lighting so users can host a party or safely gather at night. Risk Map was developed to help people navigate their environments during and in the immediate aftermath of a flood, but thinking about the larger continuum has allowed us to leverage the project for the long term. That data will also be valuable in preparedness and planning activities. This crowd-sourced project has helped map certain flood zones for the first time, showing how flood water behaves in a rapidly changing city.

Teaching

Many of these themes have been explored or expanded in studios and workshops. Studios are an opportunity to bring many minds together around complex issues. We don't need a client or a grant, so these explorations can be somewhat unrestricted, and can tackle issues and places that we think are important. Our projects rely on establishing diverse partnerships, and often studios, as a way of sharing our approach, become catalysts for forming new relationships and establishing projects. Studios also allow the lab to form relationships with students: ninety percent of the lab's research staff began as students in URL courses, and working with the lab serves as a way to continue to explore shared interests.

The studios URL leads emphasize engagement with people and places. Methods like interviewing aren't often taught in architecture school but can be incredibly fruitful, even necessary, in the contexts in which we work. In some studios this entails in-depth ethnographic interviews and conversations; in others it requires working through context.

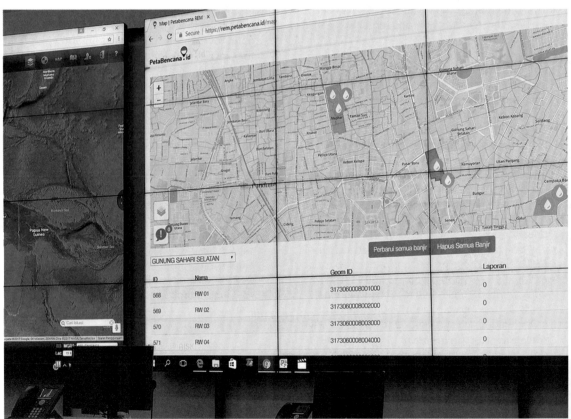

Optimism

The ability to do this work requires a certain optimism, particularly as the specter of climate change and associated disasters looms larger than ever. Researching disasters can be incredibly distressing, but we also continue to find evidence of the kindness and resilience of humanity even in the darkest of catastrophes. We believe that if design responds to social interconnections and carries the concerns of collective well-being, architecture can serve beyond its role of physical shelter. The URL aims to create lasting physical architecture and digital platforms that are embedded in their respective social, cultural, and economic contexts. While there are many problems design cannot solve, being optimistic about the potential of design, in collaboration with other fields of knowledge, allows us to establish new approaches to what at first appear to be intractable problems.

Images
P 195, 197 Top, 198: Alternatives for FEMA Disaster-Related Housing Assistance. Photographs from fieldwork in Puerto Rico, Spring 2018.
P 197 Bottom: PREPhub prototype installed at MIT, Spring 2016.
P 200: Urban Risk Map, Indonesia: This project, supported by USAID, the Indonesia's National Agency for Disaster Management, and in collaboration with the Pacific Disaster Center at the University of Hawaii, allows residents to share vital flood information using social messaging apps. Confirmed flood reports are added to a publicly available map helping to inform communities and emergency agencies of the flood situation in real-time. Currently operating in four cities, Greater Jakarta, Bandung, Surabaya, and Semarang, the flood map feeds the crowdsourced data to emergency managers and PDC's Disaster Management Early Warning platform called InAWARE through a custom-built REM (Risk Evaluation Matrix).

Projects
Alternatives for FEMA Disaster-Related Housing Assistance
Urban Risk Lab: Miho Mazereeuw, Rich Serino, David Moses, Larisa Ovalles, Lizzie Yarina, Justin Lavallee, Aditya Barve, Mayank Ojha, Jean Carlos Vega Diaz; *Digital Structures Group*: Caitlin Mueller, Assistant Professor of Architecture and Civil Engineering, Courtney Steven; *MIT DUSP*: Justin Steil, Assistant Professor of Law and Urban Planning, Mark Brennan, Aditi Mehta; *MIT Sloan School of Management*: Steven Graves, Abraham J. Siegel Professor of Management, So Han Florence Yip; *Lincoln Laboratory Humanitarian Assistance and Disaster Response Group*: Anthony Lapadula, Hayley Reynolds, Sean Winkler, Roland Weibel, Sarah Slaughter, Adam Norige

PREPhub
Urban Risk Lab: Miho Mazereeuw, David Moses, Justin Lavallee, Aditya Barve, Saeko Nomura Baird; *Past Contributors*: Evan Owens, Seungho Park, Jongwan Kwon, Lizzie Yarina, Abraham Quintero, Ananya Nandy, Alexa Jan; *MIT Lincoln Lab:* Adam Norige, Brice Maclaren, Tom Smith, Christopher Budny, Peter Klein, Andrew Weinert, Ed Orchanian. *Current Project Partners*: City of Portland, Portland General Electric, Portland State University; *Supported by* TATA Center of Technology and Design, MIT International Design Center, Council for the Arts at MIT, Seifel Fund Research Grant, Lincoln Laboratory

Urban Risk Map
Indonesia Field Team: Etienne Turpin, Pritta Andrani Widyanarko, Dika Fadmastuti, Christina Geros, Nashin Mahtani, Emir Hartato.
URL is working with Broward County, Florida in the United States and in the city of Chennai, India. The project is supported by TATA Center for Technology and Design at MIT and is focused on urban hazards vulnerability of Indian cities.

mental

Acts

Environ-

mental

Acts

Environ-

mental

Acts

Environ-

mental

How have we been taught to experience and understand our relationship to land and territory? How might architecture be thought of as an open work that allows and registers environmental change? How do we "let go" of the coast?

Challenged to consider existing and looming effects of environmental change, the projects that follow contend with the implications of change on issues of livelihood, development, governance, and nationhood. They ask how environmental harm is rendered visible and how and by whom it is experienced. The studios, seminars, and projects included here challenge modern obsessions with permanence and fixity, seeking to reshape and reimagine architectures, sites, regions, and territories that have been stabilized as if immobile.

The projects gathered here look at how landscapes have been, and could be, further transformed; they reframe these sites as political spaces, as spaces shaped by and shaping a human agenda. They struggle with violence performed onto land itself, and the repercussions of these acts on humans and non-human actors. Social, environmental, and political remnants of industrial activity are brought forward in the wake of aging infrastructures, polluted sites, and uncertain futures.

Any proposition here requires looking at long pasts and long futures to address the politics and economies embedded in these sites. Such questions require stitching together knowledge and methods from different disciplines to begin to approach issues at hand. Shifting away from the architectural object as such, the projects herein take on the systemic and infrastructural in both physical and process-based realms. They work through inherited policies, zoning, and building codes as much as they do in architectural form. They provoke us to think differently about infrastructure and its edges as integrated with social and technical considerations. These sites are recast as common spaces and public goods, as sites that still have serious implications on individuals and communities.

REVISITING "UNKNOWN QUANTITIES"
2010/2019
Peter Galison, Caroline A. Jones
Artforum
April 2010

LANDSCAPE EXPERIENCE:
SEMINAR IN LAND/ART
Seminar: History, Theory and Criticism
Instructors: Caroline A. Jones, Rebecca Uchill
Fall 2016

The word landscape always implies a subject position. Unlike the categories of "nature," "wilderness," or "ecology," landscape is something experienced (or observed, or represented, or cultivated) by human agents. We are interested precisely in that agency.

This seminar explores "land" as a genre, theme, and medium of art and architecture of the last five decades. A major opportunity afforded by the course is an optional field trip to visit major works of land art in Utah, Arizona, New Mexico, and Texas during the summer preceding the term. Focusing largely on work in the United States, the course seeks to understand how the use of land in art and architecture is bound into complicated entanglements of property and power, the inheritances of non-US traditions, and how the term "landscape" is variously deployed in the service of a range of political and philosophical positions. The work of artists, architects, and writers on art and architectural theory can offer rich insights into the tangled nexus of phenomenology, pilgrimage, and property development that has been conjured by landscape, in history and at present.

ORDER AND THE ENVIRONMENT
Option Studio
Instructors: Florian Idenburg, Sam Ghantous
Fall 2017

This architecture design studio considers the relationship between container and contained. How can architecture anticipate the objects and actions it is to house or hold?

In accelerated times, design justified through program is born dead. Programs are not stable and typically, despite most well-meaning intentions, misalign with users' behaviors. Mono-functional organizations foreclose possibility. How, then, might we order architectural space in times of flux? To this end, Umberto Eco's *Opera Aperta* (1962) describes a beautifully useful approach captured in his conjecture of openness, which characterizes an author's cultural production as a "decision to leave arrangements of some constituents of a work to the public or to chance."

The final project of the studio is the design of an archive and an exhibition space for modern and contemporary art, housed within the Nevada Museum of Art, a relatively young museum in Reno, Nevada. This institution's collections focus on art inspired by the landscape of the western United States as well as art that deals with the altered landscape. Part of this legacy is that of the Land Art movement that emerged prominently in the United States toward the 1960s and 1970s, at the height of the Cold War. The expansive landscape evoked a sense of freedom and empowerment. At the same time, concerns of the art movement centered around a rejection of commercialization in art making, and an enthusiasm for an emergent ecological movement. The movement coincided with the popular rejection of urban living. Included in these inclinations were spiritual yearnings concerning the planet Earth as home to mankind.

What is the effect of human action on our landscape? What is left of this spirit of Land Art today? How should we imagine an architectural order that can house an exhibition space and archive of art focused on this altered landscape?

MUSEUM OF LATE MODERNITY
Ammar Ahmed

The Museum of Late Modernity in Reno, Nevada is a museum of the present moment and near future. In her essay "Grids," Rosalind Krauss argues that "the grid is an emblem of modernity by being just that: the form that is ubiquitous in the art of twentieth century, while appearing nowhere, nowhere at all, in the art of the last one." The grid of the twenty-first century pervades industry and logistics inasmuch as it exists in the realm of arts. The proposed museum is a set of exertions on the grid. It is morphed, scaled, and distorted to break its own hegemony, and to reckon with estrangements, conflicts, and overlaps in those spaces.

MUSEUM OF ART AND ENVIRONMENT
Alexander Bodkin

The museum is located near an industrial park in a desert twenty-five miles outside of Reno, Nevada. It riffs on the architecture of prospector towns, generic industrial buildings, and Burning Man tents to create a desert mirage of an encampment in flux.

This project thinks through themes of control and contingency, the role and effects of time in architecture, and how a project can establish a set of parameters (form, detail, material, organization, etc.) that anticipate and register environmental change while also supporting the emergence of novel environmental conditions.

A 3.5m x 3.5m physical model of the museum at 1:100 acts as a platform for experiments relating to these themes. The experiments are documented in five videos that construct narratives within the museum site. As fictions, these narrative videos explore how humans, animals, plants, etc. might occupy and transform the museum over time. Dirt and sand are swept up by the wind and caught in deep, textured façades. Landslides gradually bury a tax-haven free-port at the bottom of a steep hill. The loose canopy flops and blows in a storm, eventually weighed down by rain that drips through to feed vegetation piles below. An annual ritual of gathering dry brush from around the museum and burning it in the chimneys overlays a cyclical, human-managed act of maintenance on the site.

CIVIC FOREST
Diana Ang, Giovanni Bellotti, Kelly Main, Alexander Wiegering
Urban Design Studio: Urbanism After Extraction–Housing, Landscape, and Infrastructure in the Katowice Agglomeration, Poland
Instructors: Marie Law Adams, Rafi Segal
Spring 2017

The current definition of "forest" as an area mainly occupied by hardwood species determines perimeters and boundaries subject to common vegetation patterns. According to this definition, forests in Poland account for thirty percent of land cover, mainly located on publicly owned land. This reading, however, fails to define the forest as a political space, as a component of the Silesian metropolis rather than its counterpart. We propose to address the forests of Silesia as new centers, able through their scale and complexity to speak of the current problems and ambitions of the metropolis.

The Civic Forest frames the collection of Silesian forests as a civic space, a space charged with a human agenda—environmental, economic, and social. In addressing the ambitions and frictions among preservation, production, and extraction, we can imagine new relations between domestic, productive, and protected spaces.

ARCHIPELAGIC SOVEREIGNTY: RE-MAPPING UNITED PACIFIC STATES OF MIGRATION
Lizzie Yarina
ARCH+ Magazine 230
August 2017

BIGHT: COASTAL URBANISM
Rafi Segal and Susannah Drake/DLANDstudio
2017

In January 2017, the Regional Plan Association (RPA) launched a design competition which called on architects, landscape architects, designers, and urban planners to demonstrate visually how policy changes, new investments, and innovative thinking proposed in the *Fourth Regional Plan: A Region Transformed* (October 2017) can transform different geographic areas in the Tri-State region and prepare them for the next twenty-five years. Rafi Segal and DLANDstudio were selected to propose visions and designs for the future of the Bight, the region's Ocean Corridor.

The Bight is the notch in the region's coast where ocean currents conspire to pile sand, forever redrawing the shore. The Bight is also an invention—a hard coastline extensively built during the twentieth century, now stiff with aging settlements determined, but ill-suited, to stand their ground against storms and sea level rise. These opposing forces, where the immovable city meets an unstoppable nature, define its uncertain future. It's time to blur this line. To relieve this tension, which threatens hundreds of miles of coast, hundreds of thousands of residents, and hundreds of billions of dollars in property losses, we propose replacing the hardened edge separating the city and nature with a new "landscape economic zone"—a buffer in which land and water commingle, creating new spaces for habitation, conservation, work, and play.

Rather than futilely trying to hold the line, the project proposes an approach of "receive, protect, adapt." Strengthen urban spines and nodes on higher ground to receive new residents at higher densities. Protect low-lying areas using the absorptive capacity of the buffer, and adapt to a more amphibious lifestyle in the zone—transforming the coastline into the new urban frontier.

The result is a less sprawling and more productive coast, made all the more resilient by tailoring homes, neighborhoods, suburbs, towns, and cities to this new reality. The transition to renewable energy and the future of work-leisure in an era of intense automation inform the reimagined Bight as a new open space for the most populous region in the United States, rather than an increasingly untenable line in the sand.

Project
Benjamin Albrecht, Susannah Drake, Greg Lindsay, Brent Ryan, Rafi Segal, Sarah Williams; Chaewon Ahn, Jan Casimir, Dennis Harvey, Mary Hohlt, Charles Huang, Xinhui Li, Chang Liu, Mary Lynch-Lloyd, Ching Ying Ngan, Zach Postone, Ellen Shakespear, Erin Wythoff

CLIMATE CHANGED: AFTER MODELS?

İrmak Turan, Jessica Varner; Rainar Aasrand, Irina Chernyakova, Sera Tolgay
Exhibition
Spring 2018

What is the feedback process between climate models and design? Since the development of the first general circulation model in the 1960s, computationally-driven models have served and continue to serve as the primary mode of understanding, representing, analyzing, communicating, and shifting the world in a climate changed. *Climate Changed: After Models?* looks at the common language and use of modeling between design and the sciences.

This exhibit positions a range of historical and future speculative modeling proposals together from the 1960s onward to explore how design has responded to climate-related models and the reality of climate change. The historical projects from the 1960s to the 1990s specifically focus on how designers, architects, engineers, consumers, and policy makers have understood the post-1960s moment as a period of changing scientific awareness around the agency of climate-related models. Coupled with a growing connection between environmental change and the built environment various changes on the ground occurred including: shifting consumer expectations, policy implementation, and projects built under the new paradigm. We ask: what happens after and between models in these projects?

By articulating the historical, present, and future role of climate-related models and illustrating their use in policy formulation and implementation, architectural practice, the protection and utilization of natural systems, and the forward-thinking planning and construction of cities, this exhibit hopes to bring multiple disciplines in conversation to discuss how the earth's climate is understood through modeling and how this informs on-the-ground practices.

CLIMAPLUS: AN EARLY DESIGN DECISION SUPPORT TOOL FOR LOW-CARBON, LOW-ENERGY BUILDINGS

Alpha Yacob Arsano
PhD Research, Building Technology
Advisor: Christoph Reinhart
Fall 2018

Mainstream building practices use extensive material and energy resources that contribute to increased greenhouse gas emissions. The mass of a pollutant emitted into the environment per unit of energy or fuel used during the operation of a building can be reduced by implementing a continuous building design process that promotes low-carbon, low-energy buildings. Successful implementation of relevant building strategies, such as cooling ventilation, thermal mass, and passive-solar heating, which can be identified early in the design process, play a great role in meeting environmental goals of a project while keeping financial goals in check.

Climate-responsive design that primarily relies on passive strategies has historically been an integral part of architecture. Buildings fully responded to their climatic context and used available natural resources to create healthy and comfortable spaces for occupants. Before the advent of mechanical building systems for heating, cooling, and ventilation in the early twentieth century, buildings responded to climatic conditions with the shape of their floor layouts, the size of windows, and envelope construction techniques. Consequently, buildings in hot and dry climates had different designs from those in hot and humid climates or cold climates.

CLIMAPLUS is an early design phase decision support workflow for maximizing passive strategies, optimizing active systems for extreme conditions where passive strategies are not applicable, and providing predictions on energy use as well as emission factors based on design decisions. The first version of the application is available: www.climaplus.net. It uses EnergyPlus and Radiance engines to run quick simulations to provide recommendations based on building energy performance and availability of solar radiation, respectively. The goal of this project is to address one of the greatest challenges architects and building system consultants face in the absence of a continuous building design workflow for the effective integration of passive building strategies.

CITIES BY THE SEA: URBANISM IN THE AGE OF SEA LEVEL RISE

Urban Design Studio
Instructors: Alan Berger, Rafi Segal, Jonah Susskind
Fall 2017

Coastal areas have been urbanizing for centuries. The expansion, building, and retrofitting of urban waterfronts must confront the urgent challenge of how to adapt to increasing floods, storms, and sea level rise. The historic dependence on the sea, for trade and exchange, is no longer a driving force in the shaping of urban waterfronts' form and infrastructure. In many cases, the relationship to the sea does not solely define a city's socioeconomic milieu. In the age of sea level rise, the sea has become a threat or risk to citizens, a thing to protect and defend against, or retreat from. Waterfront urbanism now carries a heavy burden of damage, loss, and vulnerability.

How are coastal cities responding to these challenges? How can physical and spatial design, and urban planning aid in preparing cities to adapt to these new conditions? Can these dangers also create new opportunities for cities to promote resilience, livability, and socio-equitable growth? The studio combines research and urban design around the theme of rising seas in the age of climate change for the city of Boston and its surrounding neighborhoods.

BERMANISM
Mario Giampieri, Kelly Leilani Main, Yue Wu, Juncheng Yang

Chelsea is an industrial waterfront city near Boston. The city faces a host of environmental problems, mostly stemming from years of industrial activity that have polluted the water and air. These industries had priority access to Chelsea Creek and Mystic River, disconnecting residents of the city from an essential asset.

But access to this water also has its own risks: the industrial area, located in the infill of the historic Island's End Creek, is the most vulnerable to sea level rise and pluvial flooding. Rather than reduce Chelsea's coastline with a barrier at the entrance to Island End's Creek, as many resiliency initiatives suggest, we pose a different question: What if we expanded the coastline and invited the water in?

To determine the extent of our new coastline, we identified three pieces of critical infrastructure: The New England Produce Center, the MBTA commuter rail, and Everett Avenue. To protect these three assets, we propose returning a large, low-lying swath of industrial land to coastal use and creating a multifunctional berm to emphasize connections between the now-protected and newly floodable sides of the evolving city. Protecting these three pieces of infrastructure and releasing some of the floodable land results in numerous positive consequences: access to open and recreational space, reduced and reconcentrated industrial activity, and economic growth generated by investment.

This is a new urban condition: bermanism, or the utilization of a berm not to protect as much land as possible, but as a strategic marker to differentiate areas of up-zoning (increased urban intensity) from areas of down-zoning (return to green space and recreational use). As a marker, the berm functions as the primary access point by which floodable areas are connected to those that are protected by its existence.

MONUMENTS OF MONSTERS
Malcolm Rio

Monuments of Monsters is a cultural project. It is a speculative urban park along the petroleum-dense industrial corridor of the Chelsea Creek. Facing the catastrophic effects of climate change and sea level rise, the site confronts adversarial futures: to engage in continuous efforts of fortification and risk distribution that allow for continued exploitation of the site's regional value, or, to retire the site's petroleum industries and allow for the sea to reclaim portions of the urban fabric. Simultaneous to envisioning these potential futures, the threat of inundation by sea level rise also forces the site to reconcile with its past. These petrol storage cylinders were not arbitrarily placed. They are intimately linked to the site's local context and a legacy of ecological racism.

The project proposes a hypothetical 2049 World's Fair, a year before the nominal year of the second wave of sea level rise (twenty-one inches). A Disney of New England, this future World's Fair commemorates the beginning of the end, celebrating the Anthropocene as the gold standard of resiliency discourse. At the World's Fair, the cosmopolitan citizens of the earth gather to marvel at the monuments of industry, fossil fuels, and a legacy of technology. However, visitors who come to this World Fair are confronted with the "externalities" of disregarded histories of the site, the nation, and the globe.

INFRASTRUCTURE/ARCHITECTURE LAB
Arindam Dutta
Fall 2018

PICTURESQUE PRAIRIES: PRODUCTIVE PRESERVATION ON A PETROLEUM PLANET
Tyler Ray Swingle
MArch Thesis
Advisor: Joel Lamere
Fall 2017

Fires burn bright atop the flare stacks in the distance as bison watch from behind the two-meter-high fence of the Theodore Roosevelt National Park. In this modern scene, complex geographic formations in North Dakota's Badlands have established a shared topography among an assemblage of disparate actors: engines, bison, and humans. The Bakken formation six kilometers below ground provides enough resources to encourage a deployment of oil and gas wells while the sedimentary surface, eroded from melting snow, provides "scenic" lands for tourists and prairie ecosystems for bison.

The sociopolitical distinction among actors has produced abstract borders and delineations in the form of habitats and land-use policies. Materialized through fences, these policies have created autonomous operating systems like fracture drilling and wildlife conservation, which are specified for a single or hierarchical order of actors. This not only facilitates settler practices of separation and domination but also encourages unaccountable externalities outside of the operating system.

Located between two and a half National Park units, this project embraces the multiple identities of the subterranean region by proposing a design strategy that engages the three actors as equal shareholders. Acknowledging the actors as an assemblage reveals material kinships and commitments to the geography that offer design considerations for shared spaces and memories. The project is composed of three archetypes, each weaving and entangling the actors within each other's programs and seasonal patterns. Through this built environment, the archetypes frame a physical and conceptual shared geography as a construction of landscape.

TERRA-SORTA-FIRMA: SEEKING RESILIENT URBANISM IN SOUTH FLORIDA
Urban Design Studio
Instructors: Fadi Masoud, Miho Mazereeuw
Fall 2016

With nearly twenty million residents, Florida is one of the country's fastest growing states. Its ubiquitous suburban landscape is enabled by the continued manipulation of a dynamic estuarine environment and a pervasive real-estate-driven housing pattern. Thirty-five miles of levees and two thousand hydraulic pumping stations drain 860 acres of water per day, resulting in the "world's largest wet subdivision" with $101 billion worth of property projected to be below sea level by 2030. The overall structure that defines Florida's cities emerges from the combination of hard infrastructural lines, developer driven master plans, reductive normative zoning, and rigid form-based codes. These conventional tools have proven marginally effective in dealing with the increased vulnerability caused by Florida's inherently dynamic ecological forces and constantly fluctuating environment. This renders traditional static "object-based codification," which has defined much of contemporary urban design, inadequate and in urgent need of innovation.

By recognizing that it is exactly in the process of design and physical planning that we may be the most operative and strategic agents, this studio puts front and center the agency and efficacy of urban designers' tools as they deal with issues of twenty-first century urbanism. It starts by rendering the exclusivity of building cities on dry ground insufficient, and accepts a state of constant hydrological flux—that is neither wet nor dry but always shifting—as the starting point of a novel and contextual "process-based" language for the future of Floridian urbanism.

Student teams designed projects that covered many scales ranging from large-scale landscape infrastructural systems to the design of housing prototypes of varying densities. The teams worked to develop a systemic approach that takes the hydrological extremes and ecological resonance of the context as the foundation for their formal propositions. Through the design process, students then devised a set of unique resiliency zoning, codes, land uses, programs, and typologies that are precise, yet dynamic, flexible, and responsive. These new codes and designs were collected in a compendium of urban design guidelines to be handed to the practicum's clients as they reconsider their policy documents. By incorporating the indeterminacy of the shifting broader environmental systems, with the pervasiveness and exactitude of planning code, we establish an opportunity for the instrumentality of policy to be a part of the design process and a progeny of it.

THE EVERGLADES: PERFORMATIVE GROUNDS, GROUNDS THAT PERFORM
Monica Hutton, Sam Jung, Angelos Siampakoulis

High rainfall events that produce stormwater influxes threaten the integrity of the levees in the Everglades conservation areas from breaching the retaining structure and moving water into the urban area of Broward County. Additionally, urbanization aided by the canalization of water flows, has expanded into what is called the transverse glades (Everglades that trend east-west instead of north-south).

This process has allowed development to occur in such a way that risks flooding when stormwater surges move from the Everglades Coast westward through Broward County along these transverse glades. The Everglades Coast is susceptible to a threat similar to the one that sea level rise poses for the Atlantic Coast of Broward County: potential flooding from storm surges from Lake Okeechobee and the Everglades. As a result, this edge is the other vulnerable coast. Broward County currently seeks to create more opportunities for water storage and aquifer replenishment, to bolster climate resiliency, and to foster energy security. For long, the Everglades has not been acknowledged as part of Broward County in the spatial imagination of its residents despite the fact that it constitutes two thirds of the county. This has led many to falsely consider the developed areas of Broward as constituting the entirety of the county. Our design approach seeks to intervene in the Everglades Coast to not only bolster its capacity to withstand man-made and natural disasters, but also catalyze the transformation of the spatial imaginary of Broward County residents to connect them to the immense natural treasure that is the Everglades.

THE TRANSITIONAL PLANNED UNIT DEVELOPMENTS
Giovanni Bellotti, Elaine Kim, Annie Ryan, Alexander Wiegering

Starting in the early 1990s the residential planned unit development (PUD) has been the driving force shaping urban form in Davie, Florida. The transformation of large tracts of agricultural land into repetitive rows of detached single-family housing surrounded by canals and retention ponds has transformed the county. The result is a vast landscape of single-use and insular developments that create a car-oriented environment disconnected from natural systems. The resource intensive process that is required for new PUDs also necessitates a substantially altered landscape to address flooding risks caused by rising sea levels. The result is a spectrum of flood risk for the city, with wealthier residents living in newly constructed PUDs facing lower levels of risk than their lower income neighbors to the east.

We challenge these sharp boundaries. At the same time, however, we embrace the existing control mechanisms as a way to implement changes through new negotiations both inside the PUD as well as between the PUD and surrounding soft spaces. By fostering negotiations between and among homeowners, PUDs, residential developments, natural landscapes, and commercial uses, the design strategies create opportunities for agile and strategic interventions to transform a relentlessly homogenous, inward-facing development pattern.

FLATNESS EXPANDED: INFRASTRUCTURAL SPECULATIONS
Option Studio
Instructors: Michael Maltzan, Jeremy Jih
Fall 2017

Since its founding, Los Angeles has been defined by its infrastructure. In a sea of ubiquitous suburban sprawl, infrastructure has been one of the primary drivers and organizers of the city. Although soaring freeways might be the most iconic elements, the city's freight railroads, waterways, and utilities network are equally responsible for simultaneously uniting and dividing the city. Understood as conduits of movement rather than destinations, single-use infrastructure has long defined spaces but not been able to create places within the city.

LA's current investment in its infrastructure, particularly its expanding Metro network, is radically reshaping the city physically, politically, socially, and culturally. But new stations and nearby development associated with the Metro in LA all too often rely on imported development models. While we have created functional transit nodes, we have not been able to create thriving urban destinations.

In contrast, cities like Paris, Moscow, and Washington have approached the design of their transit systems as integral civic destinations. Their networks of stations have become aesthetically significant indicators of the importance of infrastructure and they have become iconic landmarks within the city fabric. By investing in the design and architecture of these networks, these transit systems have become international emblems of the cities themselves, reflecting both the unique time and culture of these places. The challenge to architects, planners, and designers in LA is to learn from these precedents while creating an authentically LA experience. How can design move LA beyond the notion of cars in gridlock to a more fluid, multi-modal transit identity? These questions and provocations will be explored through the design of a new Metro station and Metro Maintenance Facility in the city's rapidly changing Arts District.

L.A.L.A.Z. (LOS ANGELES LEISURE ACTIVITIES ZONE)
Milap Dixit

One of the emblematic experiences of Los Angeles is the experience of being alone, together, facing the same direction. The parallel gaze, whether of the ocean or the receding freeway, is intensely individual and simultaneously collective. This project finds opportunities to both exaggerate and subvert this gaze through infrastructural form. The building appropriates the formal language and scale of the infrastructures to which it is grafted, but extends them to accommodate programs of leisure rather than utility. It aims to establish a framework for a future density that is not premised on real estate speculation or consumption but on fixing spaces of leisure and production onto existing infrastructures. The ubiquitous private plunge pool becomes the pool-as-aqueduct: extending seemingly to infinity, a private emblem is recast as public good.

TECHOS: DISASTER RESPONSES FOR PUERTO RICO
Jorge Silen Rivera, Danniely Staback, Luisel Zayas; Alexandre Beaudouin-Mackay, Gabrielle Heffernan, Catherine Lie, Jackie Lin, Cristina Solis, Courtney Stephen, Cheyenne Vandevoorde, Yifen Zhong
Workshop
Spring 2018; 2019

More than sixty days after Hurricane Maria devastated the island of Puerto Rico, the most immediate necessity was still the lack of shelter. Although many buildings survived the hurricane, a significant number were left without roofs. Despite the distribution of tarpaulins, a standard emergency aid response, many remained braced against the elements, awaiting help. As graduates of the University of Puerto Rico, we came together to help in Puerto Rico following the hurricane. We believed we could use our knowledge of the built environment and our fabrication skills to have a positive impact amidst the dire situation. As we later came to understand, a roof is not only a component of a house that requires repair and upkeep. In a post-hurricane context, a roof is the difference between staying or leaving one's home, community, even country.

The hope of the workshop was to disseminate accessible, affordable, and scalable construction practices that were appropriate for hurricane-prone areas. It was also an exercise in understanding our own capacities to organize ourselves, fundraise, consider where our efforts would be most effective, and accept that we would have to shape our project on-the-ground. We needed to quickly learn how to channel the resources at hand, use our support network at MIT, and maybe bend a few rules to accomplish this project.

For the first half of the month-long workshop, we met with local and international institutions working on disaster relief and reconstruction, conducted site visits with the University of Puerto Rico, and organized a charrette for the design. We focused on the design and detailing for a wooden roof with an integrated water collection system. Following, we spent three weeks in a community in the southwestern region of Puerto Rico where we adapted and built the timber roof structure to shelter three different houses.

REVISITING "UNKNOWN QUANTITIES" 2010/2019
Peter Galison, Caroline A. Jones

We wrote this text for Artforum in the fall of 2010, a few months after the announced capping of the Deepwater wellhead by British Petroleum and its contractors. This study (now amplified) serves as the opening salvo of a short book in progress. Invisibilities: Seeing and Unseeing the Anthropocene offers a three part analysis of the difficulties of rendering environmental harm visible—underwater, in the air, and on the ground—invisibilities that are only occasionally punctured to allow a cut into the vast scale and duration of planetary damage. Images one to three (213–215) account for the visibilities we identified in 2010. Image four (217) accounts for the sensory modes that can bloom when invisibility reigns.

Have we already forgotten? On April 20, 2010, a high-pressure methane bubble shot up through the drilling pipe of *Deepwater Horizon*, an offshore oil rig operated on behalf of British Petroleum in the Gulf of Mexico. The gas exploded and killed eleven workers; the giant rig was still burning two days later when it sank, and over the course of the next eighty-four days the ruptured mile-down well released approximately 206 million gallons of oil, constituting the largest petrochemical "spill" in history. Images played a unique role in the crisis, accompanying it at every turn but also failing, by definition, to capture that which could not be made visible. What we *could* see were tragic images of oil-coated shorebirds, sublime satellite photographs of iridescent oil slicks on the ocean surface, and stream-of-catastrophe footage that brought the wellhead gusher onto computer screens around the world. Such sights galvanized response, but as those surface images (seafloor surface, ocean surface, and shorefront) faded, both the public and the politicians were primed to declare the spill over. That we have yet to develop or popularize certain kinds of technologies of vision (for deep ocean vertical plumes, for durational models of wetland change, or for the microscopic uptake of petro dispersants inside organisms) produces specific invisibilities that fit well with corporate policy. No picture, no action.

The three types of images outlined above seem to apply to all oil spills, even those half a world away in rural China. These types reveal patterns in the visible that structure the occlusions of the invisible as well. Most familiar were those midsize close-ups of pathetic oil-drenched creatures (seagulls, pelicans, turtles, dolphins), safe in human hands.[1] Clustered under rubrics such as "Cleaning Dalian Harbor" (the

Boston Globe, in reference to the PetroChina spill that hit the North China port in July) or "Making It Right" (on BP's website),[2] these all-too-familiar spill icons combine the sad fate of individual creatures with a media-ready rescue in a perfect combination: a technological failure, a compassionate human-scale response, a documented cleanup. Never mind that only a fraction of the oil-doused birds make it to the cleanup station, or that biologists assert that only a small percentage actually survive in the medium term.[3] And forget the countervailing images that, in a ghastly parallel to the BP riggers' deaths, show us the drowning of a cleanup worker in the PetroChina spill flooding Dalian harbor. Deaths are not intended to be in the messages that accompany these images, nor are they what either BP or the environmental volunteers want to hear. If the streaming spill images have a Hollywood ending, the bird-in-cleaning is their movie poster.

Substituting sublimity for tragedy, the second type of image emerged primarily from NASA (and the less well-funded NOAA [National Oceanic and Atmospheric Administration]): pictures taken from space of colorful slicks and billowing subsurface phenomena, and spectrally enhanced views of oily incursions on the ocean surface (accompanied by excited captions such as "NASA'S MISR provides unique views of Gulf oil slick"). Mostly they provided everyday Web surfers with support for the definitive scientific judgment: Yep, it's oil. But these were also the most hauntingly beautiful of the spill images, reminding us that such distanced tragedy is the very stuff of the sublime (from Longinus to Burke to Lyotard), its technovariants a stock-in-trade of our cyberfictions and disaster films. The sublime often works to blunt political response even as it stimulates aesthetic contemplation of a distant doom. When such images fuel understandable but draconian decisions to curb all offshore drilling, those politics can be just as distant from the catastrophe's more intimate or systemic scales. The burning question of where local inhabitants are to find work when tourism, fishing, and the oil industry all collapse at once is brought to a head by the moratorium in a way that belies BP's "Making It Right—Beaches" and shadows even the Obama family's cheerful August swim off the Florida coast. It was only by setting aside the images' sublimity that data miners in the scientific and activist communities were able to take up the views from space for pragmatic modeling of the ongoing

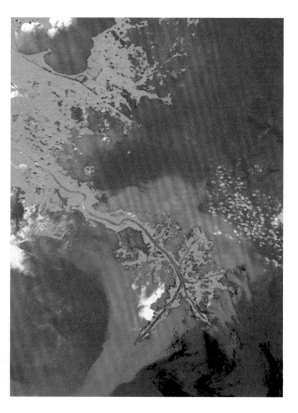

situation—will the next tropical storm dump oil balls, or spray droplets of petroleum? Will waves disperse, or deposit, the sludge? The Loop Current may have had a name before the BP disaster, but with the spill we could see what it looked like: The nine cameras on top of the NASA Terra satellite aimed at the slick from various vantage points in order to cull differentials in refracted and reflected light; they measured the parallax from their differently angled lenses and beamed the collected data to the Jet Propulsion Laboratory in Pasadena, California. There, it was parsed and recombined to create a psychedelic portrait of our oil addiction, blossoming in the lazy current coming up from the Yucatán before picking up its petrochemical load for dropping into the Gulf Stream—and into our Internet imaging algorithms.

Between the intimate scale of individual death and the sublimity of the satellite view was the webcam a mile down on the ocean floor. Of all the spill images, those provided by this camera were the only ones to be unprecedented, installing in our techno-imaginary the live feed of oil billowing from BP's broken wellhead to form its own imagistic "gusher," defeating all the technical verbiage ("static kill," "top kill," "side kill," "blowout protector") and proving so incendiary that it took considerable effort by Representative Ed Markey (D-MA) to pry it from BP's proprietary control. Grudgingly made public by BP on May 19, and later accessible from a link on the Congressional energy site, the "spillcam" darkened once the well's flow was capped on July 15, its once urgent activity now cached in YouTube archives that show pixilated documentation of the burbling ejecta. Meant to galvanize response and doubtless determinative in extending the administration's moratorium,[4] the feed's online posting was a victory for the public sphere, fueling ongoing efforts to hold BP and its numerous subcontractors financially and politically accountable. Presumably the government's sumptuous NASA slide show intended the same. And all these images and their public sources did have impact. As soon as BP released initial video of the wellhead to selected agencies on May 13 (even before it was posted online), scientists were able to revisit estimates made from satellite photos and to recalculate the flow to ninety-five thousand barrels a day (a barrel containing forty-two gallons), directly confronting the corporation's preposterous initial estimates of one thousand to five thousand daily barrels.[5] The spillcam's unprecedented imagery—so much finer in detail and information, seemingly, than any of our technologies for controlling the leak itself—was clearly the most effective in galvanizing action.

What philosophies can we generate in this millennium to build on the once-unstoppable imagery of the webcam? If the similarly pixilated "Patriot" shots from the first Gulf War were as punchy as video games, the BP webcam shots were unbearably durational, live, endless, ceaseless, hour after hour, day after day, month after month. The brief happenstance of a "spill" (a sudden event, captured in the speed of "Doc" Edgerton's strobe) was a term that couldn't possibly encompass the hemorrhaging, billowing brown crude that *kept on gushing* from the unknowable depths, beyond the visibility of our surfaces (ocean, shore, floor), into untold futures and dissolving durational extensions. Quite unlike the fast-paced news cycle with its banners and "swooshes," the spillcam offered a continuing and repetitive announcement of our ability to picture but not to stop the flow, to make images but not achieve a satisfying response (from BP, or, for that matter, from our government's mining management agency, locked as it is in the cozy embrace of the oil industry). Watching these webcam images became a form of environmental torture that we have not yet theorized or adequately examined.

These images—the pathos of bird cleaning, the sublimity of space views, the durational spewing of the Web gusher—will stand for the catastrophic failure of ever deeper wells, and of *Deepwater Horizon*. But that prophetic name demands that we keep scanning the darkening horizon of deep water, and calling for the non-images that are *implied by the visibility* only because their *invisibility* is part of a system in which the seen is supported and enabled by the unseen. Just as Foucault would have parsed "Don't ask, don't tell" as a classic instantiation of how what can be said is intimately related to what cannot be said (both controlled by dispersed and internalized modes of power), so the systems of what can be made visible are intimately tied to what cannot. In this case, statistics reveal the ratio of the seen to the unseen: Based on pressure readings from the intermediate containment cap and on detailed analysis of the diminishment in flow over time, government scientists now calculate that only twenty percent of the oil that emerged from the broken wellhead was contained, leaving an astonishing 172.2 million gallons uncontained—counted, but still unaccounted for. Manifestly, this overage has been placed into the unseen registers of the "spill." While the gusher has stopped, that should only fuel our pondering of those aspects of catastrophe that have not been made visible, those sites where our awesome technologies of the image have yet to be applied.

Over the course of the past decade, it has become increasingly evident that oil released at great depth does not all come to the surface (particularly if it is dense crude). One controlled study of an oil release conducted off the Norwegian coast indicated

CAGE   Maxx 3
THR: 0
DPT: 4840'
HDG: 016
TRN:-0.3

345 0 15 30 45 60 7
P:-5   028   R:-1
TRN:-0.4

ROV
DPT: 4937'
ALT: 69'
BTY: 5006'

OCEANEERING

Dive Number: 37

06/03/10
16:17:33

that only a relatively small amount—between two and twenty-eight percent—ever made it to the surface. The real damage is deeper, out of the camera's eye. And in the Gulf spill, to the annoyance of BP, NOAA, and the Coast Guard, chemical oceanographers have taken deepwater samples, mapped their distribution, analyzed their contents, and presented compelling evidence that vast undersea plumes of oil have formed and are drifting far from their site of origin.[6] Most scientists believe that these submerged columns were produced by quantities of dispersant (Nalco's "Corexit") injected at the wellhead. (BP reported applying one million gallons on the surface and another 721,000 gallons in subsea locations, but independent analysis of Corexit depletion estimates that yet another 965,000 gallons were deployed in unreported applications).[7] The toxic emulsifier is designed to break up the crude into tiny bits, which then take on a density close to that of water itself and either sink (from the surface slicks) or fail to rise (from the subsea emissions). No longer visible, the treated oil floats in those submerged transparent plumes, unimaged and hence largely unimagined. It may be that in the final analysis, the real role of the dispersant was to remove the spill from the camera—and with it, BP from the glare of popular and political scrutiny. The circuit—of drill, spill, "clean up," and drill again—relies on such systems of images and occlusions, in which the production of invisibility forms an aesthetic chiaroscuro to all the tragic, sublime, and subaquatic flows. Our response must be to take what's out of sight, and keep it well in mind.

1   The incredible sequence "Photographer Captures Firefighter Losing His Life Cleaning Up Dalian Oil Spills," China Hush, August 3, 2010, can be seen at www.chinahush.com/2010/08/03/photographer-captures-firefighter-losing-his-life-cleaning-up-dalian-oil-spills/.
2   For Dalian, see "Cleaning Dalian Harbor," Boston Globe, July 28, 2010, www.boston.com/bigpicture/2010/07/cleaning_dalian_harbor.html. For BP, see company website: http://bp.concerts.com/gom/MakingitRight.htm. (Link updated.)
3   See German biologist Silvia Gaus, as reported in Christine Dell'Amore, "Oil-Coated Gulf Birds Better Off Dead?," National Geographic News, June 9, 2010, news.nationalgeographic.com/news/2010/06/100608-gulf-oil-spill-birds-science-environment.
4   As early as April 30, President Obama had announced a moratorium on approving new leases for offshore rigs, but his May 27 extension of the moratorium for another six months was clearly tied to the new information emerging on the magnitude of the spill from webcam-based calculations.
5   See Janet Raloff, "BP's Estimate of Spill Rate Is Way Low, Engineer Suggests," Science News, May 19, 2010, www.sciencenews.org/view/generic/id/59381/title/BP%E2%80%99s_estimate_of_spill_rate_is_way_low_engineer_suggests.
6   The Norwegian study was called "Project Deep Spill"; United States groups extending these findings are from the University of South Florida and the University of Mississippi. "'I got lambasted by the Coast Guard and NOAA when we said there was undersea oil,' USF marine sciences dean William Hogarth said. Some officials even told him to retract USF's public announcement, he said, comparing it to being 'beat up' by federal officials." Craig Pittman, "USF Says Government Tried to Squelch Their Oil Plume Findings," St. Petersburg Times, August 10, 2010.
7   See the extensive and well-sourced Wikipedia entry "Deepwater Horizon Oil Spill," last modified September 28, 2010, especially the articles referenced in notes 171 (Mark Guarino, "In Gulf Oil Spill, How Helpful—or Damaging—Are Dispersants?," Christian Science Monitor, May 15, 2010), and 175 ("US Oil Production, Shipping Unaffected by Spill So Far," Agence France-Presse, May 1, 2010).

Images
P 213: The Aerial View: Multiple cameras on JPL's MISR instrument on NASA's Terra spacecraft were used to create two unique views of oil moving into Louisiana's coastal wetlands.
Credit: NASA/GSFC/LaRC/JPL, MISR Team

P 215 Top: The Oil-Soaked Shorebird: Plaquemines Parish Coastal Zone Director P.J. Hahn rescues a heavily oiled bird from the waters of Barataria Bay, which are laden with oil from the Deepwater Horizon oil spill, in Barataria Bay, La., Saturday, June 26, 2010.
Credit: AP Photo/Gerald Herbert

P 215 Bottom: The Wellhead Cam: Still from June 3, 2010 showing the Oceaneering firm's feed from one of its "Maxx" ROVs, focused on the "Cut Riser Leak." This still was used as figure 6 in the Plume Calculation Team report (June 21, 2010), taken from the footage provided to the Plume Team by BP and stamped with the subcontractor's watermark (Oceaneering). Note the lighter plume of methane behind the clearly defined darker crude, as well as the bubbles of methane inside the crude itself.
Credit: Plume Calculation Team, Deepwater Horizon Release, Estimate of Rate by PIV, Plume Team report to the Flow Rate Technical Group. Particle Image Velocimetry Report, July 21, 2010, http://www.usgs.gov/oilspill/. Credit: United States Geological Survey, Department of the Interior/USGS.

P 217: Invisibilities: Struggling to be made visible is the smell of "taint" in seafood (note the "nose" in this protocol for testing Gulf seafood), the impacts on public health, and the unseen pelagic life in the deep water column, flooded with oil and methane during the BP/Deepwater crisis. The brochure illustrates United States Food and Drug Administration (FDA)/National Oceanic and Atmospheric Administration (NOAA) protocol, codified June 2010; it was funded by BP/The Gulf of Mexico Research Initiative incorporating research from NOAA.
Credit: Larissa Graham, Christine Hale, Emily Maung-Douglass, Stephen Sempier, LaDon Swann, and Monica Wilson, Oil Spill Science: The Deepwater Horizon Oil Spill's Impact on Gulf Seafood, 2015, MASGP-15-014. Shown is Figure 2, page 4: "Federal and state agencies set up a method for sampling, testing, and reopening closed harvest waters. Waters were reopened when they had no visible oil present and seafood samples that were collected passed sensory and chemical testing. Credit for images: Kim Kraeer, Lucy Van Essen-Fishman, Jane Hawkey, Tracey Saxby, Diana Kleine, and Jason C. Fisher, IAN Image Library (ian.umces.edu/imagelibrary/)."

Sampling method used to reopen areas to commercial fishing after Deepwater Horizon oil spill

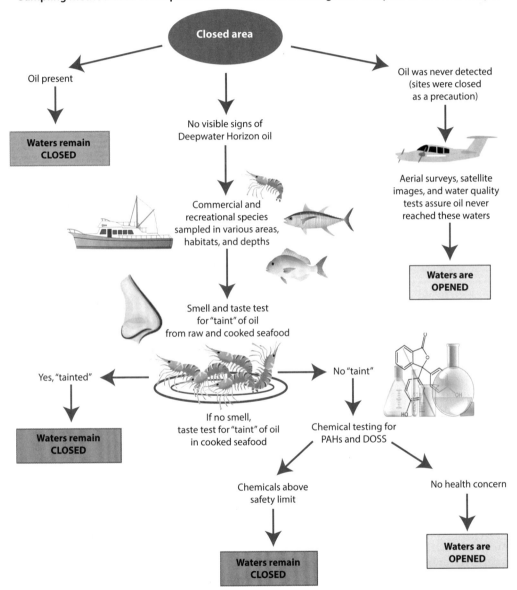

Closed area

Oil present

Waters remain
CLOSED

No visible signs of
Deepwater Horizon oil

Commercial and
recreational species
sampled in various areas,
habitats, and depths

Smell and taste test
for "taint" of oil
from raw and cooked seafood

Yes, "tainted"

Waters remain
CLOSED

If no smell,
taste test for "taint" of oil
in cooked seafood

No "taint"

Chemical testing for
PAHs and DOSS

Chemicals above
safety limit

Waters remain
CLOSED

No health concern

Waters are
OPENED

Oil was never detected
(sites were closed
as a precaution)

Aerial surveys, satellite
images, and water quality
tests assure oil never
reached these waters

Waters are
OPENED

LANDSCAPE EXPERIENCE: SEMINAR IN LAND/ART
Caroline A. Jones, Rebecca Uchill

August 21 (Sunday)
10:00 am
  All flights and people converge in Salt Lake City;
  board bus by 10:30 am.
11:00–11:45 am
  Walmart for supplies
11:45–12:00 pm
  Drive 1 hr. 10 min. to Thiokol, Promontory, UT.
12:00–12:20 pm
  Stop at Thiokol Rocket Garden for 20 min.
  Transfer to minibus at Thiokol: 9160 UT-83,
  Corinne, UT 84307
12:25–1:45 pm
  Drive through Golden Spike to *Spiral Jetty*
  (45 min.); GPS coordinates 41.438223°,
  -112.666491
1:45–3:45 pm
  Spiral Jetty
4:15–7:00 pm
  Drive to *Sun Tunnels* by way of Golden Spike (2
  hrs. 45 min.); GPS coordinates 41.303501°N,
  113.803831°W
7:00 pm
  Arrive at *Sun Tunnels*, stay 1 hr. (sunset 8:30 pm)
  Sun Tunnels self-guide
8:00–8:45 pm
  Leave *Sun Tunnels*, Drive to Montello, NV
  (40 min. drive)
7:45–8:45 pm
  Time Change (1 hr.+)
  Dinner at Montello Cowboy Bar, 443 Front
  Street, Montello, NV 89830
9:00–9:40 pm
  Time Change Again (1 hr.-),
  Drive to Wendover, Montego Bay (40 min. drive).
11:00 pm
  Arrive at Montego Bay, Wendover, NV
  Screening: *Spiral Jetty*

August 22 (Monday)
8:00 am
  Bus departs from hotel with Matthew Coolidge
8:00–11:00 am
  3.5–4 hr. tour of Center for Land Use Interpretation and Wendover area with Matthew Coolidge.
  Bring map. GPS coordinates: 40°43'51.1"N
  114°01'43.1"W
11:00–11:30 am
  Lunch at Wendover Taco Truck, Tacos el Canon
  de Juchipila, 1715 Wendover Blvd, West Wendover, NV 89835 (West of "Wendover Will" statue)

11:30 am
  Depart for *Double Negative* (Possible screening:
  Troublemakers) (5.5 hrs. to Perkins Field)
  Time Change (-1 hr.)
4:00–4:20 pm
  Meet at Perkins Field, 1110 Airport Rd, Overton,
  NV 89040, to swap to smaller vehicles.
4:15/4:30–4:45/5:00 pm
  Drive to *Double Negative* via Mormon Mesa Road
  (approx. 30 min.)
5:00–5:45/6:00 pm
  Walk to North *Double Negative* Site from Carp
  Elgin Road
5:45–7:15 pm
  Stay at *Double Negative*
7:15–8:15 pm
  Walk back to vehicles
8:15–8:45 pm
  Drive back to Perkins Field, 1110 Airport Rd,
  Overton, NV
8:45–9:00 or 9:30 pm
  Drive to hotel.
  Screening: *Troublemakers: The Story of Land Art*

August 23 (Tuesday)
8:00 am
  Depart for driving day
8:00–8:45 am
  Drive from Henderson to Hoover Dam
  (30 min. to Hoover Dam)
8:45–9:10 am
  Stop at Hoover Dam (Bus stops prior to the
  MOPT Memorial Bridge, walk across the bridge)
6:00 pm
  Navajo Council Chambers tour with Idah
  Burnside
6:30 pm
  Joined by Jonathan Perry and Church Rock
  activists
7:30–10:00 pm
  Depart, Drive to Albuquerque, NM

August 24 (Wednesday)
8:00 am
  Depart for Quemado for *Lightning Field*
  (2 hr. tour of Acoma Pueblo en route)
9:30 am
  Arrive at Acoma Pueblo
9:30–12:30 pm
  Sky City Cultural Center and Haak'u Museum,
  guided tour

12:30–2:30 pm
    Drive to Quemado, NM
    Overnight at *Lightning Field*

Aug 25 (Thursday)
9:45 am
    Pick up at *Lightning Field*
10:45 am
    Leave Quemado to Very Large Array
12:00–1:15 pm
    Very Large Array, National Radio Astronomy
    Observatory
12:00 pm
    Tour with astronomers at Very Large Array,
    Climb radio telescopes in groups.
1:15–4:00 pm
    Drive to El Paso (3 hr. 30 min.)
    Stop en route at Riverbend
7:00 pm
    Juarez Scenic Overlook
    "Scenic Drive" road, discuss border development
8:00 pm
    Grocery shop: Sprouts Farmers Market, 2036
    North Zaragoza Road, El Paso, TX 79936

August 26 (Friday)
9:15 am
    Departure for Rubin Art Center, The University
    of Texas at El Paso
10:00 am
    Meet Kerry Doyle, Director of Rubin Art Center,
    Tour border sites
12:30 pm
    Lunch and visit other sites of note
3:30–4:00 pm
    National Border Patrol Museum, 4315 Woodrow
    Bean Transmountain Drive, El Paso, TX 79924
    (then 3 hrs. to Marfa including Prada Marfa)

August 27 (Saturday)
8:30 am
    Cars depart to Chinati Foundation, S. Hill St. and
    Katherine St.
9:00 am
    Private group tour of Chinati Foundation
Afternoon
    Time to visit Marfa and Presidio County
    Museum, open until 5:00 pm (Thunderbird pool!)
6:30 pm
    Dinner
8:15 pm
    Sunset private guided tour of Robert Irwin
9:00 pm
    Check out Marfa lights (Route 67, Mitchell Flat)

August 28 (Sunday)
9:30 am
    Drive to Judd Foundation
9:50 am
    Block and studio tour of Judd Foundation
1:00 pm
    Lunch in Marfa
2:00 pm
    Drive to Austin (6 hr. 30 min.), arrive 8:30 pm
10:00 pm
    (optional) Visit to UT Austin James Turrell
    Skyspace

August 29 (Monday)
1:00 pm
    Leave Austin, drive to Houston
3:30 pm
    One car through Sharpstown to view Mary Ellen
    Carroll's *Prototype 180*
5:45 pm
    Cars depart for Rice University visit
6:00 pm
    Meet Alison Weaver, Director of Moody Center
    for the Arts, discuss "de Menil years of the Rice
    Museum." View Michael Heizer collection in the
    Engineering quadrangle (*45°, 90°, 180*).
7:30–8:19 pm
    Sunset sky sequence in James Turrell *Skyspace*,
    Rice University (reservation for 13).

August 30 (Tuesday)
10:00 am
    Exhibitions at Contemporay Arts Museum
    Houston (CAMH); Lunch at with Bill Arning,
    Director of CAMH.
7:15 pm
    Live Oak Meeting House visit (Turrell) with
    Jane Houser

August 31 (Wednesday)
9:00 am
    Look at Houston-based land art proposals and
    drawings in the Menil Collection, discuss unreal-
    ized John Gibson gallery show
10:30 am
    Rothko Chapel: Tour collection and Dan Flavin
    Richmond Hall until 1 pm, lunch on site
2:00 pm
    Project Row Houses

Images
P 220–223: Students who participated in the field trip created a collective
video, *Travelogue of the Undocumentable*, which documented their trip to
Utah, Arizona, New Mexico, and Texas. Video stills: Rainar Aasrand.

Project
The video, full course syllabus, reading list, itinerary, with hyperlinks, is
available via MIT OpenCourseWare: https://ocw.mit.edu/courses/architec-
ture/4-s67-landscape-experience-seminar-in-land-art-fall-2016/syllabus/.

The west is now a landscape of server farms, logistics warehouses, and tech titans; cowboys like Tesla boldly claim this space to help save the world, while simultaneously compromising its environmental future. A museum for art about the environment might not be able to save the world, but might it embody our cultural circumstances, our current perspectives? Might it document values and dispositions in the way it organizes its spaces and contents about our predicament?

Florian Idenburg and Sam Ghantous

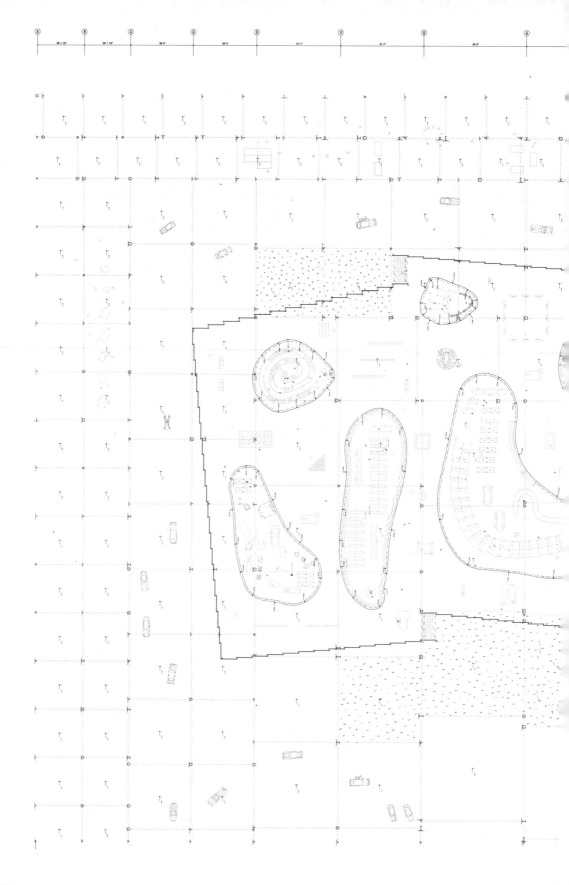

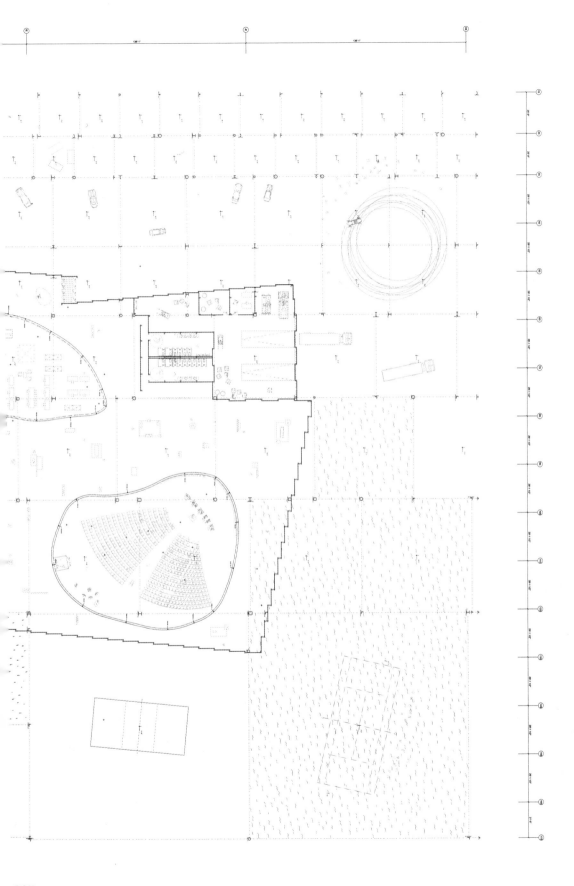

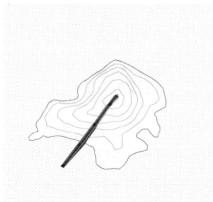

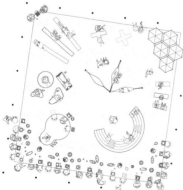

ARCHIPELAGIC SOVEREIGNTY: RE-MAPPING UNITED PACIFIC STATES OF MIGRATION
Lizzie Yarina

Close your eyes, and imagine the Pacific. Do you see an endless stretch of water and waves? A vast empty space dotted with a few tropical islands, sandy beaches, and swaying palms amongst the cyan expanses? Perhaps media narratives surrounding climate change have reframed your imaginary, and you imagine "sinking islands" and the first victims of rising seas wading through salty water with their belongings atop their heads. While the Pacific certainly is a lot of ocean—our planet's largest—it is also home to a richly diverse and interconnected set of societies, geographies, and ecologies. Oceanic authors have long challenged limited conceptions of Pacific space, most prominently Tongan-Fijian writer and anthropologist Epeli Hau'ofa, who reframed the Pacific[1] as a "sea of islands," challenging "tiny island" narratives as (post)colonial constructs:

> Nineteenth century imperialism erected boundaries that led to the contraction of Oceania, transforming a once boundless world into the Pacific islands states and territories that we know today. People were confined to their tiny spaces, isolated from each other. No longer could they travel freely to do what they had done for centuries. They were cut off from their relatives abroad, from their far-flung sources of wealth and cultural enrichment.[2]

The drawing of lines on maps—by paternalist European explorers, missionaries, and colonizers—attempted to fix a region united by mobility, migration, and flux. In response, this project explores a re-mapping of the Pacific to identify a region *united* through flows, migrations, and inherent non-fixity. These maps begin with a simple act of re-projection, re-centering the Pacific as the (non-)object of inquiry. In doing so, the work seeks to call into question not only the way the Pacific has been mapped, but how maps have limited the mobility of inherently migratory (both historically and presently) Oceanic inhabitants. If maps can fix, can alternative maps instead suggest new political formations in the Pacific, rejecting the hard boundaries established through colonialism and West-oriented modernities and reuniting a divided "sea of islands"? What might be the geopolitics of a self-determined Oceania—a Pacific universe?

In a standard map projection (Mercator, Mollweide, Lambert, Robinson), the world is centered on the Atlantic Ocean, and 0° longitude (the Prime Meridian) marks the midline of the map. The Pacific Ocean, the world's largest body of water, is squeezed to the periphery, and the many Pacific Island nations that populate this zone become dismembered, split to opposite sides of the map, or left off entirely. Global geospatial data often has a small gap around 180° longitude, running right through nations including Kiribati, Tuvalu, Fiji, and even New Zealand such that many of the maps in this collection have been sutured together across that seam. These nations are divided not only in map-space, but also in time, as the International Date Line jogs through the Pacific, separating adjacent islands into different days. A short haul-flight from Tonga to Tahiti can take you back in time a full day; Sunday in American Samoa is Monday in Samoa proper. National shifts across the international date line illustrate intentional alliances East or West. African American/i-Kiribati scholar Teresia Teaiwa notes: "On a global capitalist map of significance, Oceania's economic and politico-strategic value is derived from its between-Asia-and-America-ness"[3]; the Pacific as a non-place, simply a medium for exchange.

Modern mapmaking stems from a western history of Westphalian, continental states as relatively fixed and land-based constructs; neither of which apply in the context of the Pacific. The translation of these models to the Pacific often leaves its island occupants illegible; most Pacific Islands do not register on a scaled map. Furthermore, the "nations" themselves might be seen as fixed constructs imposed by colonizing powers and perpetuated by a high-ground ideology of what a nation-state should encompass. For example, the Gilbert and Ellice Islands Colony lumped together two (plus)[4] distinct ethnic groups, now known as Tuvalu and Kiribati[5] with a series of uninhabited islands including the Line Islands and Phoenix Islands. Following Tuvaluan independence in 1978 and Kiribati independence in 1979 the now partially inhabited archipelagoes[6] remain part of Kiribati, contributing to its sprawling oceanic territory (over 3.5 million km²).[7] The boundaries of Papua New Guinea result from the straight colonial lines drawn by the German, British and Dutch in spite of the rich matrix of languages (Papua New Guinea has the highest language diversity in the world) and cultures underneath—many of whom are fierce rivals. The centerline boundary now places Papua New Guinea in the sphere of the Pacific with West Papua attached to Southeast Asia as part of the Indonesian archipelago. Various separatist and secessionist movements attest to the contestation of these colonial lines.

Oceanic Mobility

In contrast to continental concepts of fixity and rigid borders, the history of Oceania is characterized by migrations of both occupants and landscapes. Traditional navigation devices such as Micronesian stick charts communicate an understanding of flows rather than objects; while islands were depicted, these portable maps focused on illustrating winds, currents, and swells. Fluid systems such as tidal regimes and weather patterns tie the region together through atmospherics: as the Micronesian maps suggest, the Pacific is perhaps better understood by its seas than its lands.

The Pacific is home to more than 360 coral islands, formed by reefs grown on the rim of submerging volcanic cones. While all coastlines are dynamic, coral islands such as lagoon-ringing atolls are particularly mobile, moving and evolving as a result of sediment flows, storm events, and coral life-cycles. In response to these mobile geographies, the atoll-dwellers of Micronesia and Polynesia developed fluid tactics of architecture and settlement that allow them to mobilize and adapt to changing contexts. As Oceanic researcher John Connell notes:

> In historic times atoll dwellers were extremely mobile and far from insular; men and women moved readily between islands in search of new land, disease-free sites, wives, trade goods, and so on. In this way some islands were populated, depopulated, and later repopulated. Mobility itself was responsible for demographic survival; without mobility, adaptation and change were impossible.[8]

For example, Tuvaluan architectural vernaculars were characterized by mobility/transformability that allowed for their inhabitants to physically and socially adapt to their fragile atoll ecosystems. Open floor plans with storage in rafters above allowed for flexible use; removable thatched roofs allowed for protection during storms; and flexible woven wall panels could be raised or lowered depending on weather. Land was collectively owned based on a reciprocally structured clan system, and settlements could be occupied temporally depending on resource availability.[9]

Refugees from Fluid Nations

Climate change calls into question the fixed borders of all nation states: rising seas, melting glaciers, and eroding shorelines show us that all landscapes are under migration.[10] Italy and Switzerland are currently renegotiating territory once defined by the Swiss Alps glacial watershed[11] and coastal dwellers the world over are claiming losses on disappearing shorelines. Atoll nations, with their highest points only a few meters above sea level (and with coral foundations vulnerable to increasing water temperatures) may disappear entirely. It remains unclear whether these nations will still be able to claim their oceanic territory if their lands become submerged. Without claims to land or sea, will these nations cease to exist entirely? Or might they persist as ex-situ states, like the Order of Malta (population: 3)?[12]

However, those threatened with the loss of their homelands, particularly the low-lying nations of Tuvalu and Kiribati, often reject the designation of "climate refugees." The climate refugee, as an emerging (media) construct, in fact has no legal standing and is not an official refugee status. The United Nations High Commissioner for Refugees 1951 Convention defines a "refugee" as someone who "owing to a well-founded fear of being persecuted for reasons of race, religion, nationality, membership of a particular social group or political opinion, is outside the country of his nationality, and is unable to, or owing to such fear, is unwilling to avail himself of the protection of that country." Past climate refugee claims to Australia and New Zealand have either been rejected due to the lack of a legal basis for climate refugee status, or have been accepted because the claimant identifies climate amongst a slew of other reasons for migration.

In contrast to preordained notions of refugee-hood, the leaders of Tuvalu and Kiribati have opted to negotiate their own distinct narratives surrounding climate-changed futures. Tuvalu has stood firm to a mitigation-focused stance, using their "sinking islands" imaginary as a way of pressuring larger nations to reduce emissions. Even if Tuvalu cannot prevent its own demise, this attitude does represent a claiming of agency over the future of the tiny nation. Tuvaluan UN representative Aunese Makoi Simati goes so far as to eliminate migration from the conversation: "The government doesn't push people to leave, and it doesn't have any plans for migration for climate change. Our policy is to save Tuvalu."[13] In contrast, Kiribati has embraced a program of "migration with dignity," emphasizing training and education that will facilitate migration, and even purchasing land in Fiji. In response to criticisms of this approach, i-Kiribati President Anote Tong has insisted on the importance of migration in national climate change adaptation policy: "It's not a question of surrendering—I think it's a case of being practical in the face of the limited choices that we have."[14]

The Marshall Islands, another atoll-nation have established a similar stance to Tuvalu, self-identifying as a kind of canary in the shark tank. Marshallese minister Tony de Brum takes the issue even beyond sovereignty, to liken climate change to the ending of civilizations: "Displacement of populations and destruction of cultural language and tradition is equivalent in our minds to genocide."[15] When culture is rooted in place, the destruction of place can eviscerate a culture. These statements are powerful, and it is no wonder that atoll leaders now make a kind of global circuit speaking out against the off-gassing of larger and more powerful states. And while there may seem to be a naiveté of these tiny nations attempting to halt climate change, essentially taking on the development-oriented capitalist world as we know it, perhaps atoll-nation narratives are more powerful *for* their attempt to reclaim agency over indigenous futures, rejecting the notion that American cars and Chinese coal plants thousands of miles away can destroy their entire society.

What the discourses of both Tuvalu and Kiribati reveal most clearly is a rejection of the fetishized construct of the "climate refugee." While Pacific atoll-dwellers are willing to concede themselves as "representations and representatives"[17] of climate risk, they refuse to revoke their agency as individuals and as nations in the process. For Tuvalu, this comes in the form of spurning even the possibility of displacement and associated destruction of culture and sovereignty, even if they cannot control the rising tides. In Kiribati, desire for self-determination translates to attempting control over migration processes, even when accepting migration itself as a necessary burden. Or, perhaps it is Tuvalu's smaller population and favorable migration agreements with other nations (in particular New Zealand) that allows Prime Minister Enele Sopoaga to hold up his fist and reject jumping ship, declaring "We must work together to save the world!"

Within the framework of narrow, depoliticized narratives of the climate refugee, it has been difficult for atoll-dwellers to develop alternative futures for their archipelagoes. That this narrative operates largely in the framework of Western platforms of media and geopolitics is further problematic, positioning Pacific Island states as tiny pawns in a global narrative in spite of their rich history of local, mobile adaptations. Characterizing Pacific Islanders solely as "climate refugees" confuses one type of victimization (impacted by environmental change, and complicated by contemporary passport politics) with another (how Pacific Islanders choose to respond to that change).[18] Instead of resigning themselves to these fatal destinies, Pacific nations have sought to redesign alternative and self-determined futures, in fact leveraging the legacies imposed by Western maps and nation-making.

Archipelagic Sovereignty: A Pacific Universalism?

Most island nations of the Pacific are a unique typology of microstate[19] which have emerged only in the recent post-colonial era. For the eleven independent island nations of Oceania (excluding the larger nations of Australia, New Zealand, and Papua New Guinea, as well as offshore territories of larger nations), the average population of these countries is less than a quarter of a million people, and their average land area is 5,800 square kilometers.[20] These are many of the smallest nations in the world by both population and area; the smallest, Nauru has only ten thousand people inhabiting a single ten square kilometer island. The combined surface area of these island-nations is similar to that of Rhode Island, and the sum of their eleven GDPs is still only a quarter of New Zealand's, (a small nation by most counts). Still, as independent nation-states, each has earned a seat in the UN General Assembly (Tuvalu as recently as the year 2000), and all of the other trappings of transnationally recognized sovereignty. While many of these nations might be worth less than a Manhattan penthouse, they have leveraged their sovereignty, and particularly their UN seats, to their advantage.

Sovereign nations successfully admitted into the UN gain a voting seat in the UN General Assembly due to the rule of "one state, one vote" (an allocation begrudged by larger UN members).[21] While this vote and voice is valuable in and of itself, it becomes a true force when UN member nations align their positions (and votes) in the UN towards shared interests and agendas. For Pacific Island nations, the most significant alliance is the Pacific Islands Forum (PIF), founded in 1971 as the South Pacific Forum. This intergovernmental organization is an official observer of the UN, and its member nations occupy sixteen of the 193 seats in the General Assembly (over eight percent of seats for five percent of the global population). Tiny states such as Tuvalu and Nauru play a particularly outsized role.

These votes can then be pooled towards shared Pacific Island country objectives, particularly sustainable development and climate mitigation/ adaptation agendas. Some past successes of the forum within the UN framework include establishing a provision for holding a global conference on the interests of small island developing states during the 1992 UN Conference on Environment; reinscribing New Caledonia on the UN list of non-self-governing territories; and shaping the 1982 Convention on the Law of the Seas in terms that were favorable to interests of Pacific Island nations. This is particularly significant, as it allocated all coastal nations a two hundred nautical mile Exclusive Economic Zone (EEZ) where nations have exclusive rights to marine resources (i.e., pelagic fish stocks). For some nations, the words in this document multiplied their territory more than ten-thousand-fold.

For climate-change related issues, PIF defers to AOSIS, or the Alliance of Small Island States. With forty-two UN seats, AOSIS exerts an even stronger pull; the alliance was established in 1990 with the specific agenda of exerting increased influence during the UN Convention on Climate Change (UNCCC) in the interest of small island states particularly vulnerable to climate change and seal level rise. Together they have initiated the Barbados Programme of Action for the Sustainable Development of Small Island Developing States initially launched in 1994 and signed by 125 nations, which establishes regional and local action programs to improve climate change adaptation through UN organization.

Through these coalitions, Pacific Island nations leverage the postcolonial nation-state framework for their collective benefit. Writing nearly twenty-five years ago, in his seminal essay "Our Sea of Islands" Epeli Hau'ofa advocates for a re-enlargement of Pacific space, through mobility and alliances:

It should be clear now that the world of Oceania is neither tiny nor deficient in resources. It was so only as a condition of colonial confinement that lasted less than a hundred of a history of thousands of years. […] Islanders have broken out of their confinement, are moving around and away from their homelands, not so much because their countries are poor, but because they had been unnaturally confined and severed from much of their traditional sources of wealth, and because it is in their blood to be mobile. They are once again enlarging their world, establishing new resource bases and expanded networks for circulation. Alliances are already being forged by an increasing number of islanders with the *tangata whenua* of Aotearoa and will inevitably be forged with the native Hawai'ians. It is not inconceivable that if Polynesians ever get together, their two largest homelands will be reclaimed in one form or another.[23]

The indigenous as minority make Hawaii and New Zealand unique in the context of the Pacific, and as high island metropolises, both sites serve as hubs of Pacific education and employment. As Hau'ofa notes, efforts to reclaim indigenous lands and assert indigenous values in Hawaii and Aotearoa/New Zealand have been aided by alliances with other Pacific Islanders, as highlighted by the recent He Lawenata agreement between New Zealand's Māori Party and the One Pacific group, the first ever formal agreement between Māori and Pasifika.[24] Māori are of Polynesian heritage, and are thought to have arrived in Aotearoa by canoe from the Cook Islands around 800 years ago. As a One Pacific press release notes, the alliance "… speaks with a strong clear voice that is independent, but united. It speaks of their self-determination. *Mana Motuhake!*"[25] The Māori term *mana motuhake* (with cognates across other Polynesian languages) refers to "autonomy" or "self-governance." The immigration platform under the new alliance creates a visa category for Pacific Islanders displaced by climate change and grants amnesty for Pasifika visa overstayers, suggesting a return towards unrestricted Oceanic mobilities. Free movement in the Pacific will take on increasing urgency as many home islands—in particular the four Pacific nations composed entirely of low-lying coral atolls[26]—come under threat as a result of warming waters and rising seas.

Aotearoa/New Zealand also has a history of more informal Māori/Pasifika alliances. Māori author Alice Te Punga Somerville in her book *Once We Were Pacific* explores a number of these connections, including the neologism "nesian" which emerged in early 2000s New Zealand hip-hop. An appropriation of the geographic Pacific regions of *micro*nesia, *poly*nesia, and *mela*nesia. Somerville writes "*Nesian* thereby challenges existing dominant constructions of the relationship between Indigenous and diasporic Pacific communities .… Nesian people are situated within the boundaries of one nation-state or city or neighborhood, yes, but they participate in the complexity, border crossing, linguistic differences, political positionings, and cultural nuances of the wider Pacific region."[27]

The distinct geographic/anthropolical regions in the Pacific have also been problematized in academic spheres; Manuhuia Barcham, Regina Scheyvens, and John Overton have proposed a "New Polynesian Triangle" which accommodates new, multidirectional flows which now commonly include the Western United States and Australia. They "regard this movement as a continuation of the exploratory processes that were established centuries ago in Polynesian societies."[28] Their proposal further suggests that when discussing the "Pacific" as a region, the boundaries are likely to be fuzzy.

If Pacific Islanders are united by mobility, they are also united by ties to land (in Polynesia, place-identity is termed by the cognates *whenua/fenua/ fanua/vanua*). While some of this land is placed at risk by climate change, today many in the Pacific diaspora identify with two—or many—homes. Histories of migration suggest that new places can take on meaning (or even physical material) and borrow from the old, as with the Māori cultivation of the Polynesian mulberry tree in Aotearoa to create their prized *tapa* cloth from its bark. In a recent conversation, an elderly Tuvaluan living in Auckland pondered how village spatial structures might be translated into the New Zealand context.

These actions and ideas suggest a resurgence of indigenous self-determination in the Pacific, achieved not necessarily by local or nationally specific action but by acting as a united, Universal Pacific. The accompanying maps attempt to provide one way of visualizing how the Pacific has been subdivided—and the many flows which make it connected. In doing so, the project seeks to not only inform how we perceive the Oceania, but also to destabilize our understanding of fixed boundaries upon migratory landscapes more broadly. As sea levels rise, weather patterns change, and the planet warms, more geographies are likely to change, migrations to emerge and expand. Understanding populations, geographies, and nations in conditions of flux provides a new frame for conceptualizing our destabilized Anthropocene.

"Archipelagic Sovereignty: Re-Mapping United Pacific States of Migration" was first published in German in *ARCH+ Magazine* 230: *Projekt Bauhaus 2, Architekturen der Globalisierun* (August 2017).

1   Many have also challenged the designations of "Pacific" or even "Oceania" as outside constructs. *Moana* (a polynesian term for "ocean") and *Nesia* (discussed below) have been suggested as alternatives. See Alice Te Punga Somerville, *Once Were Pacific: Māori Connections to Oceania* (Minneapolis: University of Minnesota Press, 2012).
2   Epeli Hau'ofa, "Our Sea of Islands," in *A New Oceania: Rediscovering our Sea of Islands* ed. Éric Waddell, Vijay Naidu, and Epeli Hau'ofa (Suva, Fiji: School of Social and Economic Development, 1993), 2–16.
3   Teresia Teaiwa, "Native Thoughts: A Pacific Studies Take on Cultural Studies and Diaspora," in *Indigenous Diasporas and Dislocations*, ed. Charles D. Thompson Jr. (London: Routledge, 2005), 15–36.
4   Many Banabans, now part of Kiribati, identify as a distinct culture; their language was lost with the arrival of I-Kiribati-speaking missionaries in the 1800s.
5   Banabans, indigenous to Banaba island which is now part of Kiribati was also included in the Gilbert and Ellice Islands, though Banabans also identify as ethnically distinct from Kiribati and the island is quite remote from the main Kiribati archipelago. Banabans were displaced to Rabi Island in Fiji when the island's phosphate resources were exploited by the British, and Banabans in Rabi retain seats in Kiribati parliament and dual citizenship between Fiji and Kiribati. For a detailed history see Katerina Martina Teaiwa, *Consuming Ocean Island: Stories of People and Phosphate from Banaba* (Indiana: Indiana University Press, 2014).
6   Efforts by the British to encourage settlement on these islands were largely unsuccessful due to chronic food and water shortages.
7   The international dateline, which was moved to the east side of I-Kiribati in 1995, means that it is the first country to see each new day and was the first nation to enter the new millenium.
8   John Connell, "Population, Migration, and Problems of Atoll Development in the South Pacific," *Pacific Studies* 9, no. 2 (1986): 41.
9   For details on Tuvalu's fluid vernacular, see Lizzie Yarina and Lomita Niuatui, "Fluid Vernacular," *The Site Magazine*, February 22, 2017, http://www.thesitemagazine.com/read/fluid-vernacular.
10 Brett Milligan, "Landscape Migration," *Places Journal* (2015).
11 CNN, "Melting glaciers force Italy, Swiss to redraw border," March 25, 2009, http://edition.cnn.com/2009/WORLD/europe/03/25/ italy.swtizerland.alps.border/index.html
12 The Sovereign Military Hospitaller Order of Saint John of Jerusalem of Rhodes and of Malta, or the Order of Malta for short, is the world's smallest nation, at only three full citizens (and an additional 13,000 non-citizen members), but it is also the world's only extraterritorial nation. While the Order of Malta is an extraordinary case, it suggests the possibility of future extra-territorial nations, which retain their seats in the UN, right to issue passports, and other trappings of sovereignty even if they no longer govern over sovereign territory.
13 Lydia Tomkiw, "Kiribati Climate Change Relocation Refugee Crisis? Sinking Low-Lying Island Nations In Pacific, Indian Oceans Seeking Solutions Before It's Too Late," *International Business Times*, October 11

2015: http://www.ibtimes.com/kiribati-climate-change-relocation-refugee-crisis-sinking-low-lying-island-nations-2127526.
14 "Kiribati Holds National Hearings On Climate Change," ABC News Australia, April 19, 2013: http://www.abc.net.au/news/2013-04-19/ an-kiribati-national-hearings-on-climate-change/4638512.
15 "Marshalls Likens Climate Change Migration To Cultural Genocide." Radio New Zealand, October 6, 2015: https://www.radionz.co.nz/news/ pacific/286139/marshalls-likens-climate-change-migration-to-cultural-genocide.
16 Their combined populations could fit comfortably into Michigan's "Big House" stadium.
17 Marybeth Long Martello, "Arctic Indigenous Peoples as Representations and Representatives of Climate Change," *Social Studies of Science* 38, no. 3 (2008): 351–376.
18 For more on this theme, see Lizzie Yarina, "PACIFIC RISING: Narrative Politics of the Climate Refugee," *Funambulist Magazine*, February 2017.
19 The UN defines microstates as nations with one million people or less.
20 Even with the larger nations included they represent less than one percent of the global population.
21 Michael Powles, "Making Waves in the Big Lagoon: The Influence of Pacific Island Forum Countries in the United Nations," *Revue Juridique Polynesienne* 2 (2002): 59–76.
22 Pamela S. Chasek, "Margins of Power: Coalition Building and Coalition Maintenance of the South Pacific Island States and the Alliance of Small Island States," *Review of European Community & International Environmental Law* 14. no. 2 (2005): 125–137.
23 Hau'ofa, "Our Sea of Islands," 11. *Tangata whenua* refers to the "people of the land" in Māori, which refers to the indigenous population of Aotearoa/New Zealand. Aotearoa is the Māori name for New Zealand; it translates to "Land of the long white cloud."
24 "Pasifika" is the New Zealand term for Pacific Islanders dwelling in New Zealand.
25 One Pacific press release, "One Pacific and Why the Māori Party?" July 9, 2017. Emphasis added.
26 Tuvalu, Kiribati, the Marshall Islands, and Tokelau (technically a non-self-governing territory of New Zealand). The Maldives, in the Indian Ocean, is the world's fifth atoll nation.
27 Te Punga Somerville, *Once Were Pacific: Māori Connections to Oceania*, 112.
28 Manuhuia Barcham, Regina Scheyvens, and John Overton, "New Polynesian Triangle: Rethinking Polynesian Migration and Development in the Pacific" *Asia Pacific Viewpoint*, December 2009, Vol. 50, no.3: 322–37.

Image
P 239: Contemporary Migrations. Sources: United Nations Global Migration Database; World Bank; Manuhuia Barcham et. al., "New Polynesian Triangle: Rethinking Polynesian Migration and Development in the Pacific," *Asia Pacific Viewpoint*, December 2009.

rate of migration: negative

rate of migration: positive

migration within Pacific
(lineweight indicates volume)

migration beyond Pacific

Seeing Earth Systems:
Ian McHarg

CLIMAPLUS: AN EARLY-DESIGN DECISION SUPPORT TOOL FOR LOW-CARBON, LOW-ENERGY BUILDINGS
Alpha Yacob Arsano

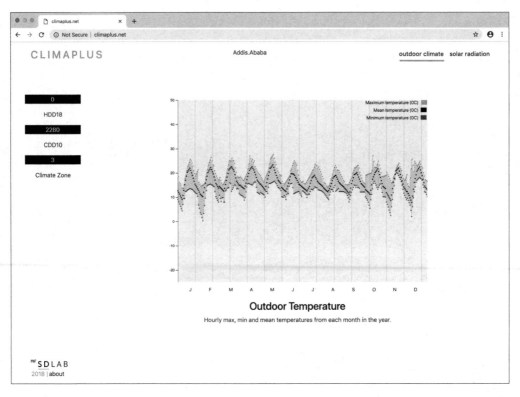

Outdoor Temperature

Hourly max, min and mean temperatures from each month in the year.

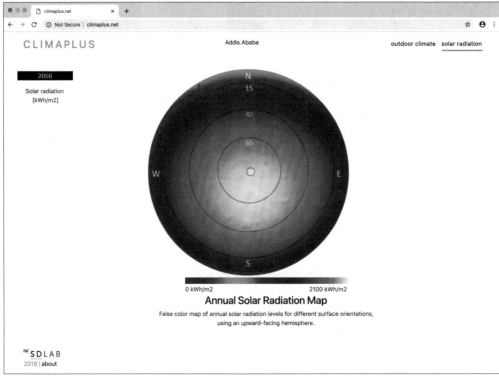

Annual Solar Radiation Map

False color map of annual solar radiation levels for different surface orientations, using an upward-facing hemisphere.

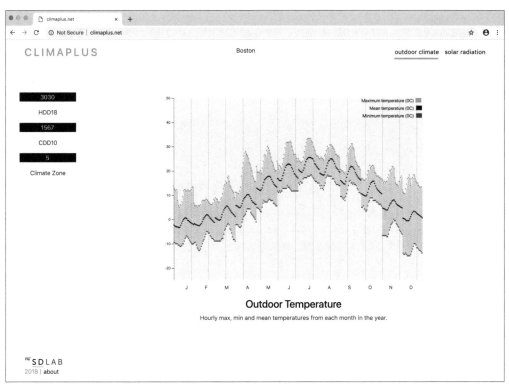

Outdoor Temperature

Hourly max, min and mean temperatures from each month in the year.

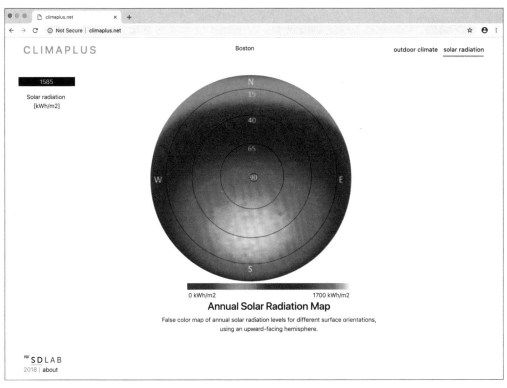

Annual Solar Radiation Map

False color map of annual solar radiation levels for different surface orientations, using an upward-facing hemisphere.

MYSTIC

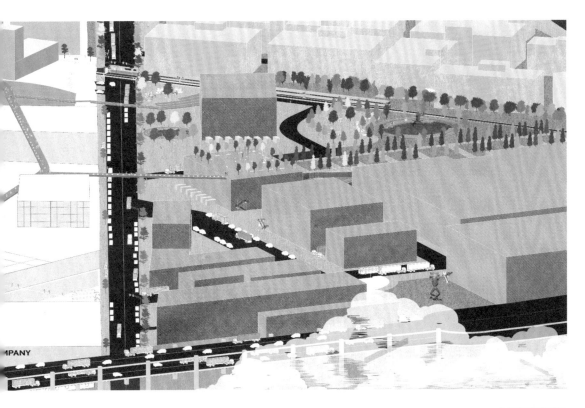

As a historian, my research has revolved around questions pertaining to institutions. What is an institution? That is to say, is it a machine that emanates diktats from on high, or is it an arrangement encompassing conventions, interests, contractual orders, what we may call a dispersed sovereignty? How is institutional functioning conceived and justified? How do they work, both in internal terms and in external terms, that is, how and why does a certain "people" consent to institutional procedures? My work delves into historical archives from the eighteenth to the twentieth century to ask and re-ask how institutions, and the people from which they garner their consent ("societies"), might be seen as mutually producing and operating what one might construe as power in its various forms. In past publications, I have looked at a nineteenth-century bureaucracy of design (*The Bureaucracy of Beauty*, 2007), MIT's mid-twentieth century history (*A Second Modernism*, edited volume, 2012), and currently a collectively edited volume on Third World development and architecture (tentatively titled *Systems and the South: Architecture in Development*) to look at how knowledge, aesthetics, and the built environment respond to aggregate, even anonymous, stimuli and drivers, forging practices and politics of various kinds.

In that light, my laboratory, MIT Infrastructure Architecture Laboratory (MIT/IAL) might be described as the antithesis of a lab: its anticipated outputs are not ersatz "solutions," but rather exercises in restating the problems that they confront. As opposed to the historian's retrospective view, MIT/IAL delves into real-time processes by deeply immersing itself in either intensive field-studies or institutional processes themselves, including governmental and political establishments. MIT/IAL looks at how "infrastructure" stands in as a proxy of power, particularly when pertaining to shifts in land relations and the consequent political and economic effects of these shifts on territorial functioning, the processes of urbanization, market and technological captures, and governmental behavior.

The term "infrastructure" has always carried a sense of neutral, transparent objectivity. When we think infrastructure, we think roads, railways, water and power supplies, or other similar such "technical" conduits for the provision of goods. We are told that society, the market, etc. has certain "essential" aggregate needs, and the state (or its private proxies) must step in to meet them at the scale of the gross population and territory within which these

needs are framed. In a time when political divisiveness and rancor appears to be undoing every other arena of agreement, "infrastructure" appears as the last thread of universality and agreement across the spectrum. The technocratic cry "Build More Infrastructure!" thus appears as if some ultimate rhetorical refuge, a discursive safe harbor allowing political leaders, bureaucrats and citizens alike to continue to entertain the fiction of a homogeneous state and an undivided sovereignty still at work beyond all the fractiousness of contemporary society. To wit, several general elections over the last decade have seen contending candidates pledge to invest in more and better infrastructure, as if this was a single "thing" or panacea that a charismatic leader could single-handedly bring into being, thus reasserting the myth of the sovereign and brushing under the carpet discussions about limited and separated powers, maps of interest, transactional domains, or, for that matter, any substantive discussion about correlations between these huge, supply-side investments and equity.

At MIT/IAL we have limited our research to a few, controlled long-term engagements that will afford us some concrete finds and outcomes rather than be swept in a relentless flurry of grant-seeking whose management becomes more time-consuming than the actual work done. Consequently, at the moment we have committed ourselves to three multi-year projects: these range from an engaged, actual planning contract with the government of India to a collaborative project that involves original Big Data creation for analysis to a focused, deep-dive study of a particular land market. The projects are as follow:

Designing Ferry Systems on the Ganges
In 2016, MIT/IAL partnered with the planning firm Thompson Design Group (TDG) to win a World Bank-funded contract with the government of India to plan ferry systems for six urban locations on the Ganges River: Varanasi, Patna, Munger, Bhagalpur, Kolkata and Haldia. Like the Yangtze, the Ganges is the cause and support for one of the world's densest riparian urban systems, encompassing a highly dense and stratified population equal to the size of that of the United States. The river provides externalities (transportation, water, soil fertility) while becoming a receptacle of externalities itself (pollution). Planning ferry systems in this context involves addressing a byzantine complex of jurisdictions:

administrative and juridical frameworks ranging from the local municipality to conurbated "metropolitan" as well as state and federal levels of government, involving multiple ministerial remits, from transport and shipping, to environment, to natural resources, to urban development. Negotiating these thickets of interests, which include control deployed by local strongmen, contending realms of expertise, financial environments, etc., infrastructure appears not as a technical presumption consistent with itself, but rather as a disaggregated collage or map of variegated interests, which a system has to impossibly imbibe and work through in order to realize itself.

Corridor Economies and Patterns of Urbanization
In collaboration with Prof. Sai Swarna Balakrishnan at Harvard's Graduate School of Design, the MIT/IAL is conducting a study on the relationships between agricultural history and patterns of urbanization. The case studies that we are using to develop a broader thesis take up the so-called "corridor": geographies resorted to by governments today (Delhi-Mumbai Industrial Corridor in India; Belt and Road Initiative across China-Central Asia) as a form of fiscal stimulus for economic growth. Its purpose will be to undo the neutral, "technical" demeanor of infrastructure projects, and focus instead on the actors, interests, knowledge frameworks, and protocols that drive them. The impetus for organizing this seminar is the prospective empirical study of India's New Economic Corridors (NECs). Straddling hundreds, if not thousands, of kilometers across multiple regions and political boundaries, these NECs—comprising concerted efforts to align road, rail, power, and water inputs into a necklace of new industrial townships—today present the driving edge of urbanization and modernization in India. Globally, infrastructural projects like the NECs today bespeak a "new arms race," where nation-states compete to stake their claims over the control of food, water, oil, and other resources not through military conquest but through competitive logistics infrastructures that seamlessly reduce the distance between desired nodes in the global supply chain. Mimicking the economic geography first identified by Jean Gottman's 1950s study of the transregional Bos-Wash corridor, India's NECs present new linear and sprawling agglomerations of field and factory, crop and city, in radically new and unfamiliar spatial-economic adjacencies.

The corridor economy also relies on the massive mobilization of natural resources such as power and water across political boundaries. In so doing, these infrastructural interventions also create institutional voids where environmental externalities can no longer be managed within existing territorial arrangements. For example, contemporary India, where we propose to do most of our fieldwork and research, faces endemic challenges of groundwater depletion, desertification, and higher carbon emissions. In contrast, the NECs today monopolize far more than their just share of these resources; an example here is Rajarhat outside Kolkata, advertised as "India's first Green City," where large amounts of water have to be continually pumped from the Hooghly River to stabilize the groundwater table in order to prevent this former swamp from sinking, taking its shiny, air-conditioned (and mostly unoccupied) corporate office buildings with it.

The socializing effects of this new geography are tremendous. The new shaping of norms of access has led to exacerbated political conflicts over water, electricity and employment. On the one hand, the NECs have tended to unevenly benefit particular politically-linked groups by enabling them to capture a surfeit of resources and restricted market opportunities in exchange for land transactions; paradoxically these very beneficiaries-middle-farmer ethnic groups such as the Jats and Patels—have erupted in vigorous political protest with new demands for affirmative action after the first wave of land monetization has worn off. Symptomatically, the strategy of protest—*bandhs*, or stoppages—has been used to shut down the very highways and railways that epitomize the NEC's key technology accumulation. On the other hand, lopsided concentration of resources in some areas has created equally large and equally ethnically-defined "megaghettos" defined by the absence of resources: pockets or enclaves of relative deprivation that further reveal stark overlaps between the map of resource-grabbing and other geographies such as ethnicity, etc., key measures of inequality in India. Examples include Mewat/Nuh in Haryana–an impoverished, lower-caste dominated area abutting the glistening skyscrapers of Gurgaon, or the Muslim principalities of Gujarat.

Economic Behavior beyond Zoning: Understanding Non-Formal Land Relations in Market Behavior
Following from the above, a third project uses funds obtained from the Samuel Tak Lee Real Estate Entrepreneurship Lab at MIT to look at land and tenurial relations as the basis of economic behavior. One example is the multi-year study of a single entrepot in the heart of Kolkata, India, called Burra Bazar, where close to one hundred billion in trading activities are carried out across a densely packed 3.2 square kilometers of space each year. The proposed research below is based upon breaking the dogma that the highest and best land value is

also the most productive. The overarching reliance of elites and governments in developing countries on "Western urban land economics" that privilege highest bidders on a rent gradient from urban center to urban periphery has paradoxically created economically uneven urban landscapes in Asia and the developing world. State-owned enterprise-driven (SOE) megaproject developments in urban cores and Special Economic Zones (SEZs) in ex-urban locations stem from investment criteria that privilege large investments, whose inflexibility towards incremental changes of use and adaptability may pose inherent barriers for the key sectors where long-term economic resilience in the developing world may be located: new (small) entrepreneurial entrants and small and medium-sized enterprises (SMEs). One measure of productivity ignored by "land economics-type" monetary measurement is the incubation function and positive externalities that cities have historically provided, positives that have been one of the core arguments for cities themselves as "engines of economies." In order to better understand these potential barriers, it is important to model correlations between "place-based" externalities (labor surpluses, co-location, interfirm linkages) created in areas where there is a high concentration of SMEs and the measurable benefits conferred by location and better infrastructure. I would argue that conventional real estate paradigms tend to narrow the range of viable enterprise and SMEs, whose collective "noise" is crucial to economic resilience for the majority of economic actors. Studying these correlations would necessarily involve the study of "informal" or "extra-legal" transactions, both in respect to real estate and the other forms of economic activity housed within it. In countries such as India or China, for instance, greater formal transparency and legal enforcement is not necessarily a stimulus for the biggest and smallest economic actors (or, for that matter, the state). This STL-funded project therefore aims to look at the potential for sub-state collaboration amongst a large diversity of economic actors, and the feasibility that might allow for urban improvements that benefit SMEs and new economic entrants. The prospect is to think about new paralegal forms of economic composition within real estate arrangements as well as infrastructural upgrades that are responsive to smaller, incremental "bottom-up" demands that are supportive of place-based externalities, and are therefore inherently better posed to aid higher productivity.

PICTURESQUE PRAIRIES: PRODUCTIVE PRESERVATION ON A PETROLEUM PLANET
Tyler Ray Swingle

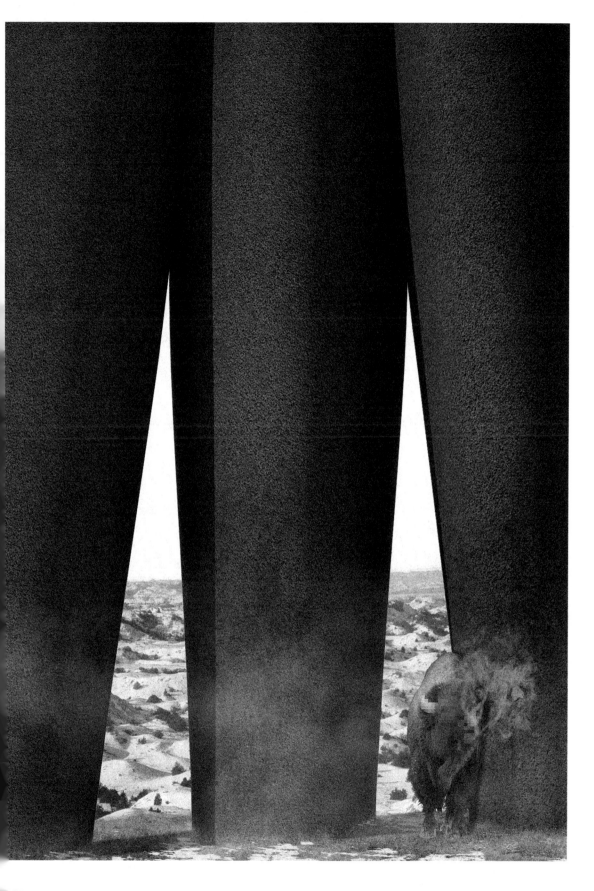

TERRA-SORTA-FIRMA: SEEKING RESILIENT URBANISM IN SOUTH FLORIDA
Studio Research

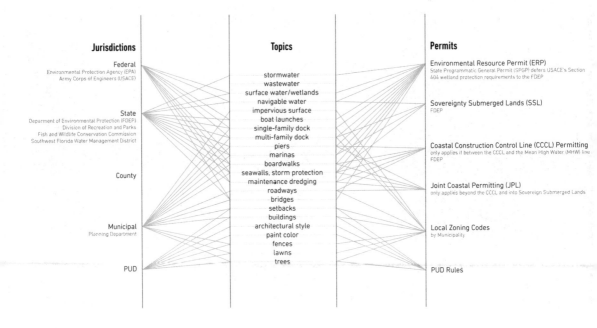

Jurisdictions

Federal
Environmental Protection Agency (EPA)
Army Corps of Engineers (USACE)

State
Deparment of Environmental Protection (FDEP)
Division of Recreation and Parks
Fish and Wildlife Conservation Commission
Southwest Florida Water Management District

County

Municipal
Planning Department

PUD

Topics

stormwater
wastewater
surface water/wetlands
navigable water
impervious surface
boat launches
single-family dock
multi-family dock
piers
marinas
boardwalks
seawalls, storm protection
maintenance dredging
roadways
bridges
setbacks
buildings
architectural style
paint color
fences
lawns
trees

Permits

Environmental Resource Permit (ERP)
State Programmatic General Permit (SPGP) defers USACE's Section
404 wetland protection requirements to the FDEP

Sovereignty Submerged Lands (SSL)
FDEP

Coastal Construction Control Line (CCCL) Permitting
only applies if between the CCCL and the Mean High Water (MHW) line
FDEP

Joint Coastal Permitting (JPL)
only applies beyond the CCCL and into Sovereign Submerged Lands

Local Zoning Codes
by Municipality

PUD Rules

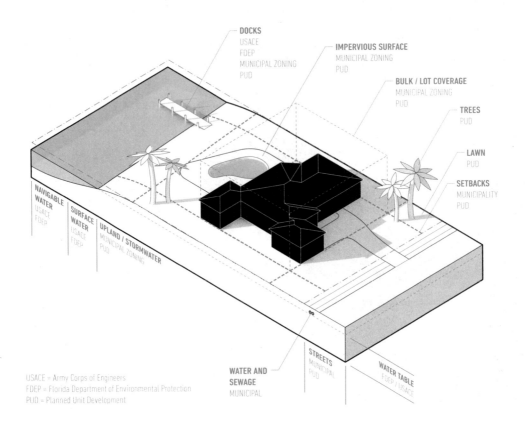

DOCKS
USACE
FDEP
MUNICIPAL ZONING
PUD

IMPERVIOUS SURFACE
MUNICIPAL ZONING
PUD

BULK / LOT COVERAGE
MUNICIPAL ZONING
PUD

TREES
PUD

LAWN
PUD

SETBACKS
MUNICIPALITY
PUD

NAVIGABLE
WATER
USACE
FDEP

SURFACE
WATER
USACE
FDEP

UPLAND / STORMWATER
MUNICIPAL ZONING
PUD

STREETS
MUNICIPAL
PUD

WATER TABLE
FDEP / USACE

WATER AND
SEWAGE
MUNICIPAL

USACE = Army Corps of Engineers
FDEP = Florida Department of Environmental Protection
PUD = Planned Unit Development

THE EVERGLADES: PERFORMATIVE GROUNDS, GROUNDS THAT PERFORM
Monica Hutton, Sam Jung, Angelos Siampakoulis

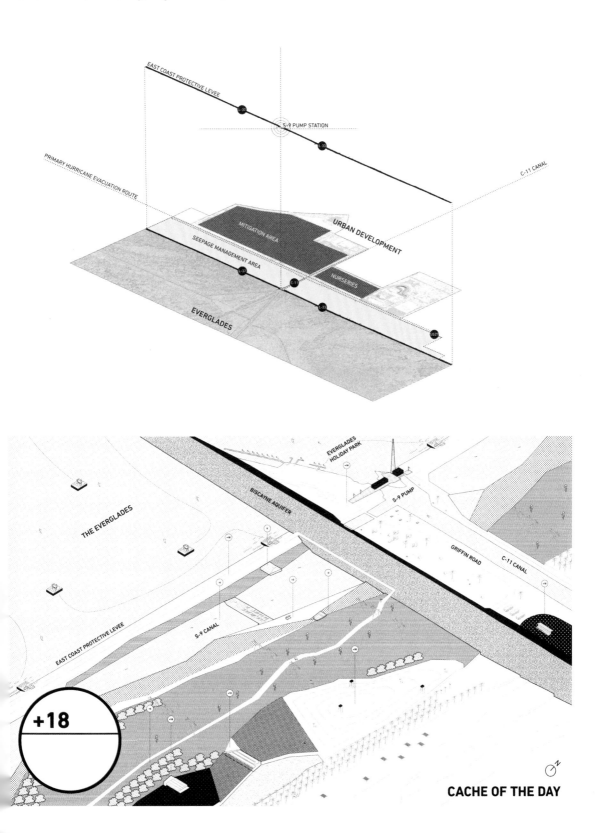

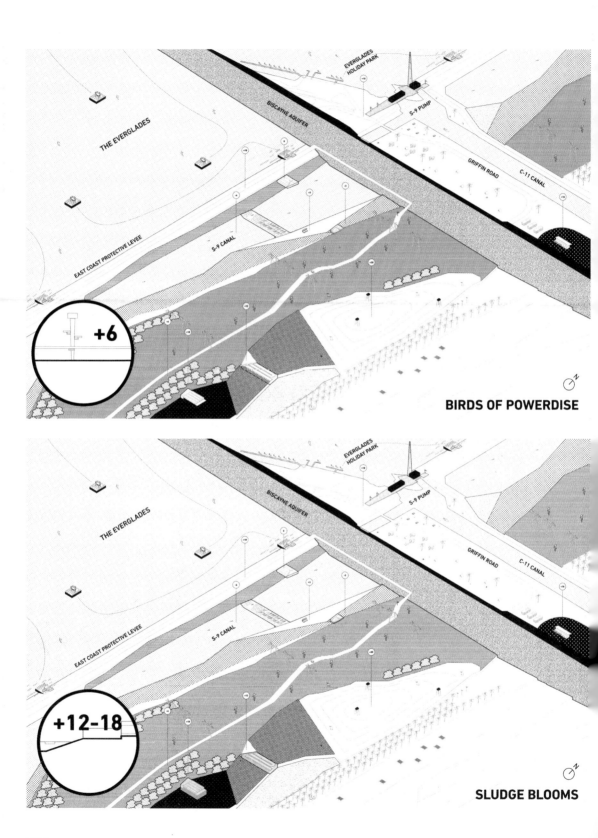

BIRDS OF POWERDISE

SLUDGE BLOOMS

THE TRANSITIONAL PLANNED UNIT DEVELOPMENTS
Giovanni Bellotti, Elaine Kim, Annie Ryan, Alexander Wiegering

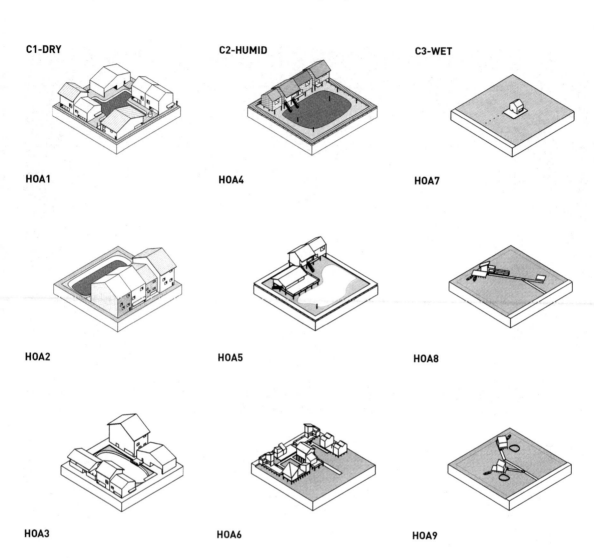

C1-DRY

C2-HUMID

C3-WET

HOA1

HOA4

HOA7

HOA2

HOA5

HOA8

HOA3

HOA6

HOA9

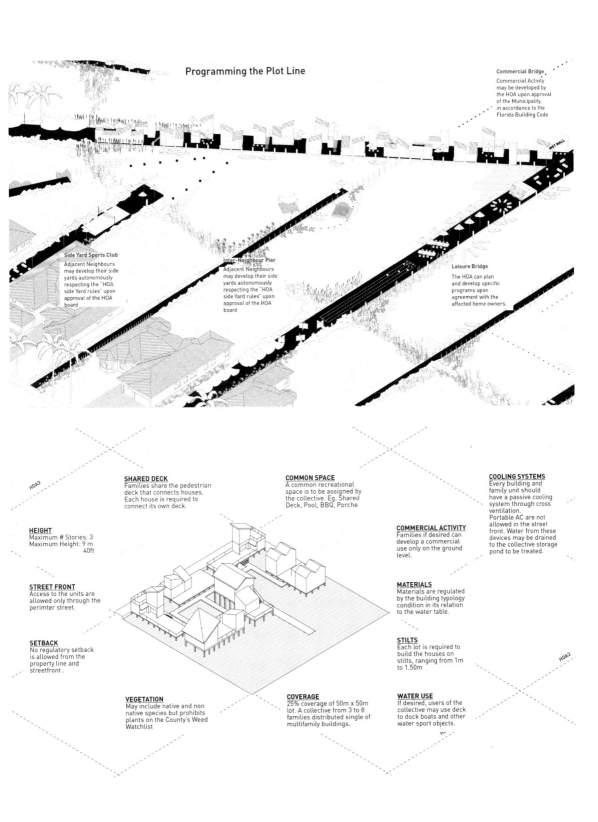

Programming the Plot Line

Commercial Bridge
Commercial Activity may be developed by the HOA upon approval of the Municipality, in accordance to the Florida Building Code

Side Yard Sports Club
Adjacent Neighbours may develop their side yards autonomously respecting the "HOA side Yard rules" upon approval of the HOA board

Inter-Neighbour Pier
Adjacent Neighbours may develop their side yards autonomously respecting the "HOA side Yard rules" upon approval of the HOA board

Leisure Bridge
The HOA can plan and develop specific programs upon agreement with the affected home owners.

WET MALL

HOA3

SHARED DECK
Families share the pedestrian deck that connects houses. Each house is required to connect its own deck.

COMMON SPACE
A common recreational space is to be assigned by the collective. Eg. Shared Deck, Pool, BBQ, Porche

COOLING SYSTEMS
Every building and family unit should have a passive cooling system through cross ventilation.
Portable AC are not allowed in the street front. Water from these devices may be drained to the collective storage pond to be treated.

HEIGHT
Maximum # Stories: 3
Maximum Height: 9 m
                40ft

COMMERCIAL ACTIVITY
Families if desired can develop a commercial use only on the ground level.

STREET FRONT
Access to the units are allowed only through the perimter street.

MATERIALS
Materials are regulated by the building typology condition in its relation to the water table.

SETBACK
No regulatory setback is allowed from the property line and streetfront .

STILTS
Each lot is required to build the houses on stilts, ranging from 1m to 1.50m

HOA3

VEGETATION
May include native and non native species but prohibits plants on the County's Weed Watchlist

COVERAGE
25% coverage of 50m x 50m lot. A collective from 3 to 8 families distributed single of multifamily buildings.

WATER USE
If desired, users of the collective may use deck to dock boats and other water sport objects.

271

TECHOS: DISASTER RESPONSES FOR PUERTO RICO
Jorge Silen Rivera, Danniely Staback, Luisel Zayas; Alexandre Beaudouin-Mackay, Gabrielle Heffernan, Catherine Lie, Jackie Lin, Cristina Solis, Courtney Stephen, Cheyenne Vandevoorde, Yifen Zhong

Discursive
Acts
Discursive
Acts
Discursive
Acts
Discursive
Acts
Discursive
Acts

How do we build new collaborations, networks, infrastructures, and support systems? How do we talk through this? How do we teach it? How are these conversations framed at MIT? The final Act gathers projects that focus on new modes and sites of knowledge production, pedagogy as a place of action, and on how new practices can be established and shared.

Each project included here bridges multiple territories of knowledge to create new work and spark change in institutional structures. They ask: How can a discipline embrace its incompleteness? How does architecture transform as it circulates? How is knowledge created, distributed, diffracted, and negotiated as it travels? What conversations could the production of an architectural artifact support? The projects and essays gathered here make space for reflection and enable dialogue; they embody a hope that these conversations lead to shared understandings and new collective identities.

We leave you with a few syllabi focused on challenging pedagogy and building conversations on design's histories and consequences, on architecture's mediation in the public realm, and on subjects long neglected and ignored. In particular, we focus on the concerted effort students and faculty have made to retool sites and systems of learning; we pull these together as preparatory acts for future pedagogies. Some are particular to MIT: the implementation of a design minor and major in the undergraduate program, for example, prompted new courses to reach students across disciplines. What we have seen in recent years is a capacity and effort to take on projects that address systemic issues in the discipline and field.

We test these questions. Experiments in Pedagogy, organized on occasion of the sesquicentennial of architecture education at MIT, opened space for a collective experiment in new inquiries and formats. It serves a mindful note to continually examine and reflect, experiment and take risks, and maintain the conversation.

CODE: SURVEY
Renée Green

Code: Survey exists as a process allowing temporary imaginary inhabitation of, or passage through, an unknowable place. In this incarnation the process has been applied to what is known as California, although other locations can by used to yield different possibilities. How might one attempt to know a place? How might one encounter a place imagined to be known? The surveying process in this instance demonstrates a form of tracing used by a highly sensitive team of polycarpous and polyglot polyhistorians, who over three years developed a methodology that encompassed searching, collecting, and exploring a variety of clues based on spoken or sung words, written words and keywords, sounds, films, and images. Photos, images, diagrams, and maps provide an index of previous moments or intentions, even if their contents aren't easily identifiable or understood by the time they are encountered. They can be examined nonetheless. Speculations can form, as well as informed attempts to decipher. Codes were assigned. Stories multiplied. The process of assembly can continue in one's imagination.

Code: Survey can be located as a website and became accessible internationally in 2006: http://www.dot.ca.gov/dist07/code_survey/intro.htm. A physical version of *Code: Survey*, made as a structure of glass, film, and steel, can be found in the Caltrans Headquarters of the California Department of Transportation in downtown Los Angeles. The work was commissioned by Caltrans and the architect Thom Mayne of Morphosis.

Images
P 284–285: Renée Green. *Code: Survey*. Caltrans District VII Headquarters, Los Angeles, 2006. Photography © Joshua White.
P 286–287: Renée Green. *Code: Survey*, detail. Caltrans District VII Headquarters, Los Angeles, 2006. Photography © Joshua White.

ARCHITECTURE MOVES
Anne Graziano, Eliyahu Keller
Thresholds 46: *Scatter!*
2018

From treatises to TED talks; postcards to propaganda; etchings to drawings, films, and blogs, architecture moves in diverse and curious ways. It is these currencies, which give architecture its agency, its authority, and life. And yet, despite the varied modes of its circulation, the majority of architecture's discursive knowledge reaches only a familiar audience. While contemporary means of information production and dispersal continue to exponentially grow and quicken, the circle of professional and discursive associations remains confined. Circulation, distribution, and access to knowledge are

not exclusive matters of the discipline. Rather they extend past architectural limits to catalyze inquiries into hidden geographies and infrastructure, restricted access, and equity.

The history of architecture has consistently seen innovation and subversion expand not only architectural theory and practice, but also the ways in which ideas are dispersed beyond established systems of circulation. With the understanding that architecture indeed moves within ever-changing boundaries, *Thresholds* 46 looks to investigate, expand, and imagine the histories, futures, means, and methods by which architecture gets around.

If half a century ago the medium was the message, now, after dozens of new mediums have expanded the manner of conversation, we wish to ask: Is the equation still so simple? Was and is the message exclusively a product of its medium? What are the architectural histories that can inform future inventions of dispersal and distribution? And how have architects, designers, artists, and scholars employed medium with message to interrogate fields of conversation and suggest new and provocative platforms for the discussion of ideas?

We wish to look at the history of architectural dissemination, while holding our gaze to a swift, saturated, and scattered connectivity. Asking, what modes of circulation were employed in various periods of history to elevate and publicize an architecture? How was architecture distributed by actors and vehicles that are both foreign to its discourse or an essential part of it? What is the power of non-architectural documents such as cartographies, letters, stamps, or money in the distribution of architectural knowledge? And what can we learn from accidents in which architectural knowledge broke loose from its constraints, reaching unimagined publics, and scattering to unintended realms?

LOW FIDELITY: FOUR INQUIRIES INTO THE ARCHITECTURAL IMAGE
Mackenzie Muhonen
Advisor: Ana Miljački
MArch Thesis
Fall 2018

Today, architectural images and their reproductions serve as stand-ins for firsthand experiences of buildings. Buildings are valued in fragments known as images. The layers of information and esoteric specificity intrinsic to design are excluded in the production of these images. This is Low Fidelity. It is a condition in which the image of the building supersedes the value of the building for which it speaks.

This thesis is an essay on maneuvering within the context of Low Fidelity. It is a four-part essay on image making within this contemporary condition. The four probes of the essay mine the contemporary state of image culture within architecture. Each of the probes engages a facet of image culture—namely, the mediums through which images are disseminated, consumed, curated, collected, uploaded, and downloaded. In doing so, the probes perform twofold. They respond to and feed content back into the networks influencing both digital and analog access to architectural information and the design process.

The architect, then, is positioned as the author of new, or perhaps recast, labors in Low Fidelity. The architect scripts the link between divergent and infinitely accessible architectural content by designing the indexes, or table of contents, that seam spatial fragments together. Architectural images and their reproductions become compositions of built-up layers of information, which are detached from their original context to gain new meaning. In Low Fidelity, then, architecture becomes a quasi-object that shifts scales, materials, and context. The labors of the architect are disembodied from the building and repositioned onto the indexes of information to destabilize the building's image.

ARCHITECTURE AFTER THE END OF WORK
Option Studio
Instructor: Keith Krumwiede
Spring 2017

> "The problem is this: How to love people who have no use."
> — Kurt Vonnegut, *God Bless You, Mr. Rosewater*

In contemporary politics both the left and the right continue to view full employment as a policy priority. Increasingly, however, questions about the nature of work in an ever-more automated world are leading political economists, technologists, and sociologists to consider the possibility of a future without work, or, more accurately, without work as it is currently defined. According to theorists Geert Lovink and Franco Berardi, the capitalist promise of "full employment turned out to be a dystopia: there is simply not enough work for everyone. Zero work is the tendency, and we should get prepared for it, which is not so bad if social expectations change, and if we accept the prospect that we'll work less and we'll have time to think about life, art, education, pleasure, love, and what have you rather than solely about profit and growth."[1] If we accept this premise, how do we prepare for a future without work?

In his recent essay "F*** Work," historian James Livingston asks, "How would human nature change as the aristocratic privilege of leisure becomes the birthright of all?"[2] In a different way, we might ask: What would it mean to live in a world where we work less? What would we do? How would we live? And, as architects, we might ultimately ask a different version of Livingston's question: How would human habitats change as the aristocratic privilege of leisure becomes the birthright of all? After all, our urbanism and architecture—including our current models of dwelling—are the product of a centuries-old economic system that segregates sites of labor and production from sites of dwelling. Under a new economic model in which individuals are freed from the requirement of work as a means of survival, it becomes necessary to speculate upon other conceptions of productivity and other forms of human association, and, consequently, to speculate upon the organization and form of such a world.

Americans define themselves through work; it builds character, or so we believe. The American Dream itself is premised on individual achievement, with the promise that our labor will be rewarded by a sense of personal fulfillment as measured by the things we collect and consume. For many, the sine qua non of the dream, our greatest collectible, is the single-family house. It is, more than any other object, the symbol of success in the United States, the tool with which we represent our achievements. To own a home, then, as we have been told over and over again, is to live the American Dream.

Across the latter half of the twentieth century—and indeed into the first decade of this century—homeownership rates advanced consistently in the US, but since the collapse of the housing market in 2008, they have been declining. The Dream, it seems, is in crisis, and the legitimating social, economic, and environmental narratives that sustained the endless reproduction of detached suburban dwellings are collapsing. According to historian John Archer, "the romanticized isolation of the individual (or nuclear family unit) in a manufactured Arcadian preserve is an increasingly untenable fiction."[3]

Increasingly, suburbs, and the detached single-family houses of which they are composed, work to isolate and separate us, to dislocate us as individuals, detached from any larger heterogeneous collective body. The common cul-de-sac is, both literally and symbolically, the end of the road, a terminus in a system. Safely sequestered within its four (or five, or six, or eight, or twelve) walls, we stand apart from the crowd, reaching out through an array of devices to make contact with those who are, more or less and more often than not, just like us. Space, meanwhile, becomes increasingly less a medium in which we mix and more a barrier that insulates us from those unlike ourselves. And as houses balloon in size, this sense of disconnection is amplified within the walls of the house itself, with each inhabitant retreating to ever more far-flung and insular private domestic retreats. The social and political consequences of this withdrawal are increasingly evident in the deterioration of civil society and the erosion of civil discourse.

But what is the alternative? Is the detached house with its resulting social detachment a prerequisite of the American Dream? Is it possible to imagine other futures for the Dream and, consequently, other futures for dwelling? What happens when personal happiness is no longer a function of economic success derived from the fruits of ones labor? In such a climate, it could be argued that the Dream, as currently defined, has no utility. Liberated from the idea that our dwellings must be understood as freestanding castles—isolated retreats from society through which we represent our individualism and secure our market share—we could instead conceive of assemblages of dwellings that collectively define a domain of mutual cooperation, interaction, and informed discourse.

But in order to credibly imagine new forms of collective dwelling, we must also imagine new social, economic, and political contexts within which we might dwell collectively. When subjected to a new set of parameters—if linked for example, as it will be in this studio, to a transformed conception of the role of work in society—each dwelling could become a cornerstone of a productive and consensual community. Even so, it is necessary to keep in mind that the Dream cannot be transformed overnight and made new out of whole cloth. It is too deeply embedded in our collective consciousness. At its core, the Dream is about security, comfort, and familiarity as much as it is about aspiration, accomplishment, and status. Any new form of dwelling, if it is to dislodge us from our long-habituated connection to the single-family detached house, must deliver a compelling new narrative that makes collective life seem both more necessary and more desirable.

The challenge of this studio then is not only to propose other possible forms of dwelling but also to tell good stories about other possible ways of living, and living together, in a world after the end of work. Often, the stories that we tell as architects are as important as the things that we make. As Lewis Mumford wrote: "The prospects of architecture are not divorced from the prospects of the community. If man is created, as the legends say, in the image of the gods, his buildings are done in the image of his own mind and institutions."[4]

The studio will begin with readings that consider alternate conceptions of work in an increasingly automated world. Through discussions and scenar-io building exercises, the class will identify possible futures visions for a post-labor economy and its impact on the shape of human communities. Concurrently we will study various key moments in the history of domestic architecture that can inform the design work of the group. Through a drawing based analysis of historic and contemporary domestic models, the studio will identify a set of inflection points in the history of dwelling that open new paths of development—both organizational and formal— for conceiving of a world without—or likely, with less—work, paths that prioritize interaction over isolation, collectivity over privacy. In the end, our objective in this studio is to study the architectural impact of a transformed political economy on our current conceptions of housing, conceptions that are, in fact, unique to the circumstances of our own historical situation.

1   Geert Lovink and Franco Berardi, "Zero Work is the Tendency, Negative Money is the Tool: To Rescue Europe from the Abyss of Racist War We Must Design Europe 2.0," *Verso Books Blog*, October 25, 2016, https://www.versobooks.com/blogs/2899-zero-work-is-the-tool-to-rescue-europe-from-the-abyss-of-racist-war-we-must-design-europe-2-0.
2   James Livingston, "F*** Work: What if Jobs are Not the Solution but the Problem?" *Aeon Essays*, November 25, 2016, https://aeon.co/essays/what-if-jobs-are-not-the-solution-but-the-problem.
3   John Archer, *Architecture and Suburbia: From English Villa to American Dream House, 1690-2000* (Minneapolis: University of Minnesota Press, 2005), 358.
4   Lewis Mumford, *Sticks and Stones: A Study of American Architecture and Civilization* (New York: Boni and Liveright, Inc., 1924), 187.

A POST-TIME WORLD
Ching Ying Ngan

Since the end of work, great cities around the world grew into twenty-four-hour cultural playgrounds. Liberated from labor and the eight-hour day, their citizens acquired ideas of time detached from efficiency and productivity. Houses were converted into workshops; creative activities engulfed the streets.

The forces of this sprawl conquered the border of the Hudson River. Jersey City, a former suburban commuter hub that fed the labor economy of Manhattan, rapidly transformed. In order to manage this public creativity, the city instituted a new planning strategy to enable the residents to maintain these lifestyles; it tested this strategy on a site composed of two empty urban blocks.

Alongside the provision of universal basic income, each individual received a space for retreat. The retreats take the form of thin vertical towers that organize and frame the cultural landscape from which they rise. The ground is turned into a volumetric, expansive landscape of cultural activities. These are housed in a series of rooms configured to stimulate diverse moods and atmospheres, rendering an environment produced by the activities of post-time life. The scale of these spaces makes the wall a building of its own, hosting smaller spaces to support a full range of cultural and social activities. In this superhouse, one can choose between thinness and thickness, between the fast and slow, between the twenty-four-hour day and the non-regimented day.

A GOOD-FOR-NOTHING MANIFESTO
Mary Lynch Lloyd

Years ago, when the most eminent class of specialists, experts, and advisors all banded together to decry the looming crisis of THE END OF WORK, we remained unmoved. Though the headlines predicted violence, boredom, melancholy, sloth, restlessness, depression, indolence, excessive languor, lustful depravity, and worst of all, a sweeping epidemic of IDLENESS AND LOSS OF IDENTITY, we simply waited and prepared for the future—a future that we knew would finally be one of our own making.

We didn't prepare for this future by training, exercising, drilling, or stockpiling. In fact, we didn't do anything to prepare. We simply ate, drank, painted, read, watched, dozed, and allowed ourselves to pursue our interests together. We can't tell if we got it right—that's part of the point—but our world now is one where it's ok to fail, it's ok to be bad at something, it's ok to enjoy being alive. This is a good-for-nothing world, in which good-for-nothingness is the highest virtue one can achieve. As Robert Filliou predicted in 1962:

> Everybody can be an artist. Everybody should. Everybody will some day as specialized good-for-something work is left more and more to machines to do. Everybody is already anyway. From now on, and forever, here on earth or in space, art is the domain of the good-for-nothing good-at-everything. (Or there will be no art, which is alright by me, provided there is fun.)[1]

Our Good-For-Nothing household consists of three large families. There are approximately twenty to thirty members in each family, and they sleep, live, relax, and pursue their interests together in different ways and in different degrees of collectivity. Our household enjoys holding good-for-nothing events at which the public can come and see what we do and participate in the myriad ways we claim our natural birthright:

good-for-nothingness. As our good-for-nothing inspiration Robert Filliou reminds us:

> The good-for-nothing world is limitless, or should be. It is yours for the taking, the making, the caressing, the beating, the drinking, the eating, the blowing, the juggling, the shitting, and so forth, and so on … .[2]

1   Robert Filliou, "GOOD-FOR-NOTHING-GOOD-AT-EVERYTHING" (c.1962), in Teaching and Learning as Performance Arts (Cologne: Verlag Gebr. Konig, 1970), 79–80.
2   Ibid.

DIGITAL STOCKHOLM SYNDROME IN THE POST-ONTOLOGICAL AGE
Mark Jarzombek
Digital Stockholm Syndrome in the Post-Ontological Age
2016

OTHER EQUATORS: MEASURES FOR AN INTERNATIONAL TRIBUNAL FOR THE RIGHTS OF NATURE
Xhulio Binjaku, Milap Dixit
MArch Thesis
Advisor: Roi Salguiero Barrio, Hashim Sarkis
Fall 2018

In 1997, the Kyoto Protocol institutionalized carbon offsetting as a market solution to emissions, allowing companies and states to offset every ton of carbon dioxide emissions with an equivalent ton of carbon dioxide sequestered somewhere else. This logic of equivalence was enabled by a set of global metrics (such as the definition of "forest" under international law) that financialized the Earth's capacity to absorb carbon. Equatorial mountains became prime targets for the production of carbon credits through pine and eucalyptus plantations.

In 2008, Ecuador became the first country to recognize the Rights of Nature, extending its jurisdiction to the scale of the planet and granting legal personhood to nonhuman entities such as mountains. More than a decade since it was first recognized, the Rights of Nature remains an elusive notion, easily absorbed into the logic of practices that reduce Nature to its exchange value. The Rights of Nature lacks an institution to specify and guarantee its functions, to measure and account for its violations, and to summon the "Nature" for whom it claims to speak. In 2018, Ecuador requested proposals for an International Tribunal with the authority to invoke universal jurisdiction for global cases related to the Rights of Nature. The Tribunal would be deployed territorially across a site of planetary significance: the Equator itself, which intersects the

Avenue of Volcanoes, a group of twenty mountains recognized as legal persons under Ecuadorian law.

The buildings of the institution make mountains legible as witnesses in courts of law by framing, measuring and collecting "units" of Nature to be used as evidence. They are the architectural expression of a paradox that underlies the very idea of the Rights of Nature: that the infinite value of Nature has to be assigned finite values in order to exist as a legal category. The legal and spatial logics used to define units of "Nature" begin to erode when they encounter the specificity of terrain, allowing the mountains to speak for themselves.

THE SWAMP SCHOOL
Nomeda and Gediminas Urbonas
Lithuanian Pavilion, Venice Architecture Biennale
Summer–Fall 2018

THE DEMISE AND AFTERLIFE OF ARTIFACTS
Pamela Karimi, Nasser Rabbat
Aggregate
2016

MEMORIAL TO ENSLAVED LABORERS, UNIVERSITY OF VIRGINIA
Höweler + Yoon Architecture: Eric Höweler, J. Meejin Yoon; Mabel O. Wilson/Studio&, Gregg Bleam Landscape Architect, Frank Dukes, Eto Otitigbe
2016–ongoing

Nestled into the sloping landscape of the "Triangle of Grass," which sits within the UNESCO World Heritage Site boundary of the University of Virginia's (UVA) grounds, the Memorial to Enslaved Laborers seeks to formally acknowledge the work and the individual lives of the enslaved African Americans who built and sustained the everyday life of the University. Founded and designed by Thomas Jefferson, UVA is considered by many to be the quintessential university campus. Yet like many of its peer institutions, the University depended on the labor and work of enslaved African American men, women, and children. Constructed of local granite, "Virginia Mist," the Memorial will create a space to gather, reflect, acknowledge, and honor the enslaved laborers who contributed to the University. Scholars estimate that at least 5,000 enslaved African Americans worked on the grounds, with many in residence, starting with the construction of the Lawn in 1817 and lasting through the end of the Civil War in 1865.

As visitors to the Memorial will experience, its physical form seeks to capture the complex and challenging lives of the enslaved through the duality of this painful chapter of history: lives oppressed by the violence of bondage, but also lives that bear witness to the perseverance of the human spirit. The Memorial captures these dualities in its circular form that references both the "Ring Shout," a dance practiced by enslaved African Americans that celebrates spiritual liberation, and a broken shackle that signals the end of physical bondage. These dual conditions form two nested rings that break when they meet the ground; this break opens a circle that welcomes gathering.

Within the Triangle of Grass, the Memorial is oriented tangent to two paths. The first path leads from the Memorial in the direction of the North Star, which for the enslaved led to freedom. The second path aligns with the sunset on March 3rd, which commemorates the day that Union troops emancipated the local enslaved community at the close of the Civil War. The communities of Charlottesville and the University will observe this important event through the newly instituted Liberation and Freedom Day on March 3rd through the city. Also sharing the same north/west orientation is the Memorial's grove of gingko trees that harkens back to the area's previous use as a productive landscape of fruits and vegetables tended to by enslaved laborers. The trees also evoke the spaces of "hush harbors" that were clearings in the forest where enslaved African Americans convened for religious rituals and communal gatherings and to arrange escape. In early spring the Memorial's central gathering space will bloom with blue snow drops, symbolically marking Liberation and Freedom Day.

The Memorial encourages multiple visitor experiences. As people walk along the memorial's path the interior granite wall rises to a height of eight feet. This wall will bear the inscriptions of the known and unknown names of the estimated 5,000 persons who worked on grounds; current research has uncovered at least 1,000 (mostly first) names of enslaved persons. Running parallel to the wall of names, a smaller ring of granite incorporates a bench for individuals to rest and reflect. The smaller ring also hosts a water table with a timeline of the history of slavery at UVA etched into the stone. For peoples of African descent, water was used for libations in religious ceremonies and waterways served as routes to freedom for the enslaved. At the Memorial's center, a circle of grass creates a welcoming gathering space for commemorative ceremonies, for use as an outdoor classroom, or as a larger community forum for performances that mine the rich African American history of song and voice. The Memorial will be a central element of an ongoing educational and commemorative effort to honor the lives of enslaved men, women and children who lived and labored at the University.

Image
P 315 Top: Eto Otitigbe, *Becoming Visible*, 2012. Courtesy of the artist.

DESIGN ACROSS SCALES
Neri Oxman, J. Meejin Yoon
Syllabus
Spring 2018, first taught Spring 2013

DESIGN: THE HISTORY OF MAKING THINGS
Timothy Hyde, Kristel Smentek
Syllabus, Undergraduate/Design Minor
Spring 2017

CURATING ARCHITECTURE: ON EXHIBITING,
RESEARCH, AND CRITICISM OF ARCHITECTURE
Ana Miljački
Syllabus
Spring 2015

QUEER SPACE: EXPLORATIONS IN ART AND
ARCHITECTURE
Jackson Davidow
Syllabus, Tufts Experimental College
Spring 2018

IS ARCHITECTURAL HISTORY GETTING ANY
BIGGER?
Timothy Hyde
Architectural Research Quarterly
2017

A CURRICULUM FOR MUD: COMPOSITION
FOR MASSACHUSETTS (OUR BELOVED KIN);
THOREAU (THE RE-ENSLAVEMENT OF
ANTHONY BURNS); DISCORPORATE (THE
INSTITUTE IN THIRDS)
Nolan Oswald Dennis
Studio: Art, Culture and Technology
Spring 2018

a curriculum for mud is conceived as a transmutation
system for books and other printed matter, a process
for turning colonial and anti-colonial thinking into
mud. The work is inspired by Audre Lorde's essay
*The Master's Tools will Never Dismantle the Master's
House* (1979), and the imperative "to make common cause with those others identified as outside
the structures in order to define and seek a world in
which we can all flourish"—a process of getting dirty,
liberating theory from the clean world of academic
work and approaching learning as a form composting and as a strategy for survival. *a curriculum for
mud* is quite simply a system for turning books and
other printed matter into earth, and then later that
earth reading as if it was a book—in cooperation with
a community of earthworms (*eisenia fetid*a).

a curriculum for mud takes mud, the soft sticky
matter resulting from the mixture of earth and water,
as the object and the target of decolonial study. The
work is a series of models, apparatuses, and systems engaged in the formation of a knowledge-body
in relation to the earth as an ecological, sociological, and colonial tragedy (as tragedy increasingly
becomes farce). *a curriculum for mud* proposes that
the sociological and ecological politics of land-own-
ership and land-use are realized through practices of
thinking with and through the material agency of the
land itself. These practices draw from non-Western
practices of commoning (especially *ubuntu*); practices of land-stewardship; of reading the land (as
if text); of writing the land; and of relations to the
whole-earth as a series of interdependent, active
agents in a community (which includes human, animal, plant, and planetary agencies as social actors).

In other words, if practices of decolonial study
demand we imagine the world *otherwise* and in
modes of alterity to the existing states of knowledge,
a curriculum for mud insists that to think *world* beyond the boundaries of authorized and legitimized
forms of knowledge, we have to think with the *world*
that lies beyond the boundaries of institutions of
knowledge. This includes the vast majority of people of color excluded from these institutions; the
methodologies and practices of knowledge which
are excluded; but also includes finding other ways
of thinking with the land, the water, the micro-
and macro-biological agencies entangled in our
world-body.

EXPERIMENTS IN PEDAGOGY
Mark Jarzombek, J. Meejin Yoon; Renée Caso,
Irina Chernyakova, Danniely Staback
Fall 2018

Image
P 283: William R. Ware, *An Outline of a Course of Architectural Instruction*
(Boston: John Wilson and Sons, 1866). Courtesy MIT Museum.

AN

OUTLINE

OF A

COURSE OF ARCHITECTURAL INSTRUCTION.

BY

WILLIAM R. WARE,

PROFESSOR OF ARCHITECTURE IN THE SCHOOL OF THE
MASSACHUSETTS INSTITUTE OF TECHNOLOGY.

PRINTED FOR PRIVATE DISTRIBUTION.

BOSTON:
PRESS OF JOHN WILSON AND SONS.
1866.

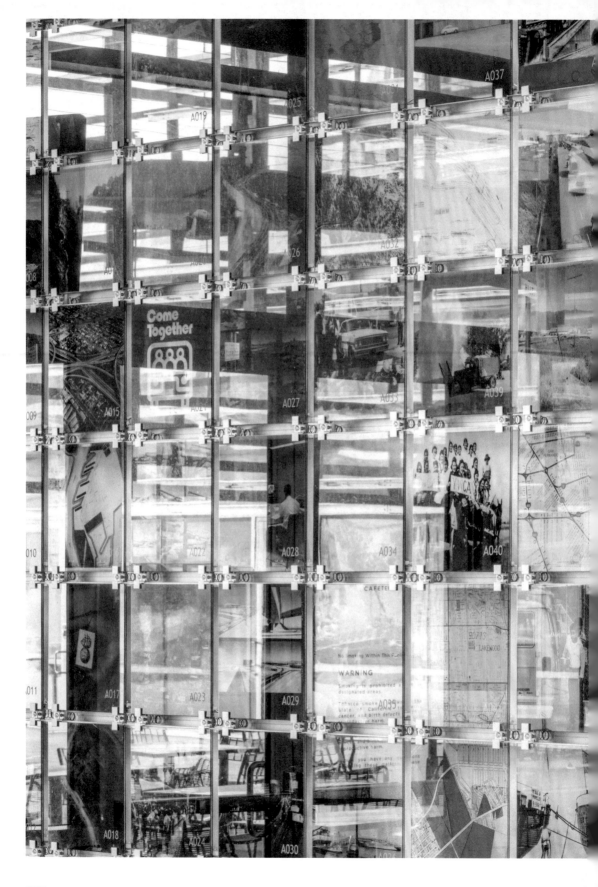

ARCHITECTURE MOVES
Anne Graziano, Eliyahu Keller

The fundamental issue of architecture is that does it affect the spirit or doesn't it. If it doesn't affect the spirit, it's building. If it affects the spirit, it's architecture. And architecture doesn't necessarily mean that it's the final form of a complete building. A drawing to me is a completer piece of architecture, a building is a completer piece of architecture, a photograph of a drawing or a photograph of an architecture is a piece of architecture; each act is individually an act of architecture.[1]
—John Hejduk, *The Education of an Architect*

Speaking to poet David Shapiro, John Hejduk recollects an argument with fellow architect Peter Eisenman, addressing the nomadic character of his work and the criticism it has received. After looking at Hejduk's *House for a Musician and House for a Painter,* Eisenman, according to Hejduk's story, states that these structures "are not architecture, because you can't get in them." Confident that his designed creatures are unequivocally "architecture," the furious Hejduk points his finger at his interviewer—standing in for Eisenman in this reenactment—and declares with conviction: "YOU can't get in them!" He then, more calmly, follows with an explanation: "In other words, he was not in the position to get into them, because he did not understand them. You can only get into something if you understand, or are willing to."[2]

The question raised by this conversation regarding the definition of what is or is not architecture—as nonsensical as it may sound to a person not familiar with architecture's disciplinary anxieties—is not new to architects or architectural scholars. This pseudo-existential inquiry into the definitive essence of the discipline is one that has eluded absolute answers, fostering endless propositions to come forth—the most common approach being one of negation: perhaps we do not know what architecture is, but we can surely tell you what it's not!

We, however, are not here to give or even attempt to find an answer to this question. Rather, and following Hejduk, we too acknowledge that architecture is by no means only "building." The two anecdotes shared by Hejduk stipulate not only that architecture exists in other, perhaps less traditional, forms, but also point to the fact that the answer to what is and isn't architecture is a matter of perspective, point of entry, and approach. It is not only, as Eisenman would have it, a matter of whether one *can* enter architecture or not, but rather of how one enters it: how one reconceptualizes what it means to approach a seemingly unintelligible thing and how, by entering differently, one broadens the category of what is or could be architecture.

The starting point for *Scatter!* is simple: buildings, for the most part, are immobile; architecture isn't. Like Hejduk's nomadic architecture-on-wheels, architecture moves, it mutates, it gets around. It does so in loud forms and subversive whispers, it finds accidental alleys into places unknown to its creators, it is mediated through walls and drawings, thoughts and poems, space, and time. True, architecture's traditional objects—namely buildings—are inert, yet architecture itself does not stand still. In the words of anthropologist Tim Ingold, "For things to interact they must be immersed in a kind of force-field set up by the currents of the media that surround them"; this "force-field" nurtures and disperses architecture into newfound motility and life. If it were not for such mobilizing agents and "cut out from these currents—that is, reduced to objects," the still pieces of architecture "would be dead."[3]

Whether through its imagery or discourses, architecture finds its way to places and people that exceed the physical limits of its sites; in fact, it expands on the very notion of what the site of its operation is. These become more than plots marked by building codes, regulations, and municipal lines—although, paraphrasing the pre-Socratic Heraclitus, here too architecture is present.[4] Rather, its sites expand beyond the traditional realm of the built work, its fragments move and shape various aspects of human culture in its travels. Through inquiries, public displays, political co-option, or with the assistance of other disciplines, architecture shakes loose from its creator's stabilizing will in surprising and curious ways. Here architecture forges new networks and establishes agency through a variety of mediums, no longer static as concrete, steel, or glass. Rather, and not unlike information, it becomes nimble, agile, and dynamic. Here, it manages to escape the exclusive clubs to which it is typically confined, dodging the figures and masters of its institutional dissemination who decide what is or isn't architecture. Here, it is able to reach unfamiliar and unexpected spaces, exerting newfound power in subtle, and at times, surreptitious ways.

Throughout history, these moves and movements have been a vital form of architecture, the most potent way by which it has entered, and was circulated and witnessed around the world. As texts and treatises, in rules and regulations, within dreams and stories, or on coins, bills, and stamps, architecture possessed power beyond the building. In such spaces, it could multiply and transform its material presence into a variety of other means, and create ripples that would sound its echoes beyond the limits of its physical sites. Still, and despite the exponential increase of its dispersal in a wired world, architecture and its discourse continue to be confined to its physicality as building while its rhetoric mostly resonates within its self-reproducing, restricted circles.

Scatter! serves as a call for action. It asks for a recognition of the many ways in which architecture moves, and for a heightened awareness to the moves that architecture makes. Like the observation made by the architectural theorist Albena Yaneva and philosopher Bruno Latour that "the problem with buildings is that they look desperately static," Scatter! demands an appreciation for the commonly recognized yet rarely expressed fact that "a building is not a static object but a moving project."[5] But this would be a limited premise. Expanding on Latour's and Yaneva's manifesto-like appeal, Scatter! urges for more than a retroactive inspection of static buildings or intricate representations of architectural works. In addition to these pleas, Scatter! charts, suggestively, the vast and almost limitless ocean in which architecture and its representatives could and should operate.

Scatter! is a command, equipped with exclamation. It demands to not only see architecture as moving, but to direct its movement, to use its moves, to move it with conviction. Still, to scatter implies that one must always be aware of chance. Like a hand grasping a pile of sand and directing it toward the wind, Scatter! intends to facilitate a more complex, layered, and inclusive notion of dissemination, while always leaving space for a storm to suddenly surge, and send the sands of architecture to places unknown.

The essays, contributions, proposals, and creative projects in this volume all begin at this port of departure and travel through their own itineraries to sites both anticipated and unexpected. They point to the history of architecture's appearance in places, documents, and spheres, some of which have been traditionally recognized, while others overlooked. Piercing through language, code, image, and sound, the discrete works assembled in this collection are now bound together and become associated with one another before being offered up to the wind. Such potent collectives both make their individual components more unique and powerful, while creating a web of relations through which a social and communal will gains an ability and power to pursue change.[6] These become malleable associations between objects, ideas, institutions, and individuals; ones that although always at the edge of anarchy, as Alexis de Tocqueville suggests, have the potential to become a powerful means of agency and action, of political capacity, and a link between disparate and supposedly disconnected peers.[7]

The tables have finally turned. Our hand has reached to the sand and gathered a collection that is as beautifully accidental as it is a result of our own intentions and contemplations. With the shared knowledge that architecture can indeed be entered in numerous ways and can indeed exist outside a fixed building, each piece within this collection presents and represents a distinct yet mutual point of entry; each work asks the reader to consider it as architecture, and in doing so expands the capacity of architecture: "each act is individually an act of architecture." We now raise our palm towards the sky and ask you, the winds, to do with it what we cannot. Scatter!

"Architecture Moves" is the introduction to Thresholds 46: Scatter! edited by Anne Graziano and Eliyahu Keller (Cambridge, MA: SA+P Press/MIT Press, 2018).

1   Education of an Architect: Voices from the Cooper Union. Directed by Kim Shkapich. (The Cooper Union, New York, NY: Michael Blackwood Productions, 1993).
2   John Hejduk: Builder of Worlds. Directed by Michael Blackwood. (New York, NY: Michael Blackwood Productions, 1992).
3   Tim Ingold, "When ANT Meets SPIDER: Social Theory for Arthropods" in Being Alive: Essays on Movement, Knowledge and Description, (New York: Routledge, 2011), 89–94.
4   "... for here too, the Gods are present." In Aristotle, De Partibus Animalium, Book 5, Chapter I.
5   Bruno Latour and Albena Yaneva, "Give me a Gun and I will Make All Buildings Move: An ANT's View of Architecture," in Reto Geiser, ed., Explorations in Architecture: Teaching, Design, Research (Basel: Birkhäuser, 2008), 80–89.
6   Georg Simmel, Conflict; The Web of Group-Affiliations (New York: Free Press, 1964).
7   Alexis de Tocqueville, "Of Political Associations in the United States," Democracy in America, Vol. II, Part 2, Chapter 4.

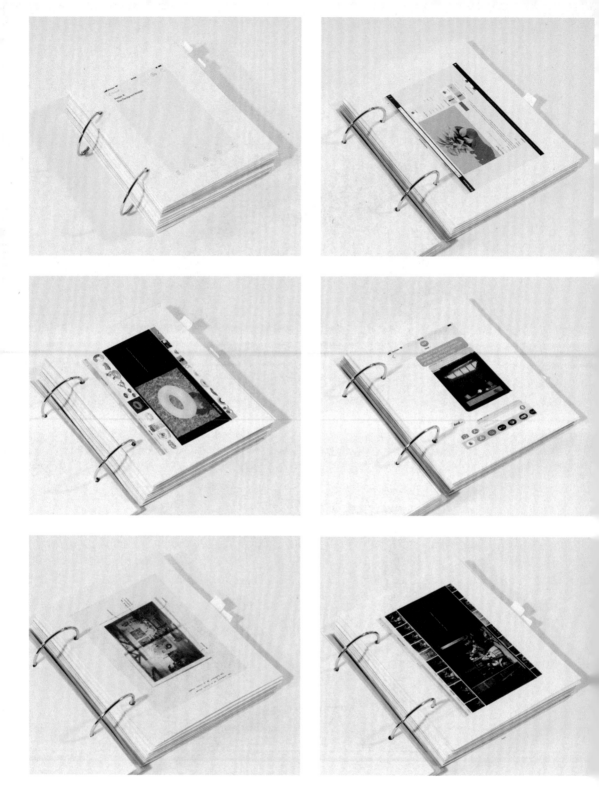

A POST-TIME WORLD
Ching Ying Ngan

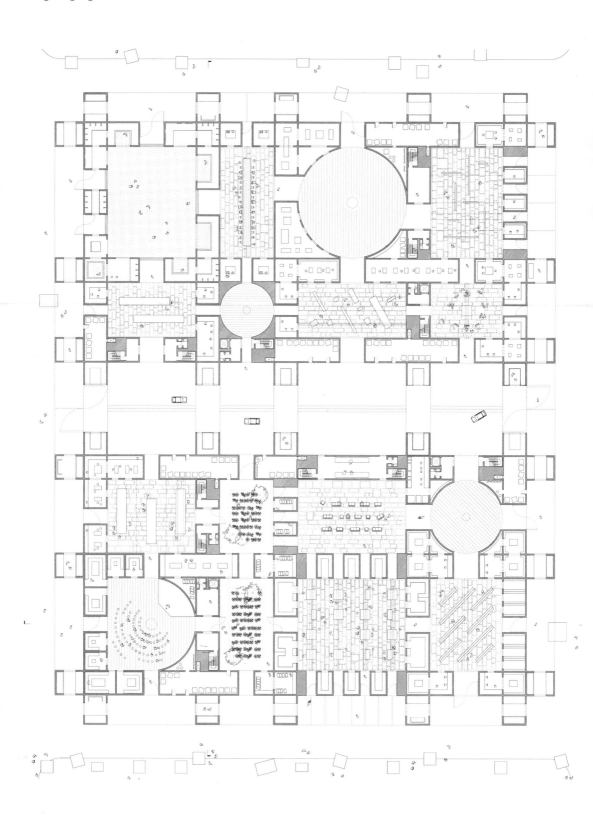

295

We didn't prepare for this future by training, exercising, drilling, or stockpiling. In fact, we didn't do anything to prepare. We simply ate, drank, painted, read, watched, dozed, and allowed ourselves to pursue our interests together. We can't tell if we got it right—that's part of the point—but our world now is one where it's ok to fail, it's ok to be bad at something, it's ok to enjoy being alive. This is a good-for-nothing world, in which good-for-nothingness is the highest virtue one can achieve.

Mary Lynch-Lloyd

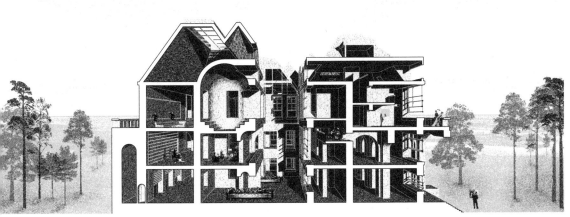

DIGITAL STOCKHOLM SYNDROME IN THE POST-ONTOLOGICAL AGE
Mark Jarzombek

Data is a compulsive self-propagator. All data equals more data. This can be summarized as the Second Law of Thermodynamics:

"Data" = Data Surplus > Data Processing

The incongruity of surplus and process is not a design flaw, but a design requirement to produce the necessary friction that holds the post-ontological together. The more the better, meaning that data as a system of comprehension is just one small step back from its own incomprehensibility.

The endless task of elastic, approximate modeling, adjusting for the (in)human, constitutes humanity in all its newly, productive glory. Like the Heisenberg Principle, the closer the deities seem to get to modeling our activities, the more elusive and vulnerable those activities become—are designed to become—even if in some cases, the endgame exposes the actual inhuman of the (in)human.

$$\text{Human} = \Delta = \Delta 1 = \Delta 2 = \Delta 3 = \Delta n = \text{Data}$$

The result is a circularity that creates a perpetual, low-intensity torture of the social-civilizational body.

The more data, the greater the addiction by the data-demanding deities, the more disruption is required. But these disruptions have to be fed into the system in precise amounts. The results can never dehumanize us completely or else the great deities that produce the algorithms would face a backlash that can easily "go viral"—such as when we discovered that Samsung televisions could possibly spy on our conversations.

Before Buddha invented renunciation, before Christians invented martyrdom, before Mohammed invented the jihad, before the Hebrews invented monotheism, before Plato invented the dreaded cave in which we supposedly live, blind to the presence of all that is Good, people talked to each other in freer ways. They talked to dead ancestors, to rocks, to trees, to animals, to spirits. A Being-Global world returns us to ancient possibilities, repressed under centuries and layers of civilizational ideologies and naturalized, self-mutilations. I can talk with my grandmother; but I can also talk with my refrigerator, washing machine, thermostat, car ignition, all of which can send me messages and suggestions. At MIT they are developing a special toilet. Soon even my shit will have something to say.

Paranoia is not a symptom that needs to be cured even though we will continue to operate in those standard modernist terms. It is the operating system (in the computational sense of functions needed to control and synchronize a computer activities). But unlike an OSes in my computer, paranoia is biologically based and thus its normalization has to be produced internal to the needs and desires of life itself. Biology does not work, in other words, with "upgrades." Upgrades are not the actual cause of paranoia—though it may seem that way—but the external modifiers of a paranoidic technology that must deny the crisis of potential collapse. Paranoia is the key requirement of this bio-technical process. It is the blood system that keeps the three post-ontological, thermodynamical equations in play.

An ontological crust, a place where our traditional sense of identity toward the outside condenses, contains our sense of Self. This crust can be loose, flexible, even compliant, or it can harden into identity politics and fundamentalism. This onto-crust is fed just as much from the outside—as in standard encounters with other (in)humans—as it is from the inside. Inside: not as in desire and passions—the interiorities of old—but as the known/unknown organization of energies that infuses its prerogatives into our sense of Being.

Our onto-crust hooks itself into the flesh of the digital, draining energy from it, for its psychic purposes. Paranoia rests below the surface of the onto-crust. The harder the crust gets, the more likely it will fissure, allowing paranoia to leak out. Flowing to the surface, paranoia spreads out over us, defining us. It is no longer an illness, but the everyday, the everywhere.

Excerpts from Mark Jarzombek, *Digital Stockholm Syndrome in the Post-Onto-logical Age* (Minneapolis: University of Minnesota Press, 2016).

P 299: "Diagram of the post-ontological condition: The Realm of Deities and Demi-Gods," *Digital Stockholm Syndrome*, 55.

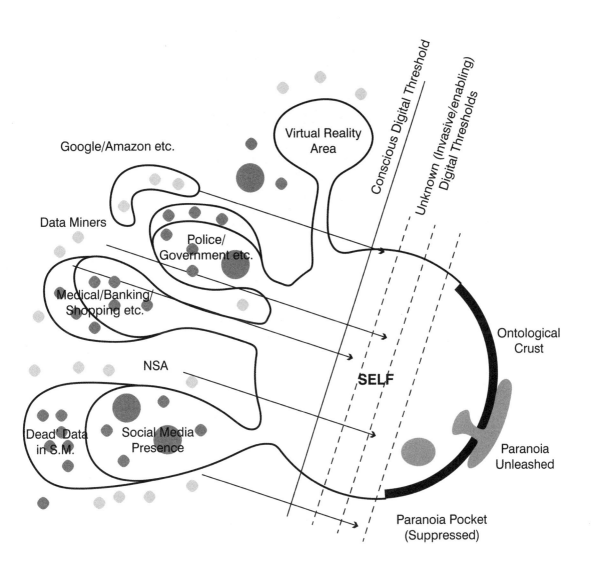

Google/Amazon etc.

Virtual Reality
Area

Conscious Digital Threshold

Unknown (Invasive/enabling)
Digital Thresholds

Data Miners

Police/
Government etc.

Medical/Banking/
Shopping etc.

Ontological
Crust

NSA

SELF

Dead' Data
in S.M.

Social Media
Presence

Paranoia
Unleashed

Paranoia Pocket
(Suppressed)

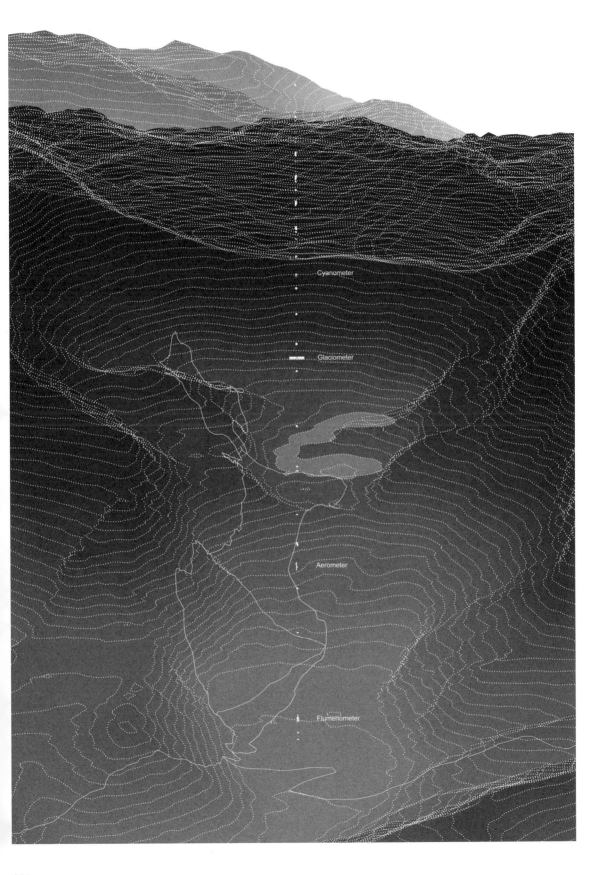

Cyanometer

Glaciometer

Aerometer

Flumeriometer

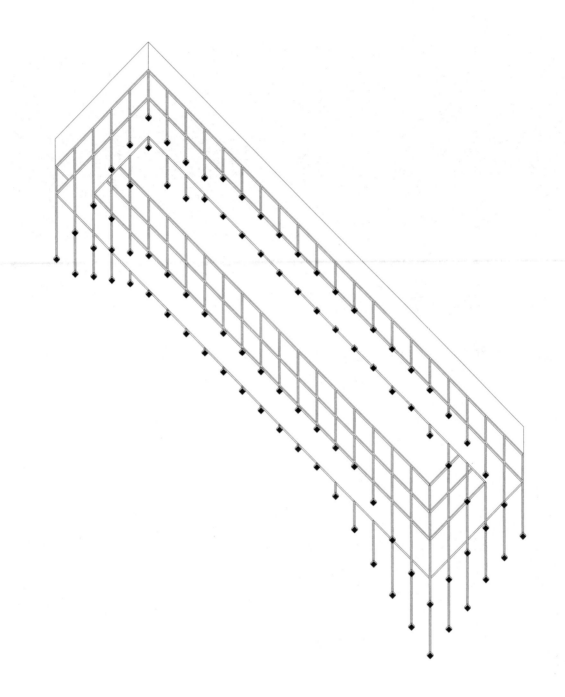

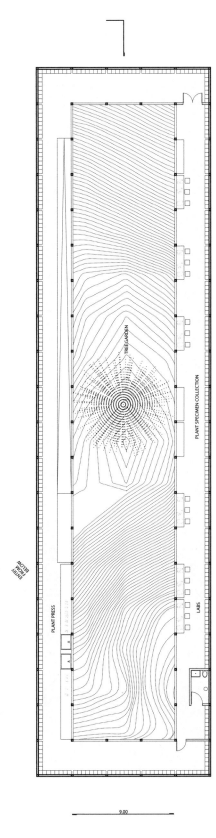

ENTRY FROM BELOW

PLANT PRESS

TREE GARDEN

PLANT SPECIMEN COLLECTION

LABS

9.00

THE SWAMP SCHOOL
Nomeda and Gediminas Urbonas

"Hope and the future for me are not in lawns and cultivated fields, not in towns and cities, but in the impervious and quaking swamps," maintained Henry David Thoreau, who loved to write about wetlands and to be written by them.

Today, valorizing the swamp over solid ground as well as exploring its complex web of interactions appears to be far from romantic clichés. We cannot get back to the marshes; there is no objectively fixed environment. In a time marked by existential threats of war and climate change, the *Swamp School* is a learning environment that sets up a cross-disciplinary dialogue to challenge conventional concepts of territory, reorganize identities, and envision the role of the immaterial in architecture, art, and nature.

The challenge of the swamp is not about rediscovering a true identity, but rather about valuing the intrinsic hybridity of the human. Blurring the line between human and nature, the swamp prompts us to reimagine our relationships and potential exchanges in the post-human turn. Just as, along Bruno Latour's lines, we have never been modern, the swamps have never retreated. They remain in the background as an invisible symbiosis of different forms of life, as an interaction of elements and organisms, as a part of our denigrated premodern subconscious of urbanized fears and nightmarish dreams. These signal an exposure to the danger of the unknown and induce into fluid motion both abjection and attraction to the uncanny.

So how do swamps foster a shift in thinking? In what ways do the wetlands provoke our repressed imagination? How could swamps benefit architecture, given that every construction project begins with land reclamation? Venice itself has a swampy past and uncertain future. Its ancient inhabitants moved from the mainland to the nearby marshes; they found refuge on the sandy islands.

The "floating city" was built by constructing a solid foundation of wooden stakes and platforms to stabilize the moving environment of the wetlands. The swamps, however, did not cease to exist. They colonized the city from within, the same way the city's structures intervened into the waters.

In fact, swamps have always been bigger than us. They are each interactions of several networks, combining heterogeneous forces and multiple layers into complex biosystems. Together, these layers and networks act as a brain that exceeds predefined bodily limits and infiltrates our living environments. Our technological engagements, based on the flux of information through digital networks, might get inspiration from its organizational structure—reminiscent of the cybernetic dream of Stafford Beer—a viable system organized in such a way as to meet the demands of surviving in a changing environment.

In this context, the theme of "immaterial materiality," as formulated by El Lissitzky, is an important point of reference. The materiality of the swamp is both present and absent; it accumulates persistence of objects by constantly setting them in motion as well as producing multiple spatial articulations. It opens an imaginary space for continuous transformations. Swampy environments remind us of the immateriality that is always at stake in every materiality, even that of architecture. The reconsideration of wetlands challenges both the material and mental architecture of the human. It serves as a reminder of the danger of reduction, present in every formal language preoccupied with pragmatic considerations, and a reminder to celebrate the informality and incompleteness of its objects.

The task of the Swamp School tutors and interlocutors is to elaborate on our capacities to engage the environmental impacts we currently face and point to how following a different course in and with the swamp could reshape the world in which we live. The heterotopic swamp prompts perspectives on these new conditions for the ecological and built environment, ripe for imagination and dialogue on possible futures.

The Swamp School contributes to a body of work that fosters architecture's utopian energy to confront the changing climate and shifting ground. Inscribed within the tradition of ideas and attempts to redefine architecture by overcoming its materiality, the Swamp School aims to be in conversation with projects such as: Juan Downey's *Invisible Architecture*, Yves Klein's *Air Architectures*, Yona Friedman's *Spatial Cities*, Frei Otto's *Suspended City*, Archigram's *Walking City* and *Plug-in City*, Superstudio's *Continuous Monument*, the aerial and oceanic architectures of the Japanese Metabolists, and Cedric Price's *Fun Palace*, among many others.

The School connects the swamp as a real space, a viable and occupiable space, and then pivots to use its physical qualities (murky, thick, confusing, amorphous, unnavigable, still, or stagnant in its timeless-ness—like the twilight zone or a dream world, yet fertile!) as a metaphor for the headspace, hallucinatory state, emotion-laden process of thinking about the possibilities in the swamp. The swamp is global and primordial; it opens a cosmology to reframe space, time, causality, and freedom.

A problematic space becomes a perfect place to reflect on problematic divisions. On what basis is ownership or territory defined? Which occupants of a place are agents and which are witnesses? Where can a new language be found, and what new aesthetic can it offer? What is material and what is not? What is the relationship between matter and imagination? How is materiality revealed in architecture? What is tomorrow? Perhaps today we must celebrate the long-maligned swamp!

Building from a network of international institutions, the Swamp School brings together experimental work by scholars, artists, and designers on intersectional topics including transnational and speculative architecture, feminist and queer theory, posthumanism, ecology, materialism, visual studies and imagination, cybernetics, physics, sociology, and the commons to argue for conviviality—living together—and sympoiesis—making together in imagining the future.

The School is made up of three chapters that progress through ways of learning: transmitting, sensing, and cohabitating. The sessions bring participants together to experience a new, maybe disorienting, environment. In this new place, participants' senses are heightened and their experience of the environment is attuned to imagine new forms for adaptation in the future. In order for the swamp to be successfully occupied, we not only need to imagine new architectures, but more importantly, new social contracts.

Swamp Radio: On Transmitting
Date: May 23–27, 2018
Sound is a powerful force in organizing space. After all, it is sounds (not visuals) that mark dramatic shifts from one world to another in non-linear ways. Sound is simultaenous, immersive, and resonant; allowing things to respond to one another. Acoustic vibrations resonate inside the body, producing a spectrum of affects, pleasures, and fears. Sound expands our external world, too—the urban environment, nature, and outer space. Scientists and artists listen to the universe, as radio signals drift far beyond our planet after transmission. This chapter engages participants in acoustic space explorations, radio experiments, environmental field recordings, acoustic immersions, and biodata sonification.

Futurity Island: On Symbio-poetics
Date: June 26–30, 2018
Inspired by discussions on radical imagination, indigenous thought, collective intelligence, and plural ecology (symbio-poesis), this chapter invites participants to develop new habits of thought for the era of environmental crisis. The Futurity Island provides participants a space to speculate on urban and material futures, and to probe the usefulness of the concept "sympoiesis" in imagining and working together in radical interdisciplinarity toward desirable futures.

Commonism: On Cohabitation
Date: September 24–29, 2018
Through contributions by theorists, designers, and artists, this chapter interrogates the commons as an ideology—an aesthetic of the real—as a way of giving a form to society and our contemporary human condition. With an understanding of aesthetics as "the art of thinking beautifully," as a way of seeing a better, more beautiful world, this chapter learns from reciprocating movements for the commons to ask: How is the commons constituted in society. how does it shape our reality of living together, and what strategies and what aesthetics do artistic commoners follow?

Images
P 306–309: Swamp Radio field trips with Jana Winderen (306–307) and Nicole L'Huillier (308–309), Venice, Italy, 2018. Photos by Norbert Tukaj.

Project
"The Swamp School" was first published as the introduction to *The Swamp School: Manual*. The Swamp School, curated by Nomeda and Gediminas Urbonas, is the Lithuanian Pavilion at the 2018 Venice International Architecture Biennale. It was on view in Venice May 25–November 25, 2018. www.swamp.lt

THE DEMISE AND AFTERLIFE OF ARTIFACTS
Pamela Karimi, Nasser Rabbat

The radical group known as the Islamic State in Iraq and Syria (ISIS) has obliterated or threatened to obliterate many historic sites and artifacts in Iraq and Syria. The losses include more than 40 major cultural heritage sites, such as the Mosul Museum and the archeological sites of Nineveh, Nimrud, Hatra, and Ashur in Iraq and Palmyra in Syria, with at least 14 sites destroyed in 2014 and 27 in 2015. By late 2015, the Islamic State (as it has become known with its expansion beyond Syria and Iraq) reached Libya, posing serious threats to the country's Greek and Roman antiquities and prehistoric artwork. Following the recent liberation of ISIS-controlled areas in northern Iraq, researchers at the American Schools of Oriental Research Cultural Heritage Initiatives reported that extensive destruction has taken place at two capital cities of ancient Mesopotamia. Throughout 2016 the quantity and range of demolitions have relatively slowed; however, the ISIS threats are still imminent.

To address the devastating effects of all destructions of ancient and medieval monuments in the Middle East, Pamela Karimi and Nasser Rabbat invited prominent scholars to contribute original essays that document, quantify, and theorize this demolition. The essays presented take a long historical view that encompasses instances of destruction of the cultural heritage in the Middle East from the Napoléonic invasion of Egypt in 1798 to the demolition spree of ISIS today. However, the volume does not aim to provide a chronological survey of destruction. Rather, it engages the idea of demolition itself by exploring the agency of ancient monuments in today's cultures, and the ways in which this agential capacity has been enacted or rejected through acts of violence, care, or indifference.

What is the impact of obliterating architectural remains on the recounting of history? Why are architectural monuments or iconic artifacts anthropomorphized, and thus their destruction seen as "slaughter"? What is the afterlife of an architectural monument following its "slaughter"? Can ancient monuments and relics "act" autonomously and/ or in absentia? If they do, should they be deemed "actants" or non-human sources of action (in the Latourian sense of the term)? As such, in what ways are they part of our lives and social networks, and how should we make sense of them in both material and semiotic ways? And, considering the worldwide reaction to the destruction of Middle Eastern monuments, how and why does the mainstream media foreground and sensationalize it? What are the consequences of dispersing images and videos of the destruction to millions of people around the world on media outlets and social media networks? Finally, why is the general public so obsessed with images of ruins?

These issues can be addressed through various lenses. For example, we can attribute the acts of destruction to ideological stands or contemplate the act of deliberate erasure in a more philosophical sense. Alternatively, we may emphasize the weight of history on destruction from deliberate colonial acts of vengeance to religiously motivated iconoclasm.

The Motives behind the Destruction of Cultural Heritage in the Middle East
Destruction of architecture and art objects is an ancient practice. From Troy and Tenochtitlan to Dresden and Munich and on to Bamiyan and Palmyra today, the obliteration of historic cities and heritage sites has taken place throughout history and across cultures. In the West, such events as the Protestant Reformation led to the destruction of many churches and religious furnishings. Later, massive aerial bombing was the major cause of cultural heritage destruction. During WWII, aerial attacks destroyed a substantial portion of Europe's historically significant buildings and museums. In Germany alone, not only major architectural monuments, but also entire cities, most famously Dresden after its firebombing in February of 1945, were obliterated.[1] A comparison of Nazi pre-WWII aerial photographs of Germany's old inner cities with photographs from the 1960s and 1970s reveals the fate of these cities: from splendid baroque and gothic urban fabric to ruins and ultimately to the postwar utilitarian architecture.[2]

The Nazis targeted Warsaw's buildings and monuments for the sake of removing the cultural and historical identity of the Polish people.[3] However, only a handful of the twentieth century military conflicts sought the destruction of significant buildings for the sake of destroying them alone.[4] In most cases, the main objective was to kill those who occupied the particular target site or building or to eliminate the function to which the building was put to use, such as manufacturing or storage of strategic material. Sometimes, the destruction of certain monuments, such as national memorials and government headquarters, was meant to weaken the morale of the "enemy," but that was the exception rather than the general aim of bombing. In contrast, the militant group known as the Islamic State in Iraq and Syria (ISIS) today aims to erase certain buildings and artifacts based on their specific meaning according to the militants' own obscurantist interpretation. In other words, for ISIS, the ravaging of irreplaceable antiquities in Syria and Iraq is dictated by an understanding of their deviant referential significance much like the relentless slaughter of "undesirable" people (such as those deemed unbelievers, members of ethnic minorities, and homosexuals) is doctrinally justified.

This determined and extremely myopic orthodoxy has attracted the attention of the world. It also has earned the modern Middle East a hot spot in the mainstream media as the place where a twisted ideology is supposedly driving the dreadful and deliberate demolition of historic monuments. Additionally, many commentators use these destructions as another example of the incongruity between "our" values and "theirs," and they conclude that the war in the Middle East is a war between the international community trying to defend universal values and a threatening "Islamic world" intent on destroying them.[5]

In Defense of Artifacts

In contrast to the recent accounts of destruction, the history of the Middle East is actually replete with instances of co-existence between ethnic and religious communities as well as examples of continued endorsement and support for ancient monuments from Antiquity to the Islamic periods. Indeed, the history of the evolution of material things in the Middle East confirms philosopher Bruno Latour's claim that, "[h]umans are not the ones who arbitrarily add the 'symbolic dimension' to pure material forces. These forces are as transcendent, active, agitated, spiritual, as we are."[6] For example, despite assaults during the invasion of the Sasanian Empire by the Arab army, the Arch of Ctesiphon (the capital city of the Parthian and Sasanian Empires, 247 BCE–224 CE and 224–651 CE, respectively) survived, as an "actant" or non-human source of action, to borrow again from Latour, became an epitome of monumentality in architecture and literature, and inspired the building of the grand *iwans* in many palaces and congregational mosques across the Islamic world. Likewise, the cross-axial orthogonal layout of the Roman city gave shape to many early Islamic towns.[7]

Such gradual and subtle forms of appropriation, improvisation, and acceptance have been continually coupled with heroic acts of saving and conserving down to the present day. During the Iranian revolution of 1979, when the aforementioned Ayatollah Khalkhali called for bringing down the Tomb of Cyrus and the remains of the 2,000-year-old Persepolis, he and his "band of thugs" were reportedly driven off by stone-throwing residents from nearby villages.[8] As early as 2012, with help from the Smithsonian Institute, Syrian specialists were able to create a wall around one of the most important ancient mosaic museums in Syria. Maamoun Abdulkarim, the Director General of Antiquities and Museums in Syria, reported that a significant portion of museum objects were concealed, thanks to the efforts of a team of Syria specialists, some of whom lost their lives to either the Assad regime or to ISIS.[9] Notable is Qassem Yehya, a young scholar who was killed by a stray mortar as he was busy at work at the Damascus citadel.[10] A week after Yehya's death, Khaled al-Asaad, a prominent antiquities scholar of the ancient city of Palmyra, was executed by Islamic State militants, who then went on to display his beheaded body on a pole in a main square of Palmyra.[11] Al-Asaad had reportedly refused to direct ISIS to the location where valuable artifacts from the historic site were hidden away. Such heroic acts confirm that the desire to terminate the life of the ancient monument always competes with the desire to keep it alive, albeit under the harshest of circumstances. Even when the monuments are gone and the artifacts looted, the images, memories, and heroic stories associated with them carry on.

The destructions that occurred during WWII, or in the 1990s wars in the Balkans, forced many specialists, politicians, and even ordinary people to become more conscious of the value of Europe's multi-layered histories. It is hoped that the same lessons will be learned from the recent and current destructions of cultural heritage in the Middle East. While rules and regulations regarding the protection of important heritage sites ought to be more rigorously defined and defended, we must also not lose sight of the destruction of cultural heritage in more remote, or lesser-known areas. Equally essential are ordinary built environments that are meaningful to people on the ground rather than to the international community and world heritage organizations. The more modern and insignificant the damaged buildings—or, what historian Nick Yablon calls "untimely ruins"—the better reminders of the sufferings of their occupants.[12] Thus we must ensure that several damaged buildings are kept as such to denote the pain of their human occupants for generations to come. These "untimely ruins" will stand as chief reminders, because as environmental historian Rebecca Solnit asserts, "[m]emory is always incomplete, always imperfect, always falling into ruin; but the ruins themselves … are … our links to what came before, our guide to situating ourselves in a land-scape of time."[13] And hopefully these ruins will not be perceived as mere sites of grief, but of far-reaching promises, hence forging a new revolutionary future, to borrow from Walter Benjamin's "Theses on the Philosophy of History."[14] Finally, it is hoped that more novel avenues of inquiry are opened for historians to study the destructions in systematic and theoretical-ly stimulating ways. Indeed, this collection aspires to bolster the emerging body of literature that is enrich-ing our understanding of the many motives behind the destruction of Middle Eastern architecture and its cultural heritage and ways to counter them.

Excerpts from "The Demise and Afterlife of Artifacts," edited by Pamela Karimi and Nasser Rabbat, *The Aggregate* website (Transparent Peer Reviewed), Volume 3, December 12, 2016. Accessed August 5, 2018, http://we-aggregate.org/piece/the-demise-and-afterlife-of-artifacts.

1   For more on the destructions in Germany during WWII, see W. G. Se-bald, *On the Natural History of Destruction,* trans. Anthea Bell (New York: Modern Library Publishers, 2004).
2   For images and more information regarding 3000 aerial photographs whose negatives were recently discovered in a box inside an attic in the northern German city of Kiel, see Kate Connolly, "A Lost Heritage: Nazi Pictures Reveal Full Devastation Wreaked by Allied Bombers," *The Guardian,* July 9, 2008, accessed May 19, 2016, http://www.theguard-ian.com/world/2008/jul/10/secondworldwar.germany.
3   Known as the planned destruction of Warsaw, these aerial attacks by the Nazis happened shortly after the 1944 Warsaw Uprising. Norman Da-vies, et al., "Warsaw: National Capital, Poland," *Encyclopedia Britannica,* accessed May 10, 2015, http://www.britannica.com/place/Warsaw.
4   It is worth mentioning that it is not always violence that leads to destruction. (Architectural) design itself might prompt violence. For an array of "violent" designs and provocative texts about them, see, Paola Antonelli and Jamer Hunt, *Design and Violence* (New York: The Museum of Modern Art, 2015).
5   Sarah Aziza, "Critics of ISIS are Perpetuating its Ideals," *Middle East Eye,* January 14, 2016, accessed January 15, 2016, http://www.middleeasteye.net/columns/critics-isis-areperpetuating-its-ide-als-1902302542. Aziza highlights a series of problematic examples, including Richard Lourie's "ISIL has Launched a World War: The Radical Group is Drawing the World's Major Powers into an Openended Struggle," *Al-Jazeera America,* December 31, 2015, accessed January 15, 2016, http://america.aljazeera.com/opinions/2015/12/isil-has-launched-a-world-war.html.
6   Bruno Latour, *We Have Never Been Modern* (Cambridge, MA: Harvard University Press, 1993), 128.
7   See, for example, Oleg Grabar, "Iwan," *Encyclopedia of Islam* IV (1973), 287–288; Nasser Rabbat, "The Iwans of the Madrasa of Sultan Hasan," in *Mamluk History Through Architecture: Building, Culture, and Politics in Mamluk Egypt and Syria* (London: I. B. Tauris, 2010), 104–111; Hugh Kennedy, "From Polis to Madina: Urban Change in Late Antique and Early Islamic Syria," *Past & Present: A Journal of Historical Studies* 106 (1985): 3–27.
8   Elaine Sciolino, *Persian Mirrors: The Elusive Face of Iran* (New York: Touchstone, 2000), 168.
9   Tim McGirk, "Syrians Race to Save Ancient City's Treasures from ISIS," *National Geographic,* July 15, 2015, accessed May 18, 2016, https://news.nationalgeographic.com/2015/07/150710-palmyra-syria-isis-loot-ing-museum-archaeology/.
10   Pádraig Belton, "A Tribute to Khaled al-Asaad, the Archaeologist Killed by ISIS in Palmyra," *Apollo: The International Art Magazine,* August 20, 2015, accessed August 2, 2016, https://www.apollo-magazine.com/a-tribute-to-khaled-al-asaad-the-archaeologist-killed-by-isis-in-palmy-ra/.
11   See further, Nasser Rabbat, "They Shoot Historians, Don't They?" *Art-forum,* November 2015, accessed August 1, 2016, http://artforum.com/inprint/issue=201509&id=55521.
12   Nick Yablon, *Untimely Ruins: An Archeology of American Urban Moderni-ty, 1819–1919* (Chicago: The University of Chicago Press, 2009).
13   Rebecca Solnit, *Storming the Gates of Paradise: Landscapes for Politics* (Berkeley and Los Angeles: University of California Press, 2007), 354. Reprinted partially as "The Ruins of Memory," in *Ruins: Documents of Contemporary Art,* ed. Brian Dillon (Cambridge, MA: MIT Press, 2011), 150–152.
14   Walter Benjamin, "Theses on the Philosophy of History," in *Walter Benjamin: Illuminations,* ed. Hannah Arendt, trans. Harry Zohn (London: Fontana, 1992), 245–255. Cited in Brian Dillon, "Introduction: A Short History of Decay," in *Ruins,* 18.

Images
P 313 Top: The ruins of a Jewish house in Yazd, Iran. Photograph by Pamela Karimi, 2007.
P 313 Bottom: The reconstruction of the entrance to the temple of Bel nears completion in Trafalgar Square. Photograph, showing only a portion of the arch under construction, by Pamela Karimi, 2016.

Memorials evoke the past through representational strategies that use figures, names, places, and dates. To commemorate slavery challenges these strategies because the violence used to dehumanize the enslaved all but erased their presence—images, names, places, and dates—from the historical record. This absence transformed how we as architects designed the Memorial for Enslaved Laborers at the University of Virginia. In lieu of historical evidence for the estimated 4,000 to 5,000 enslaved at UVA, our inventive approach seeks to humanize and vivify the lives of the enslaved community who built, maintained, and lived at the University.

Mabel Wilson

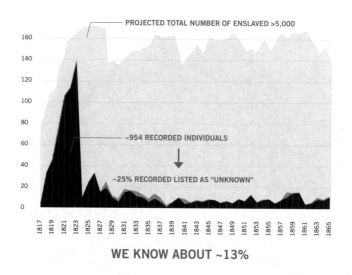

PROJECTED TOTAL NUMBER OF ENSLAVED >5,000

~954 RECORDED INDIVIDUALS

↓

~25% RECORDED LISTED AS "UNKNOWN"

WE KNOW ABOUT ~13%

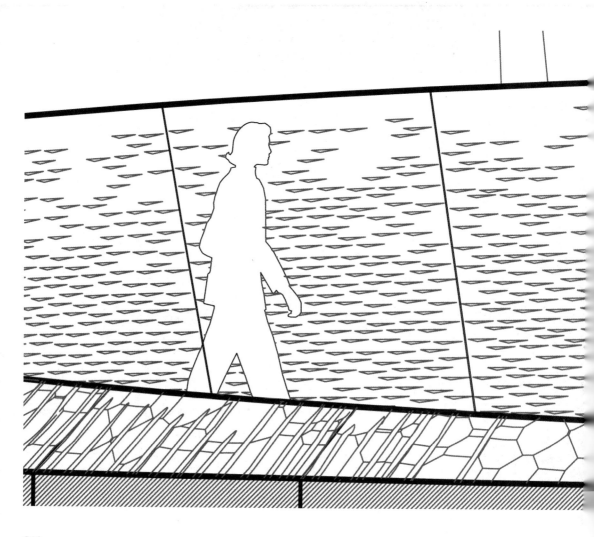

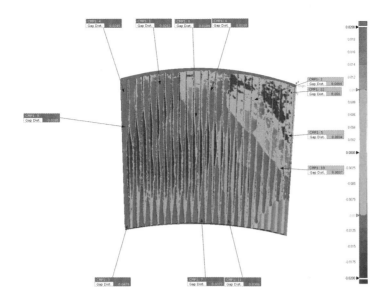

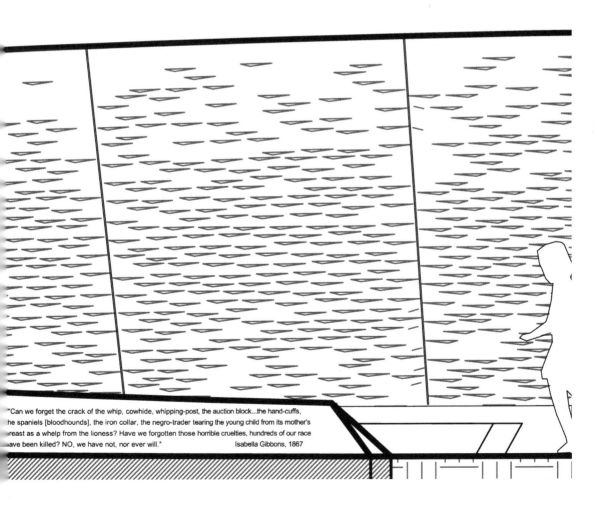

"Can we forget the crack of the whip, cowhide, whipping-post, the auction block...the hand-cuffs, the spaniels [bloodhounds], the iron collar, the negro-trader tearing the young child from its mother's breast as a whelp from the lioness? Have we forgotten those horrible cruelties, hundreds of our race have been killed? NO, we have not, nor ever will."   Isabella Gibbons, 1867

Excerpt of Names Recorded

Full Names:
Sally Cottrell Cole
Mary Fletcher
Patsy Fossett
Isabella Gibbons
William Gibbons
Jane Payne

Partial Names:
Aaron, male (no last name known)
Albert, male (no last name known)
Alfred, male (no last name known)
Anatomical Lewis, male (no last name known)
Arthur, male (no last name known)
Barnet, male (no last name known)
Barrett, male (no last name known)
Ben, male (no last name known)
Ben, male (no last name known)
Ben, male (no last name known)
Bob, male (no last name known)
Charles, male (no last name known)
Commodore Lewis Davey, male (no last name known)
David, male (no last name known)
Dick, male (no last name known)
Dick, male (no last name known)

Fielding, male (no last name known)
Fleming, male (no last name known)
Frank, male (no last name known)
George, male (no last name known)
German, male (no last name known)
Gleaves, male (no last name known)
Grandma Kidda, female (no last name known)
Guy, male (no last name known)
Harry, male (no last name known)
Harry of A.S.B., male (no last name known)
Henry, male (no last name known)
Humphrey, male (no last name known)
Isacah, male (no last name known)
Isham, male (no last name known)
Jack of A.S.B., male (no last name known)
Jackson, male (no last name known)—a young boy
     rented on a per-day basis
Jacob, male (no last name known)
Jacob, male (no last name known)
James, male (no last name known)
Jef, male (no last name known)
Jim, male (no last name known)

DESIGN ACROSS SCALES
Neri Oxman, J. Meejin Yoon

Inspired by Charles and Ray Eames' canonical *Powers of Ten*, the course explores the relationship between science and engineering through the lens of design. It examines how transformations in science and technology have influenced design thinking, and vice versa. It offers interdisciplinary tools and methods to represent, model, design, and fabricate objects, machines, and systems. Structured as core lectures and lab sessions, the course is organized thematically with topics such as information design, user interaction, digital fabrication, and design ethics.

The course creates a new pedagogical paradigm for learning and education, which cuts across various disciplines and scales to demonstrate that design is not a discipline, but a way of looking at the world; one that promotes the synthesis of interdisciplinary knowledge across scales in order to create objects and systems for the greater good. This is partly due to the fact that big, real-world challenges —such as the race to cure cancer, the Mars landing mission and the challenge to design sustainable cities and buildings—require, perhaps more than ever, an interdisciplinary skillset combined with an ability to operate across multiple scales with creativity.

The history of design innovation provides endless examples of cross-disciplinary innovations and individuals. Buckminster Fuller, for instance, was a designer, a futurist, an inventor, an author, and a systems theorist. His designs based on the geodesic dome have inspired not only generations of designers, architects, engineers, and urban planners but also chemists, material scientists, and physicists, who were inspired by his representation of the physical world. Charles and Ray Eames were mid-century designers working at a range of scales and in a variety of media, from furniture and military aircraft parts to films and exhibitions. Their experiments in design fabrication and cultural media provide significant references for design education. An example of the value of learning across disciplines today is found in Siddhartha Mukherjee's book, *Emperor of All Maladies: A Biography of Cancer,* which tells the story of how the process of inventing cell dyes to trace the growth of cancerous tissues was actually inspired by textile design.

Design has expanded to include a broad range of scales and disciplines, shifting from the production of objects to the design of experiences, data, networks, territories, and social frameworks. Designers are no longer exclusively committed to design autonomous objects (buildings, cars, furniture, and household products), but rather are conceiving and testing whole ecologies of design experiences (robotic construction systems, transportation systems, health care experiences, water distribution, and clean energy). This has prompted Tim Brown, CEO of the design consultancy firm IDEO to state, "Design is too important to be left to designers." The scope of design ecologies is so broad and so integrated with other disciplines that all disciplines benefit from design inquiry and methods to tackle the new breadth of design problems at hand. Interdisciplinary teams must work together to design the systems, experiences, environments, and futures for our increasingly complex world. Design Across Scales responds to this challenge: it is not a traditional design course for designers, but a design course about culture, science, and technology serving as a foundation for all students regardless of major.

Design Across Scales: Introduction
- Philip Morrison and Phyllis Morrison, *Powers of Ten: A Book About the Relative Size of Things in the Universe and the Effect of Adding Another Zero* (Redding, Conn: Scientific American Library, 1982).
- Tim Brown, "Getting Under Your Skin," in *Change by Design* (New York: HarperCollins, 2009), 13–28.

Design and Research
- Paola Antonelli, et al., *Design and the Elastic Mind* (New York and London: Thames & Hudson, 2008).
- Neri Oxman, "Age of Entanglement," *Journal of Design and Science* (January 2016), https://jods.mitpress.mit.edu/pub/ageofentanglement.

Design and Practice
- John and Marilyn Neuhart, *Eames Design* (New York: H.N. Abrams, 1989).
- Bruce Mau and Jennifer Leonard, *Massive Change* (London: Phaidon, 2004).
- William McDonough and Michael Braungart, *Cradle to Cradle: Remaking the Way We Make Things* (New York: North Point Press, 2002).

Design Through Agency
Guest: Prof. Allan Chochinov, SVA MFA in Products of Design Program Chair and Co-Founder, Core 77
- Choose from some of the following: https://medium.com/@chochinov/top-reads-of-2017-8a7691f73586.

Design of Interfaces
Guest: John Snavely, Principal Design Manager, XBox
- Edith Ackermann, "Experiences of Artifacts," in *Key Works on Radical Constructivism* (Sense Publishers, 2007).
- Ted Chiang, *The Lifecycle of Software Objects*, (Subterranean, 2010).
- George Lakoff and Mark Johnson, "Orienting Metaphors," in *Metaphors We Live By* (Chicago: University of Chicago Press, 1980).
- Bill Moggridge, *Designing Interactions* (MIT Press, 2007).
- Donald Norman, "Natural User Interfaces are Not Natural," *ACM Computer Human Interaction* 17, no. 3 (2010).

Design of Representation
- Julie Steele and Noah P.N. Iliinsky, *Beautiful Visualization: Looking at Data Through the Eyes of Experts* (Sebastopol, CA: O'Reilly, 2010), Chapters 2 and 12.
- Edward Tufte, *Envisioning Information* (Cheshire, Conn: Graphic Press, 1990).
- Marshall McLuhan, "The Medium is the Message," in *Understanding Media: The Extensions of Man* (New York: Signet, 1964).

Design of Discovery
Guest: James Weaver, Senior Research Scientist, Hansjorg Wyss Institute for Biologically Inspired Engineering, Harvard University
- James Weaver et al., "Hierarchical Assembly of the Siliceous Skeletal Lattice of the Hexactinellid Sponge Euplectella aspergillum." *Journal of Structural Biology* 158 (2007): 93–106.
- Ali Miserez et al., "Effects of Laminate Architecture on Fracture Resistance of Sponge Biosilica: Lessons from Nature," *Advanced Functional Materials* 18 (2008): 1–8.
- Li Wen et al., "Biomimetic Shark Skin: Design, Fabrication and Hydrodynamic Function," *The Journal of Experimental Biology* (2014), 217.
- Nicholas W. Bartlett et al., "A 3D-printed, Functionally Graded Soft Robot Powered by Combustion," *Science* 349, no. 6244 (July 2015).

Design of Life
Guest: David Sun Kong, Technical Staff, MIT Lincoln Laboratory
- Gaymon Bennett, "Nature Natured and Nature Denatured," in *Synthetic Future: Can We Create What We Want Out of Synthetic Biology?*, Hastings Center Report 44, no. 6 (2014): S38–S39.
- Drew Endy, "Foundations for Engineering Biology," *Nature* 438, no. 7067 (November 2005), 449–453.
- Alexandra Daisy Ginsberg, et al., *Synthetic Aesthetics* (Cambridge, MA: MIT Press, 2014).

Design of Systems
Guest: Carlo Ratti, Professor of Urban Technologies and Planning; Director, SENSEable City Lab, MIT
- Carlo Ratti and Matthew Claudel, *Open Source Architecture* (London: Thames & Hudson, 2015).
- Dietmar Offenhuber and Carlo Ratti, *Decoding the City: Urbanism in the Age of Big Data* (Basel: Birkhauser Verlag, 2014).
- Carlo Ratti and Matthew Claudel, *The City of Tomorrow: Sensors, Networks, Hackers, and the Future of Urban Life* (New Haven: Yale University Press, 2016).

Design of Experience
Guest: Lee Moreau; Principal, Continuum
- Susan Weinschenk, *100 Things Every Designer Needs to Know About People* (Berkeley: New Readers, 2011).
- Hugh Dubberly, "How Do You Design?" *Dubberly Design Office*, 2005, http://www.dubberly.com/articles/how-do-you-design.html.
- Jakob Schneider and Marc Stickdorn, *This is Service Design*, thisisservicedesignthinking.com.
- Michael Rock, "F*#k Content," *2x4.org*, 2009, http://www.2x4.org/ideas/2/fuck-content/.

Design for Humanity
Guest: Nicholas Negroponte; Co-Founder, MIT Media Lab
- Nicholas Negroponte, Forum Response, "Can Technology End Poverty?" *Boston Review* 35, no. 6 (2010).
- Aaron Watson, "Future Perfect," *Acuity*, 2016.
- *Design for the Other 90%* (New York: Cooper-Hewitt, National Design Museum, Smithsonian Organization, 2007).

DESIGN: THE HISTORY OF MAKING THINGS
Timothy Hyde, Kristel Smentek

The term design has many meanings, but at its core it refers to the human capacity to shape the environment we inhabit. Design is as old as humanity itself and studying its history provides a way to think critically about the past through the lens of design.

To think critically about design is to understand not only its history of successes, but also its missteps and its unintended consequences. This course examines all three aspects, following themes in the history of design with an emphasis on design for organized manufacture from the eighteenth century to the present. Though its focus is on Euro-American theory and practice, we seek to situate both in their global contexts, contexts that range from early modern transcontinental trade to imperialism to contemporary globalization.

Questions the course will pose include: How have the processes and products of design been shaped by new technological possibilities, whether the discovery of silk, the invention of the automatic loom, or the development of the computer? How have constraints, whether material, legislative, or aesthetic, impacted design? What role has design played in globalizing capitalist consumer desire, and how, in turn, has it been mobilized in the service of alternative economic and political systems? What are the ethics of design in an age of inequality and environmental crisis? Finally, how have the meanings we assign to design been mediated by magazines, exhibitions, corporate communication, glossy design monographs, and advertising?

Introduction
What do we mean when we talk about design?
- John Heskett, "What is Design?" and "The Historical Evolution of Design," in *Design: A Very Short Introduction* (Oxford: Oxford University Press, 2005), 1–23.

Taking the Longer View, 1: Sit! The Body Accommodated
- Margaret Campbell, "From Cure Chair to Chaise Longue," *Journal of Design History* 12, no. 4 (1999): 327–343.
- Cliff Kuang, "The Secret History of the Aeron Chair," *Slate*, November 5, 2012, https://slate.com/human-interest/2012/11/aeron-chair-history-herman-millers-office-staple-was-originally-designed-for-the-elderly.html.

Communication and Design
Taking the Longer View, 2: Communication Design: From Moveable Type to Pentagram
- Jorge Frascara, "Graphic Design: Fine Art or Social Science?" *Design Issues* 5, no. 1 (Autumn 1988): 18–29.
- Michael Bierut, "How to Think Like a Designer," filmed February 2015 at DesignIndaba, Cape Town, South Africa, video, 39:15, https://www.youtube.com/watch?v=RanfCx18gi4.

Design Before Designers
Design in the Age of Discovery
- Bernard Siegert, "Waterlines: Striated and Smooth Spaces as Techniques of Ship Design," in *Cultural Techniques: Grids, Filters, Doors, and Other Articulations of the Real* (New York: Fordham University Press, 2014): 147–163.

Design Before Designers, continued
Learning from China: Mass Production before Industrialization
- Lothar Ledderose, "Factory Art," in *Ten Thousand Things: Module and Mass Production in Chinese Art* (Princeton: Princeton University Press, 2000).

Motifs and Materials: Transpacific and Transatlantic Migrations
- Madeleine Dobie, "Oriental Veneers," in *Trading Paces: Colonization and Slavery in Eighteenth-Century French Culture* (Ithaca: Cornell University Press, 2010).

Factory Production and Industrialization: Design for Manufacture
The Loom and the Pot: Design and the Factory
- Adrian Forty, "Images of Progress," in *Objects of Desire: Design and Society since 1750*, rev. ed. (London: Thames and London, 1992).

Nations by Design: Worlds of Consumption
- Owen Jones, *Grammar of Ornament, 1856* (London, 1986). Read introduction; propositions; chapters on Arabian, Turkish, Moorish, Persian, Indian, Hindu ornament; and Leaves and Flowers from Nature.

Fashion and Color

Taking the Longer View, 3: Fashion as Design Technology

- Nicholas de Monchaux, *Spacesuit: Fashioning Apollo* (Cambridge, MA: MIT Press, 2011).

Taking the Longer View, 4: Chroma: Color and/in Design

- Michel Pastoreau, "The Favorite Color," and "Blue Today," in *Blue: The History of a Color* (Princeton and Oxford: Princeton University Press, 2001).
- Pantone Color of the Year, 2018: https://www. pantone.com/color-of-the-year-2018.

Design and Modernity

Design Against Industry

- Charles Harvey and Jon Press, "John Ruskin and the Ethical Foundations of Morris & Company, 1861–96," *Journal of Business Ethics* 14, no. 3 (March 1995): 181–194.

MIT's Office of Design Services

- Guest lecture by Gary van Zante, Curator of Architecture, Design and Photography, MIT Museum, and Julia Meer, Humboldt University, Berlin, and Volkswagen Foundation Fellow, MIT
- "Jacqueline S. Casey (1927–1992)," in Steven Heller and Greg D'Onofrio, *The Moderns* (New York: Abrams, 2017), 140–143.
- Silas H. Rhodes, "Campus Advertising in the USA," *Graphis* 22, no. 124 (1966): 148–167.

Total Design

The Bauhaus

- Anni Albers, *Selected Writings on Design* (Hanover: Wesleyan University Press, 2000).

The Socialist Object: Design Behind the Iron Curtain

- Christina Kaier, *Imagine No Possessions: The Socialist Objects of Russian Constructivism* (Cambridge, MA: MIT Press, 2005).

Design and Postwar Internationalism

Materials of Modernism: Wood, Plastic, and Beyond

- Eeva-Liisa Pelkonen, "Organic Lines," in *Alvar Aalto: Architecture, Modernity, and Geopolitics* (New Haven: Yale University Press, 2009), 142–157.

Cities and Corporations

Design for Cities: Street Furniture in the Modern City

- Eleanor Herring, *Street Furniture Design: Contesting Modernism in Post-War Britain* (London, 2016).

The Eames and the Corporatization of Design

- Reyner Banham, "The Great Gizmo," *Industrial Design* (September 1965): 48–59.

Critical Design

Radical Design in the 1960s

- *Italy: The New Domestic Landscape. Achievements and Problems of Italian Design*, ed. Emilio Ambasz, (New York: NY Graphic Society, 1972).

Design, Disability, and Social Imagination

- Guest lecture by artist and designer Sara Hendren

After the Industrial Economy

Design and the Global Economy

- Hazel Clark, "Back to the Future, or Forward? Hong Kong Design, Image, and Branding," *Design Issues* 25, no. 3 (Summer 2009): 11–29.

Designing Experience

- Joseph Pine, *The Experience Economy* (Cambridge, MA: Harvard Business Review Press, 2011).

Futures and Conclusions

Designing Futures: Responsible Design in an Age of Affluenza

- *Design as Future-Making*, ed. Susan Yelavich and Barbara Adams (London and New York: Bloomsbury Academic, 2014).
- *Disobedient Objects: How-To Guides* (Victoria & Albert Museum, 2014), http://www.vam.ac.uk/ content/exhibitions/disobedient-objects/ how-to-guides/.

Return to the Question: What is Design?

CURATING ARCHITECTURE: ON EXHIBITING, RESEARCH, AND CRITICISM OF ARCHITECTURE
Ana Miljački

Architectural exhibitions have been important sites of testing, dissemination, and consensus building in the field. Just as much as the narrative of architectural modernism is hard to imagine without MoMA's 1932 International Style exhibition, the early definitions of architectural postmodernism were deeply indebted to the first Venice Biennale of Architecture in 1980, titled *The Presence of the Past*. Equally importantly, the cultural exchange and competition during the Cold War played out in part on the grounds of international expositions and trade fairs, the early 1990s digital turn is unimaginable without its mesmerizing 1:1 installations, and architectural green-washing got its most in-depth critical review in *Behind the Green Door* at the 2014 Oslo Architecture Triennale. With the exception of a few narrowly focused studies (of the Eames' exhibition work, the activities of the United Stated Information Agency, or of MoMA's architecture program) and several recent critical re-enactments (such as the remaking of *Italy, the New Domestic Landscape*), architectural exhibition and curation have yet to receive the kind of historiographic treatment on par with anything in the art world.

The contemporary view of architectural exhibitions' potential for disciplinary contribution varies among curators, who see them as platforms for atmospherics (Urbach), for contextualization (Zardini), for activism (Bergdoll), and for storytelling (Cohen). Although this seminar is designed to pay close attention to the ways in which such curatorial conceptions are reflected in specific curatorial works, its key assumption is that architectural exhibitions are a form of publishing of both architectural research and criticism, and thus a specific mode of producing reflections on the discipline, which provide an equally specific set of symptoms, lineages, and historical traces that will allow us to reconstruct both the explicit and the unconscious political and cultural haunts of the field. Through a series of case studies that start with the inaugural exhibitions of architectural modernism and end with the most recent Venice Architecture Biennale, this seminar will examine the historical, political, and institutional conditions in which specific exhibitions were conceived and mounted, their contribution to seminal disciplinary conversations, and their critical reception. Curating Architecture will be run as a discussion class; its conclusions are open-ended. The course aims to both construct a sophisticated view of architectural curatorship and to use the history of architectural exhibitions as a datum for studying the changing disciplinary definitions and roles of research, criticism, and curating.

On Curating …

As an Object of Study
- Helene Lipstadt, "Architectural Publications, Competitions, and Exhibitions," in *Architecture and its Image: Four Centuries of Representation* ed. Eve Blau and Edward Kaufman (Montreal: Canadian Center for Architecture, 1989), 109–137.
- Jean-Louis Cohen, "Exhibitionist Revisionism: Exposing Architectural History," *Journal of the Society of Architectural Historians* 58, no. 3 (September 1999): 316–325.
- Hubert Damisch, "A Very Special Museum," in *Skyline: The Narcissistic City* (Stanford: Stanford University Press, 2001), 49–67.
- Yve-Alain Bois, Denis Hollier, Rosalind Krauss and Jean-Louis Cohen, "A Conversation with Jean-Louis Cohen," *October* 89 (Summer, 1999): 3–18.
- Sylvia Lavin, "Showing Work," *Log* 20, *Curating Architecture* (Fall 2010): 5–10.
- Mirko Zardini, "Exhibiting and Collecting Ideas: A Montreal Perspective," *Log* 20, *Curating Architecture* (Fall 2010): 77–84.
- Henry Urbach, "Exhibition as Atmosphere," *Log* 20, *Curating Architecture* (Fall 2010): 11–17.
- Jean-Louis Cohen, "Mirror of Dreams," *Log* 20, *Curating Architecture* (Fall 2010): 49–53.
- Hélène Jannière "Architecture Criticism: Identifying an Object of Study" *OASE* 81 *Constructing Criticism* (June 2010): 33–58.

As Representing (Utopia)—Constructions of Architectural Modernism: "Utopia" on the Wall and 1:1
Cases: *Proun Room* (1923); The Bauhaus Exhibit and L'Esprit Nouveau Pavilion (1925); Weissenhof Siedlung (1927)
- Eva Forgacs, "Definitive Space: The Many Utopias of El Lissitzky's Proun Room," in *Situating El Lissitzky: Vitebsk, Berlin, Moscow* (Los Angeles: Getty Research Institute, 2003), 47–75.
- John G. Hatch, "Some Adaptations of Relativity in the 1920s and the Birth of Abstract Architecture," *Architecture, Mathematics and Perspective* (Basel: Birkhäuser, 2010), 131–147.
- Richard Pommer and Christian Otto,

"Proclaiming Weissenhof: Werkbund Management of the Press," in *Weissenhof 1927 and the Modern Movement in Architecture* (Chicago: University of Chicago Press, 1991), 131–144.

- Richard Difford, "Infinite Horizons: Le Corbusier, the Pavillon de l'Esprit Nouveau Dioramas and the Science of Visual Distance," *The Journal of Architecture* 14 no. 3 (2009): 295–323.
- Beatriz Colomina, "The Media House," *Assemblage* 27, *Tulane Papers: The Politics of Contemporary Architectural Discourse* (August 1995): 55–66.
- "Mies Van Der Rohe 'Barcelona Pavilion' to be Reconstructed," *MoMA* n. 27 (1983): 2.
- Matei Calinescu, "The Idea of the Avant-Garde," in *Five Faces of Modernity: Modernism, Avant-Garde, Decadence, Kitsch, Postmodernism* (Durham: Duke University Press, 1987), 112–125, 132.

As Codifying (Style)—MoMA's Role in Disseminating Narratives of Architectural Modernism
Cases: *Modern Architecture: International Exhibition* (1932) and *The Bauhaus, 1919-1928* (1938), at MoMA
Guest: Rebecca Uchill

- Henry Russell Hitchcock and Philip Johnson, *The International Style* (New York: W.W. Norton & Company, 1997 [1932]).
- MoMA, Press Release, "Modern Architecture: International Exhibition," February 7, 1932, https://www.moma.org/documents/moma_press-release_324957.pdf.
- MoMA, Press Release, "The Bauhaus, 1919–1928," December 2, 1938, https://www.moma.org/documents/moma_press-release_325130.pdf.
- Henry Matthews, "The Promotion of Modern Architecture by the Museum of Modern Art in the 1930s," *Journal of Design History* 7, no. 1 (1994): 43–59.
- Henry-Russell Hitchock, Jr., "Architectural Criticism," *Shelter* 2, no. 3 (April 1932): 2.
- Knud Lönberg-Holm, "Two Shows: A Comment on the Aesthetic Racket," *Shelter* 2, no. 3 (April 1932): 16–17.
- Lewis Mumford, Henry Wright, Raymond M. Hood, George Howe, and Harvey Wiley Corbett, "Symposium: The International Architectural Exhibition," *Shelter* 2, no. 3 (April 1932): 3–9.
- Frank Lloyd Wright, "Of Thee I Sing," *Shelter* 2, no. 3 (April 1932): 10–12.
- Herbert Bayer, "Fundamentals of Exhibition Design," *PM* 6, no. 2 (December 1939–January 1940): 17–25.
- William H. Jordy, "The International Style in the 1930s," *JSAH* 24, no. 1 (1965): 10–14.
- Manfredo Tafuri, "The Crisis of Utopia," in *Architecture and Utopia* (Cambridge, MA: MIT Press, 1976), 125–149.

As Collecting (Cultural Artifacts)—The Independent Group: Situating Architecture in the Expanded Field of Cultural Production
Cases: *Parallel of Life and Art* (1953), *This is Tomorrow* (1956), and *The House of Tomorrow* (1956)

- Alaistair Grieve, "Towards an Art of the Environment," *The Burlington Magazine*, 132 (1990): 773–781.
- Alastair Grieve, "'This is Tomorrow', a Remarkable Exhibition Born from Contention," *The Burlington Magazine* 136, no. 1093 (April 1994): 225–232.
- Julian Myers, "The Future as Fetish," *October* 94 (Autumn, 2000): 62–88.
- Lawrence Alloway, "London: Beyond Painting and Sculpture," *Art News* 55, no. 9 (September 1956): 64.
- Reyner Banham, "This is Tomorrow," *Architectural Review* 120 (September 1956): 187.
- Reyner Banham, "Not Quite Architecture, Not Quite Painting Either," *Architects' Journal* 124 (August 16, 1956): 217.
- Alison and Peter Smithson, "The Parallels of Art and Life," and Reyner Banham, "The New Brutalism," *Architectural Review* (December 1955) reprinted in *As Found: The Discovery of the Ordinary*, eds. Claude Lichtenstein and Thomas Schregenberger (Zürich: Lars Müller Publishers 2001): 38-45; 128–135.
- Alison and Peter Smithson, "But Today, We Collect Ads," *Ark* 18 (1956) reproduced in *L'Architecture d'Aujourd'hui* 344 (January, February 2003): 44–45.
- Jean Baudrillard, *The System of Objects* (New York: Verso, 1996): 3–29.

As Persuading—United States Information Agency (USIA), Expos and the Cold War Design of Lifestyle and Media
Cases: Expos in Brussels (1958), Montreal (1967), and Osaka (1970)

- David Riesman, "The Nylon War," in *Abundance for What?* (New York: Doubleday, 1964), 67–80.
- Greg Castillo, "Better Living through Modernism," in *Cold War at the Home Front* (Minneapolis: University of Minnesota Press, 2010), 59–86.
- Office of Public Information, "Facts About the American National Exhibition in Moscow" 1959: 1–8.
- Beatriz Colomina, "Enclosed by Images: The

Eameses' Multimedia Architecture," *Grey Room* 2 (Winter 2001): 5–29.

- Héléne Lipstadt, "Natural Overlap: Charles and Ray Eames and the Federal Government," in *The Work of Charles and Ray Eames: A Legacy of Invention* (New York: Harry N. Abrams, 1997): 160–166.
- Judith Shatnoff, "Expo 67: A Multiple Vision," *Film Quarterly* 21, no. 1 (Autumn, 1967): 2–13.
- Marshall McLuhan, "The Invisible Environment: The Future of an Erosion," *Perspecta* 11 (1967): 161–167.
- Umberto Eco, "A Theory of Expositions," *Dot Zero* no. 4, World's Fairs (Summer 1967): 5–10.
- Anne Collins Goodyear, "Expo '70 as Watershed: The Politics of American Art and Technology," in David Crowley and Jane Pavitt, eds., *Cold War Modern: Design 1945–1979*, (London: V&A Publishing, 2008), 198–203.

As Activism—The Specter of 1968
Cases: Milan Triennale (1968); *Italy: The New Domestic Landscape* (1972)
Guest: Mark Wasiuta

- Paola Nicolin, "Beyond the Failure: Notes on the XIVth Triennale," *Log* (2008): 87–100.
- Anty Pansera, Anna Venturelli, and Antonio C. Mastrobuono, "The Triennale of Milan: Past, Present, and Future," *Design Issues* (1985): 23–32.
- Mirko Zardini, "Milan (Italy) 1968," *Team 10 Meetings*, http://www.team10online.org/team10/meetings/1968-milan.htm.
- Hans Ulrich Obrist, "Triennale di Milano 68: A Case Study and Beyond; Arata Isozaki's Electric Labyrinth: A 'MA' of Images," in *Iconoclash,* eds. Bruno Latour and Peter Weibel (Cambridge, MA: MIT Press, 2002).
- David Hirsch, "Exhibit Design: The Example of the Triennale," *Progressive Architecture* 49 (October 1968): 214–217.
- Adolfo Natalini, "Italy: The New Domestic Landscape," *Architectural Design* 42 (August 1972): 469–473.
- Ada Louise Huxtable, "Italian Design Show Appraised: Ambiguous but Beautiful," *New York Times*, May 26, 1972.
- Robert Jensen, "Italian Design Show at MoMA: A Postmortem," *Artforum* 11 (October 1972): 85.
- Andrea Branzi, "Radical Architecture: Refusing the Disciplinary Role," *Casabella* 386 (1974): 46.
- Emilio Ambasz, "The Designs of Freedom," *Perspecta* 13/14 (1971): 363–365.
- Pier Vittorio Aureli, *The Project of Autonomy* (Princeton: Princeton Architectural Press, 2008), 69–83.

- Felicity Scott, "Italian Design and the New Political Landscape," in *Architecture or Techno-Utopia: Politics after Modernism* (Cambridge, MA: MIT Press, 2007), 117–150.

As Monetizing (Drawings)—And Now We Collect Drawings: The Other Narrative of Autonomy
Cases: *Architecture I* (1977) and *Houses for Sale* (1980) at Leo Castelli, NYC
Guest: Jordan Kauffman

- Paul Goldberger, "Architectural Drawings Raised to an Art," *New York Times*, December 12, 1977, 50.
- Ada Louise Huxtable, "Architectural Drawings as Gallery Art," *New York Times*, October 23, 1977, 27.
- Colin Rowe, "Introduction," in *Five Architects* (Oxford: Oxford University Press, 1975), 3–9.
- Michael Sorkin, "Drawings for Sale," *Village Voice*, (November 12–18, 1980), 85–86.
- Robin Evans, "In Front of Lines That Leave Nothing Behind," *AA Files* 6 (London: Architectural Association, 1983), 88–96.
- Stanford Anderson, "Architectural Design as System of Research Programs," *Design Studies* 5, no. 3 (July 1984), reprinted *Architecture Theory Since 1968,* ed. Michael Hays (Cambridge, MA: MIT Press, 2015).
- Hal Foster, "Pastiche/Prototype/Purity: "Houses for Sale," *Artforum* 19, no. 7 (March 1988): 77–79.
- Fredric Jameson, "Postmodernism and Consumer Society," in *The Cultural Turn: Selected Writings on the Postmodern, 1983-1998* (New York: Verso, 1998), 1–20.

As Criticism—Critique of Corporate Modernism
Cases: *Architectural Works by Skidmore, Owings & Merrill* (1950), *The Architecture of the École des Beaux-Arts* (1975), and *Transformations in Modern Architecture* (1979), all at MoMA
Guest: Michael Kubo

- Henry-Russell Hitchcock, "The Architecture of Bureaucracy and the Architecture of Genius," *Architectural Review* 101, (January 1947): 3–6.
- Sigfried Giedion, "The Experiment of S.O.M.," *Bauen + Wohnen* 12 (April 1957).
- MoMA, Press Release, "Ecole des Beaux-Arts," April 30, 1975, https://www.moma.org/calendar/exhibitions/2483.
- Norman Neuerburg, "The Architecture of the Ecole des Beaux-Arts by Arthur Drexler," *Journal of the Society of Architectural Historians* 38, no.1 (March 1979): 85–86.
- Arthur Drexler, "Introduction," in *Transformations in Modern Architecture* (New York: MoMA, 1979).

- Arthur Drexler, "On Transformations," *Skyline* (Summer 1979).
- Felicity Scott, "When Systems Fail: Arthur Drexler and the Postmodern Turn," *Perspecta* 35: *Building Codes* (2005): 134–153.
- Manfredo Tafuri and Francesco Dal Co, "The International Panorama in the Fifties and Sixties," *Modern Architecture* 2 (New York: Electa/Rizzoli, 1976), 339–363.
- Reinhold Martin, "Introduction" and "Organizational Complex," in *The Organizational Complex* (Cambridge, MA: MIT Press, 2005), 2–41.

As/Of History—Defining the Terms of Architectural Postmodernism

Cases: *The Presence of the Past* (1980) and *Roma Interrotta* (1978) at the Venice Architecture Biennale

- Paolo Porthoghesi, "The End of Prohibitionism," and Charles Jencks, "Toward Radical Eclecticism," in *The Presence of the Past: First International Exhibition of Architecture* (London: Academy Editions, 1980): 9–13.
- Marco De Michelis, "Architecture Meets in Venice," *Log* 20 (Fall 2010): 29–34.
- Robert A.M. Stern, "La Strada Novissima," *Log* 20 (Fall 2010): 35–38
- Charles Jencks, "La Strada Novissima: The 1980 Venice Biennale," *Domus* 610 (October 1980), https://www.domusweb.it/en/from-the-archive/2012/08/25/-em-la-strada-novissima-em--the-1980-venice-biennale.html.
- Lea-Catherine Szacka, "Historicism versus Communication: The Basic Debate of the 1980 Biennale," *Architectural Design*, 213 (September 2011).
- Michael Graves, "Roman Interventions," and Alan Chimacoff, "Roma Interrotta Reviewed," *Architectural Design* 49, no. 3, (1979): 2–5, 7–8.
- Jürgen Habermas, "Modernity—An Incomplete Project," in *Postmodern Culture,* ed. Hal Foster, (London: Pluto Press, 1985), 3–15.
- Manfredo Tafuri, "There is No Criticism, Only History," *Design Book Review*, no. 9 (Spring 1986): 8–11.
- Alan Colquhoun, "Three Kinds of Historicism," *Modernity and the Classical Tradition: Architectural Essays, 1980-87* (Cambridge: MA, MIT Press, 1991), 3–31.

As Research—The Rise of the Research Exhibit: The Questions of "Evidence" and "Matters of Concern"

Cases: *Iconoclash* (2002) and *Making Things Public* (2004) at ZKM

- Paul Basu and Sharon Macdonald, "Introduction: Experiments in Exhibition, Ethnography, Art and Science" and Peter Weibel and Bruno Latour, "Experimenting with Representation: Iconoclash and Making Things Public," in *Exhibition Experiments*, ed. Sharon Macdonald and Paul Basu (Oxford: Blackwell, 2007), 94–108.
- Yve-Alain Bois, "Iconoclash: Yve-Alain Bois Responds," *Artforum International* 44, no. 9 (2006): 24.
- Bruno Latour, "From Realpolitik to Dingpolitik, or How to Make Things Public," in *Making Things Public: Atmospheres of Democracy* (Cambridge, MA: MIT Press, 2005).
- Bruno Latour, "From the World of Science to the World of Research?" *Science* 280, no. 5361 (April 1998): 208–209.
- Eyal Weizman, "Introduction," *Forensis: The Architecture of Public Truth* (Berlin: Sternberg Press, 2014), 9–32.
- Lionel Devlieger, "Note From The Editor," *Behind the Green Door: A Critical Look at Sustainable Architecture through 600 Objects by Rotor* (Oslo Architecture Triennale, 2014), 3–8.
- Charles Jencks with Rem Koolhaas, *Log* 32 (Fall 2014): 62–63.
- Marco De Michelis, "Fundamentals," *Log* 32 (Fall 2014): 93–102.
- Silvia Lavin, "Too Much Information," *Artforum* (September 2014): 347–353, 398.

Images
P 325: *OfficeUS*, June 4–November 23, 2014, United States Pavilion at the Venice Architecture Biennale, Venice, Italy. Curated by Eva Franch i Gilabert, Ana Miljački, Ashley Schafer. Photos courtesy David Sundberg/ESTO and Storefront for Art and Architecture.
P 328 Top: *Un/Fair Use*, September 10–January 25, 2016, AIANY Center for Architecture, New York, NY. Curated by Ana Miljački and Sarah Hirschman.
P 328 Bottom: *Fair Use: An Architectural Timeline*, February 22–March 8, 2013, MIT Architecture Keller Gallery, Cambridge, MA. Curated by Ana Miljački and Sarah Hirschman with Kyle Barker, Christianna Bonin, Kyle Coburn, Daniela Covarrubias, Juan Jofre, Nicholas Polansky, Kelly Presutti.

QUEER SPACE: EXPLORATIONS IN ART AND ARCHITECTURE
Jackson Davidow

What is "queer space"? How have art and architecture shaped, and been shaped by, queer understandings and experiences of space?

This seminar will consider these questions across queer history and theory from the disciplinary vantage points of art, architecture, and visual culture. We will examine how a range of artists, architects, curators, critics, and other cultural practitioners have developed aesthetic and political strategies to engage with their spatial and built environments. In so doing, we will also think about how queer people have used, interrogated the limits of, and laid claim to spaces that have been hostile to gender and sexual dissidents.

Beyond ruminating on queer spatial aesthetics and form, we will navigate spaces of queer world-making and production (e.g., bathhouses, nightclubs, cruising grounds, alternative art venues, domestic settings, archives, memorials, the internet). In turn, we will explore spaces of queer appropriation and intervention (e.g., museums, campuses, streets, cityscapes, environments, borderlines). We will also consider the queer dimensions of space, and queers in space, as they relate to concepts of diaspora, (de)colonization, globalization, and gentrification. Throughout the course, we will pay close attention to how race, class, and nationality function alongside and intersectionally with queer gender and sexuality.

It is often assumed that the fields of art history, architectural history, and visual cultural studies have little to contribute with regard to queer studies, which tends to be dominated by literary, film, and performance studies. At the same time, the disciplines of architecture and art history regularly pass over scholarship that engages with queer topics. Even though there have been vital contributions to queer art and architectural history since the early 1990s, much of this material is underappreciated, and it is rarely taught, especially at the undergraduate level. For these reasons, this course seeks to unearth some alternative intellectual and aesthetic genealogies for thinking queerness and culture in relation to space and the built environment. Interdisciplinary in nature, the course will appeal to students with interests in art and architectural history, women's, gender, and sexuality studies, among other fields. Cultural practitioners, including artists, architects, and filmmakers, are also encouraged to participate.

Welcome and Course Overview
- Lauren Berlant and Michael Warner, "Sex in Public," *Critical Inquiry* 24, no. 2 (1998): 547–66.
- Aaron Betsky, "Some Queer Constructs," in *Queer Space: Architecture and Same-Sex Desire* (New York: William Morrow & Co, 1997), 2–15.
- Jennifer Doyle, "Queer Wallpaper," in *A Companion to Contemporary Art since 1945*, ed. Amelia Jones (Oxford: Blackwell Publishing, 2006), 343–55.

Introductory Frameworks
What is "queer space"? What does this concept mean to you? What is its historiography like in queer theory, art, and architecture? How have these disciplines historically treated questions of (non-normative) gender and sexuality? How does the space vs. time treatment in queer theory play out in art and visual culture? What insights can the disciplinary perspectives of art and architecture offer us? How does context affect queer experience and articulation? How are "queer" and "trans" used differently as critical and theoretical terms, as well as modes of identification? How does queer space become complicated and nuanced as a concept in relation to race, class, and nationality?
- Lucas Crawford, "Foundations and Ruins: Why Don't Transgender and Architecture Get Along?" in *Transgender Architectonics: The Shape of Change in Modernist Space*, (Burlington: Ashgate, 2015), 19–38.
- Alpesh Kantilal Patel, "Space/Site: Writing Queer Feminist Transnational South Asian Art Histories," in *Productive Failure: Writing Queer Transnational South Asian Art Histories*, (Manchester: Manchester University Press, 2017), 109–50.
- John Paul Ricco, "Preface" and "Minor," in *The Logic of the Lure*, (Chicago: University of Chicago Press, 2002), xix–29.
- Joel Sanders, "From Stud to Stalled! Architecture in Transition," *Log* 41 (Fall 2017): 145–54.

Networks and New Subjectivities
Have notions of queer space morphed with the rise of new media technologies and digital culture? How has the internet impacted the production of art and architecture? How has it impacted modes of queer sociality, subjectivity, and resistance? Are there histories of queer artistic networks in which we might situate our contemporary moment?

- Gwen Allen, "The Magazine as Mirror: FILE, 1972–89," in *Artists' Magazines: An Alternative Space for Art* (Cambridge, MA: MIT Press, 2011), 147–74.
- Tom Roach, "Becoming Fungible: Queer Intimacies in Social Media," *Qui Parle* 23, no. 2 (2015): 55–87.
- Andrés Jaque, "Grindr Archiurbanism," *Log* 41 (Fall 2017): 74–84.
- Tavia Nyong'o, "Queer Africa and the Fantasy of Virtual Participation," *WSQ: Women's Studies Quarterly* 40, no. 1–2 (2012): 40–63.

Cruising and the Spatialization of Sex
In what ways have queer sex and eroticism had spatial dimensions across history? How has architecture contributed to the development (and erasure) of certain sexual subjectivities and practices? What roles have art and architecture played in processes of queer world-making in counterpublics? What roles have they played in social control, in policing gender and sexuality?
- Allan Berubé, "The History of the Gay Bathhouse," in *Policing Public Sex: Queer Politics and the Future of AIDS Activism*, ed. Dangerous Bedfellows, (Boston, MA: South End Press, 1996), 187–220.
- Amelia Jones, "The City/Wandering, Neurasthenic Subjects," in *Irrational Modernism: A Neurasthenic History of New York Dada*, (Cambridge, MA: MIT Press, 2004), 168–233.
- Carlos Motta and Joshua Lubin-Levy, eds., *Petite Mort: Recollections of a Queer Public* (New York: Forever & Today, 2011).
- Sarah Schulman, "Making Love Making Art: Living and Dying Performance in the 1980s," in *This Will Have Been: Art, Love & Politics in the 1980s*, ed. Helen Molesworth (New Haven: Yale University Press, 2012), 414–23.

Domesticities
How have queers inhabited, aesthetically articulated, and visually represented their domestic spaces? How have they subverted and embraced traditional gendered and sexualized understandings of domestic space? Is there a relationship between domesticity, interiority, and identity? How have art, architecture, and interior design worked together to create domestic experiences? What is the significance of collecting and curatorial practice? Under what circumstances do domestic lives become publicly disseminated and exhibited? How might this change our understandings of the artist and their oeuvre?
- Tirza True Latimer, "Looking like a Lesbian: Portraiture and Sexual Identity in 1920s Paris," in *The Modern Woman Revisited: Paris between the Wars*, eds. Whitney Chadwick and Tirza True Latimer (New Brunswick, NJ: Rutgers University Press, 2003),127–44.
- Richard Meyer, "Mapplethorpe's Living Room: Photography and the Furnishing of Desire," *Art History* 24, no. 2 (2001): 292–311.
- John Potvin, "Men of a Different Sort: The Seven Deadly Sins of the Modern Bachelor," in *Bachelors of a Different Sort: Queer Aesthetics, Material Culture and the Modern Interior in Britain* (Manchester: Manchester University Press, 2014), 1–36.
- Paul B. Preciado, "Manifesto for an Indoor Man: The Awakening of the Playboy's Domestic Consciousness," in *Pornotopia: An Essay on Playboy's Architecture and Biopolitics* (New York: Zone Books, 2014), 29–49.
- Olivier Vallerand, "Home Is the Place We All Share," *Journal of Architectural Education* 67, no. 1 (2013): 64–75.

Alternative Spaces of Making and World-Making
What sites, spaces, and surfaces have queer artists and publics sought out to make and view art that might transgress social norms? How have these spaces facilitated and catalyzed new forms of art? How did these spaces enable particular modes of queer sociality? How do questions of race and class factor into our understandings of access and participation?
- Fiona Anderson, "Cruising the Queer Ruins of New York's Abandoned Waterfront," *Performance Research* 20, no. 3 (2015): 135–44.
- Julia Bryan-Wilson, "'Out to See Video': EZTV's Queer Microcinema in West Hollywood," *Grey Room* 56 (2014): 56–89.
- Raquel Gutiérrez, "A Vessel Among Vessels: For Laura Aguilar," *The New Inquiry*, June 18, 2018, https://thenewinquiry.com/a-vessel-among-vessels-for-laura-aguilar/.
- Ricardo Montez, "'Trade' Marks: LA2, Keith Haring, and a Queer Economy of Collaboration." *GLQ: A Journal of Lesbian & Gay Studies* 12, no. 3 (2006): 425–40.
- Kevin D. Murphy, "'Secure from All Intrusion': Heterotopia, Queer Space, and the Turn-of-the-Twentieth-Century American Resort," *Winterthur Portfolio* 43, no. 2–3 (2009): 185–228.

Queer Abstraction and Spatial Aesthetics

How can artworks and objects offer up queer theorizations of space? What spatial and aesthetic vocabularies have artists and critics relied on to evoke queer gender and sexuality in their work? What are the spatial connotations of queer abstraction? In our close readings of artworks, is it still possible to attend to the actual spaces of artistic production, dissemination, and reception?

- Julia Bryan-Wilson, "Queerly Made: Harmony Hammond's Floorpieces," *The Journal of Modern Craft* 2, no. 1 (2009): 59–79.
- David Getsy, "Introduction: 'New' Genders and Sculpture in the 1960s," in *Abstract Bodies: Sixties Sculpture in the Expanded Field of Gender*, (New Haven: Yale University Press, 2015), 1–41.
- Lex Morgan Lancaster, "The Wipe: Sadie Benning's Queer Abstraction," *Discourse* 39, no. 1 (Winter 2017): 92–116.
- Jacob R. Moore, "Full Disclosure: Speaking Personally at the New York City AIDS Memorial," *The Avery Review* 12, (December 2015), http://averyreview.com/issues/12/full-disclosure.
- James Rondeau, "'The Cage-Bed of Dreams': Hélio Oiticica and the Evolution of the Barracão," in *Hélio Oiticica: To Organize Delirium*, eds. Lynn Zelevansky, Elisabeth Sussman, James Rondeau, and Donna De Salvo (Munich: Prestel, 2016) 110–30.

Intergenerational Memory, History, the Archive

What is the importance of queer monuments and memorials? How have they brought to light histories of trauma, oppression, and erasure? Do they function differently from archives and exhibitions? What potential do they have for intergenerational contact and learning? What continuities and discontinuities come into view? What is an archive? When have artists intervened queerly in archival practices and spaces? When have they instigated their own? What has this afforded them aesthetically, politically, institutionally?

- Christophe Castiglia and Christopher Reed, "For Time Immemorial: Marking Time in the Built Environment," in *If Memory Serves: Gay Men, AIDS, and the Promise of the Queer Past* (Minneapolis: University of Minnesota Press, 2011), 73–112.
- Gayatri Gopinath, "Queer Visual Excavations: Akram Zaatari, Hashem El Madani, and the Reframing of History in Lebanon," *Journal of Middle East Women's Studies* 13, no. 2 (2017): 326–36.
- José Esteban Muñoz, "Ephemera as Evidence: Introductory Notes to Queer Acts," *Women & Performance: A Journal of Feminist Theory* 8, no. 2 (1996): 5–16.
- Robert Summers, "Queer Archives, Queer Movements: The Visual and Bodily Archives of Vaginal Davis," *Radical History Review* 122 (2015): 47–53.
- Kylie Thomas, "Rage Against the State: Political Funerals and Queer Visual Activism in Post-Apartheid South Africa," in *Public Art in South Africa: Bronze Warriors and Plastic Presidents*, ed. Brenda Schmahmann and Kim Miller (Bloomington: Indiana University Press, 2017), 265–83.

Spaces of Resistance and Activism

How have activist programs engaged with their environments to push for social change? What resonances and citations are there today? How did the AIDS crisis usher in new politicized understandings of space and the public sphere? Can art history and criticism be considered a form of activism?

- Douglas Crimp, *AIDS Demo Graphics* (Seattle: Bay Press, 1990).
- Kate Eichhorn, "Eros, Thanatos, Xerox," in *Adjusted Margin: Xerography, Art, and Activism in the Late Twentieth Century* (Cambridge, MA: MIT Press, 2016), 113–46.
- Kobena Mercer, "Where the Streets Have No Name: A Democracy of Multiple Public Spheres," in *This Will Have Been: Art, Love & Politics in the 1980s*, ed. Helen Molesworth (New Haven: Yale University Press, 2012), 134–47.
- Erin Silver, "Epilogue: Out of the Boxes and into the Streets: Translating Queer and Feminist Activism into Queer Feminist Art History," in *Otherwise: Imagining Queer Feminist Art Histories*, eds. Amelia Jones and Erin Silver, (Manchester: Manchester University Press, 2016), 372–84.

Diasporas, Borders, Globalization

How have queer artists used their work to address tender issues surrounding globalization, diasporas, and national borders? How have they conceived these topics in spatial terms? Has queer space been articulated differently on local, national, and global levels? Do Euro-American theorizations of queerness translate to other global cultural contexts? In what ways is art a privileged site for interrogating and undoing Westernist/universalist notions of gender and sexual difference and dissidence?

- Bobby Benedicto, "Queer Space in the Ruins of Dictatorship Architecture," *Social Text* 31, no. 4 (2013): 25–47.
- Huey Copeland, "Glenn Ligon and the Matter of Fugitivity," in *Bound to Appear: Art, Slavery, and the Site of Blackness in Multicultural America*, (Chicago: University of Chicago Press, 2013), 109–152.
- Gil Z. Hochberg, "'Check Me Out': Queer

Encounters in Sharif Waked's Chic Point: Fashion for Israeli Checkpoints," *GLQ: A Journal of Lesbian and Gay Studies* 16, no. 4 (2010): 577–98.
- Amelia Jones, "'Traitor Prophets': Asco's Art as a Politics of the in-Between," in *Asco: Elite of the Obscure: A Retrospective, 1972–1987*, eds. C. Ondine Chavoya and Rita González, (Ostfildern: Hatje Cantz, 2011).

Possibilities for a Queer Museum

When and how did mainstream galleries and museums begin to show queer art? What tactics have curators and artists cultivated to queer exhibition practice? What is at stake when queer art becomes institutionally validated, institutionalized, and normalized?

- Nicholas Gamso, "Fascist Intrigue and the Homo-Spatial Imaginary," *Log* 41 (Fall 2017): 113–22.
- Catherine Lord, "The Anthropologist's Shadow: The Closet, the Warehouse, the Lesbian as Artifact," in *Space, Site, Intervention: Situating Installation Art*, ed. Erika Suderburg (Minneapolis: University of Minnesota Press, 2000), 297–316.
- Christina Sharpe, "Isaac Julien's *The Attendant* and the Sadomasochism of Everyday Black Life," in *Monstrous Intimacies: Making Post-Slavery Subjects* (Durham: Duke University Press, 2010), 111–52.
- Jennifer Tyburczy, "Introduction: All Museums Are Sex Museums," in *Sex Museums: The Politics and Performance of Display* (Chicago: University of Chicago Press, 2015), 1–37.

View

Isaac Julien's *The Attendant* (1993). Available here: http://www.ubu.com/film/julien_attendant.html.

IS ARCHITECTURAL HISTORY GETTING ANY BIGGER?
Timothy Hyde

It is by chance that just-published obituaries of the American architectural historian Vincent Scully are open on my screen as I begin to write an article for this issue of *arq*, but the juxtaposition seems significant. Scully passed away at the age of ninety-seven, a long scholarly life to bookend the present subject of this issue of *arq*: the journal's coming of age in its twenty-first year. That one of these is a biological age and the other a temporal duration distinguishes them, of course, but the juxtaposition nevertheless illuminates in a curious way the question of when and whether architectural history will enter into maturity.

Scully's death, occurring so recently, is a reminder that the discipline is not terribly old, with only a few intellectual generations needed to skip back to the turn of the twentieth century. Heinrich Wölfflin died in 1945 and Scully started writing his dissertation the following year, under the supervision of Henry-Russell Hitchcock. James Ackerman (who died only a year ago) co-taught with Scully in those graduate student years while being advised by Richard Krautheimer, who had completed his own dissertation under Paul Frankl. Students of both Scully and Ackerman are, of course, alive and well today, adjusting the contours of the field with their books, articles, and lectures. Similarly, students taught by Manfredo Tafuri have a present standing in the field, and Tafuri (who died the year before *arq* published its first issue), anchors a short chain linking himself, Giulio Carlo Argan, and Lionello Venturi, Wölfflin's contemporary. Other architectural historians could serve equally to reveal the same point: that the scope of the development of architectural history is perhaps more limited than chronological age might suggest, and certainly that in comparison to the existence of its presumed subject matter—architecture—has barely made it to infancy.

Without diminishing the hours of archival labor, fieldwork, cogitation, and writing that have been undertaken over the past century and a half, and without understating the contributions to knowledge and understanding those efforts have produced, the implication should be admitted: there really isn't very much architectural history. Not that many architectural historians, not that many books, not that much history, relatively speaking. Especially when set against comparative measures, such as linear feet of library shelving allotted to literature, for example, or the grant funding allocated to physics; when viewed against the overall context of architectural production that has taken place around it during its one-hundred-and-fifty formative years. This isn't to say, necessarily, that architectural history is marginal, for it has attained points of instrumentality and effect along the way, but the admission is the necessary starting point for reflection on the future of the discipline, because architectural history needs to think about how to get bigger.

Incompleteness
The ambition to provide broad accountings and summary explanations, as formalized in universities by the textbook and by the institution of the survey course, accompanied architectural history from the start. Auguste Choisy, for example, made such an attempt, to be followed by Sigfried Giedeon's sweeping textual panoramas and Nikolaus Pevsner's nimble narratives, shorter in their chronologies but even more insistent upon their syntheses. Over the past few decades, new accounts have been placed alongside these by historians brave enough to write surveys and textbooks, variously covering architecture over a period of several centuries, architecture from all around the globe, or architecture from all times and places. Even the most generous publisher will allot only a certain number of pages to such books, so even these surveys, more precise and more rigorously theorised than their predecessors, are episodic, edited to use exemplars to stand for tendencies they represent and sets in which they are included.

Put simply, architectural history has long depended upon a strategy of extrapolation. Unable to achieve any comprehensive collation of its subject matter, the discipline's historical narratives have coalesced into categories sustained by extrapolative approaches. They embed discrete architectural works within aesthetic or technological movements, or use nation-states as isomorphs of architecture's geography, or employ monographic studies of individuals as corollaries of durations of social time. From the necessity of employing the organization and presentation of selections, architectural history has over the past century made habitual and conventional what should actually be startling and problematic. That the claims of the discipline are based upon an incomplete knowledge is not in itself the issue—what area of historical enquiry, indeed what discipline, does not share in this? Rather, the issue lies in the fact that architectural history has, as a discipline, failed to theorize sufficiently the incompleteness of its knowledge.

The disciplinary guilt needn't be evenly shared. Many classicists and medievalists have been clear enough about the constraints faced in fully constructing their subjects. It is perhaps the modernists who, possibly too close to the nineteenth century's illusory impression of a complete archive and to technologies of reproduction, need most urgently to confront the problematic condition of incompleteness. And yet, the reflexive response to the problem—to fill in more information, to seek out the missing buildings, the unknown architects, the unstudied cities and territories—should be recognized as itself being a modernist response, one which, while well-intentioned and undoubtedly helpful, does not address the underlying methodological crisis. Nor would another familiar response, that of reinforcing disciplinary boundaries so that they contain only already-extant categories—a response that is becoming less common, but which is by no means extinct.

One potential opening toward an expansion of the discipline of architectural history, in its materials and its subjects but more so in its epistemological capacity to address incompleteness, might be signalled not by the modernist response but by taking up the theoretical concern for deeper histories. The current conceptual scope of deep history addresses materials and boundaries of time that precede architecture itself, so mere appropriation of the perspective would not address a specific disciplinary concern. But the deliberate conceptualization of distance and duration could suggest a means of fashioning historiographic frameworks that are more loosely attached to their particulate subjects.

Invisibility

What other evolutions of the discipline might have come to pass had the enquiries into the history of architecture emerged and been consolidated not from within art history but another field—intellectual history, say, or from a science such as chemistry? Such counterfactual possibilities are hard to conjure in any great detail, though the cause is less their short-sightedness in themselves than the relentlessness of the aesthetic priority that has attached to architectural history since its relatively recent emergence from art history. But to the extent that such alternative narratives can be conceived and deployed as speculative inquiries, they point toward the myriad non-aesthetic, and more specifically non-visual, dimensions through which architecture and its understanding are approached.

Text has accompanied the visual and physical appearance of architecture, of course, so that textuality has been an accomplice of the phenomenal in architectural interpretation, no matter that the two are often stood in opposition to one another. From their initially subordinate relation within conclusions drawn by architectural history, text and textuality came to hold, by the end of the twentieth century, a position of near independence from architectural appearance within some disciplinary arguments. If this development opened the clear possibility of an emphasis in architectural history upon the non-visual, or even a non-visual architectural history, it was only a provisional step away from visibility, given that text remained conventional communicative language, and textuality remained the textuality of literary criticism and linguistics.

Through this opening, however, different potentialities of textuality have entered into the compass of architectural history. Contracts, specifications, legislation, and other instrumental texts of legal reasoning have, for example, begun to receive increasing attention as necessary materials of architectural history, even to the extent that, in some arguments, the specification surpasses the drawing as the evidentiary ground of interpretation. Such texts, however removed from the visual sphere, retain at least the recognizability of everyday communicative language. That is not likely to be the case for the next expansion of architectural history's attention, into the mediums of the digital age, algorithms, scripts, and machine codes. Some groundbreaking work notwithstanding, in the context of the overall field of architectural history, the pervasiveness of computation within architecture of the last half-century has barely been acknowledged, taken as a decisive criterion only in consideration of architects whose work is explicitly "about" computation.

Yet the presence of the digital has been widespread for some time, whether in design, communication, manufacture, or in other realms of architectural production. So, if the historian examining the nineteenth century needed to read French and German and to be able to navigate the documentary realm of bureaucracy, the historian of the twentieth century and beyond needs a fluency in computational languages as well as a knowledge of the material supports of the digital: magnetic cores, silicon chips, and fibre-optics. The expansion of architectural history is an expansion toward invisibilities, and it is not clear that the discipline has yet formulated even primitive, let alone adequate, tools to work with invisibility. It will not likely be sufficient merely to translate tools devised for realms of visibility. For example, the phenomenological approaches premised upon human experience will not elucidate the molecular materiality of architecture and its significance (though some theorists are

Alongside monographs could appear data sets; alongside Scully's anthropocentric empathetic encounters with buildings could appear visualizations of molecular change; alongside Tafuri's contextualizing narratives of contingency could be a new literature of intermittent documentation, closer in conception to a seismograph than a Pevsnerian narrative.

Timothy Hyde

attempting such a bridge using claims of neuroscience). Architectural history can certainly seize upon this all-but-unexplored territory of architectural understanding, but must first admit a disciplinary unpreparedness in order to shift effort and resources toward a new objective.

Invention

From its foundational endeavour of evaluating and explicating the origins and significances of architectural forms, the discipline of architectural history assembled an armature of connections to disciplinary neighbors, in philosophy, in engineering, and in literature. From these connections developed the fuller scope of what would now be defined as the potential for interdisciplinarity, in which architectural history traded concepts and arguments with these adjacent fields, while retaining its privileges as an interpreter of the architectural profession and the built environment. But it has not only been broad disciplinary overlaps that have shaped the development of architectural history; the influences have been conveyed more instrumentally through techniques: the empirical routines of archaeology, for example, or the operations of archival conservation and recording, or quantitative regimes of calculation and computation. These techniques, encoded with their own rules, potentials, and limits, contribute their own capacities to bring architectural objects into the requisite degree of presence such that they can become objects of architectural history.

The objects of architectural history are not found, but invented; not only in the sense that they are designed, conjured up through the motivated actions of persons and institutions, but invented in the sense that they are designated as the proper materials of disciplinary enquiry and resolution. Unlike the geologist seeking out and discovering the autonomous materials to be placed under scrutiny, the historian is engaged in a process of summoning from disparate materials a coherent (or at least provisionally coherent) entity to be situated, examined, and questioned. For the architectural historian specifically, this process is carried out with borrowed techniques, and by understanding these borrowed techniques as the tools through which it encounters its objects, architectural history would confront a quite challenging possibility: that architectural history is not a discipline in and of itself, but is the collection and remainder of potentials defined in and by the techniques other disciplines.

Continued rehearsals of claims to a disciplinary core or to a disciplinary irreducibility do more to threaten disciplinary persistence than to enhance it, precisely because they postpone a moment of reckoning. By contrast, an embrace of inventiveness,

as represented by all of these prior acts of borrowing, might authorise a new moment of disciplinary expansion. For architectural history to be bigger–in the sense of a capacity to engage a wider array of materials and also in the sense of greater maturity that enables it to resolve its current methodological deficiencies—for the discipline to be bigger, a willing experimentation in novel assemblies of techniques would offer a way to invent different kinds of objects of enquiry. Alongside monographs could appear data sets; alongside Scully's anthropocentric empathetic encounters with buildings could appear visualizations of molecular change; alongside Tafuri's contextualizing narratives of contingency could be a new literature of intermittent documentation, closer in conception to a seismograph than a Pevsnerian narrative.

Bigger and bigger

The route to disciplinary growth is in some aspects obvious: more doctoral students, more academic appointments in universities and research assignments in institutions around the world, more books and articles; a natural growth, however compromised by current trends within academic spheres of funding and publishing. But, of course, disciplinary growth is not merely a numerical measure. Although this issue of *arq*, as the journal's speculative coming of age, provokes from me an assessment of the smallness or—maintaining the chronological metaphor—the immaturity of architectural history, the prognosis, like that for any minor, should be optimistic. For by recognizing that the discipline is presently quite circumscribed, and quite modest in its aspirations, a different tone can be forged, of encouragement and speculation. Though the expansion of architectural history is by no means a given, and is unlikely to be a painless transformation, the obstacles are largely self-imposed. By declaring an end to its childhood, and by seeing what paths are open toward many futures, architectural history can become bigger and bigger.

"Is Architectural History Getting Any Bigger?" by Timothy Hyde was first published in *arq*, *Architectural Research Quarterly* 21, no. 4 (December 2017): 347–350, https://doi.org/10.1017/S1359135518000106. © Cambridge University Press, reproduced with permission.

A CURRICULUM FOR MUD: COMPOSITION FOR MASSACHUSETTS (OUR BELOVED KIN); THOREAU (THE RE-ENSLAVEMENT OF ANTHONY BURNS); DISCORPORATE (THE INSTITUTE IN THIRDS)
Nolan Oswald Dennis

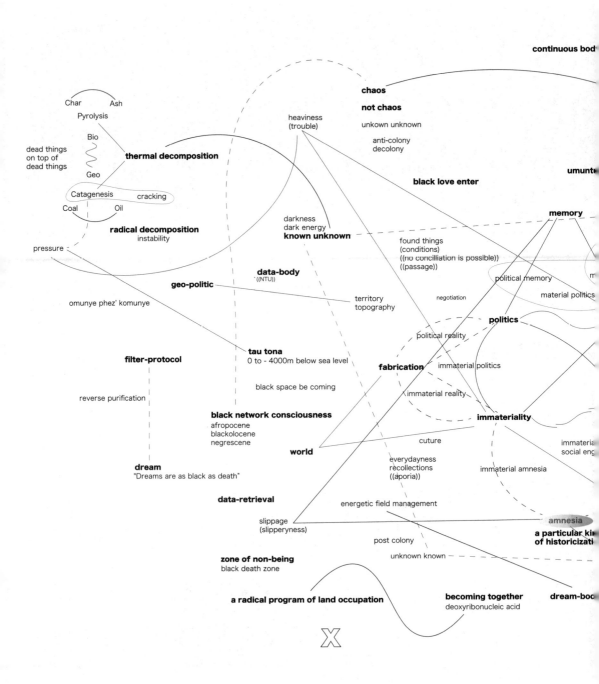

continuous bod

chaos

not chaos

unkown unknown

anti-colony
decolony

Char   Ash

Pyrolysis

Bio

dead things
on top of
dead things

thermal decomposition

Geo

Catagenesis   cracking

Coal   Oil

heaviness
(trouble)

black love enter

umunt

memory

darkness
dark energy
known unknown

found things
(conditions)
((no concilliation is possible))
((passage))

political memory

m

material politics

radical decomposition
instability

pressure

data-body
`((NTU))

geo-politic

territory
topography

negotiation

politics

omunye phez' komunye

political reality

tau tona
0 to - 4000m below sea level

fabrication

immaterial politics

filter-protocol

black space be coming

immaterial reality

immateriality

reverse purification

black network consciousness
afropocene
blackolocene
negrescene

world

cuture

immateria
social eng

dream
"Dreams are as black as death"

everydayness
recollections
((aporia))

immaterial amnesia

data-retrieval

energetic field management

slippage
(slipperyness)

amnesia

post colony

a particular ki
of historicizati

zone of non-being
black death zone

unknown known

a radical program of land occupation

becoming together
deoxyribonucleic acid

dream-boo

X

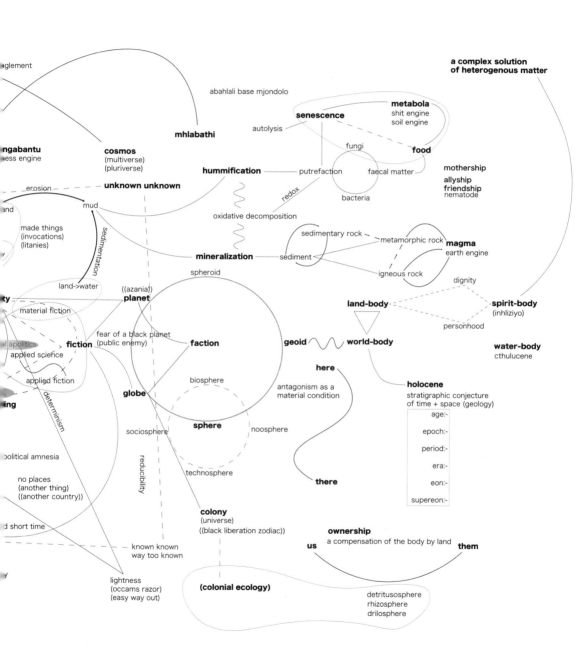

EXPERIMENTS IN PEDAGOGY
Mark Jarzombek, J. Meejin Yoon; Renée Caso, Irina Chernyakova, Danniely Staback

The Experiments in Pedagogy are tests and provocations organized on occasion of marking 150 years of architecture education at MIT in Fall 2018. Selected from an open call, the Experiments are invitation to students and faculty to investigate and test new models and modes of inquiry and teaching. Organized under a single subject number, students select up to four Experiments to fulfill an open elective. Each takes a unique format, from weekend field trips and workshops to half-semester workshops. Each Experiment includes a public event open to all.

Space/Dance Studio
Mark Jarzombek and Richard Colton with the Neave Trio and Guy Bigland

Earth on Display: The Anthropocene Museum of Natural History
Rania Ghosn

Agit Arch Experiments
Ana Miljacki/Critical Broadcasting Lab with Ann Lui and Mimi Zeiger; Luke Bulman; Felicity Scott and Mark Wasiuta

Fear and Wonder: The Shape of the Future
Liam Young

Transensational Objects: Methods for Inclusive Design
Maroula Bacharidou and Athina Papadopoulou

Robotic Force Printing
Philippe Block and Philip Yuan with Zain Karsan at Tongji University

Structural Upcycling
Caitlin Mueller, Feliz Amtsberg, Yijiang Huang, Demi Fang, Paul Mayencourt, and Daniel Marshall with Jason Detwiler and the City of Somerville

Paper Space: Creative Writing and Architecture
Stratton Coffman and Sarah Wagner with Garnette Cadogan, Dorothea Lasky, and Ken Urban

Virtual Reality Design 2.0
Eytan Mann and Çağrı Zaman

Self/Work/Place/Thing
Rosalyne Shieh

Architectural Access: Code and Care
Gabriel Cira and Emily Watlington with Wendy Jacob and Sara Hendren; Valerie Fletcher and David Gissen; Meryl Alper and MIT Biomechatronics (Matt Carney and Lisa Freed); and Aimi Hamraie, David Mitchell, and Sharon Snyder

Monuments in Perspective
Erin Genia

Visualizing 150 Years of Architecture at MIT
E Roon Kang and Richard The

Captivating Character
Brandon Clifford, Jennifer Leung, and Hans Tursack (Core 1 Studio) with Joshua Longo

Images
P 343: Rodrigo Escandón Cesarman, Nof Nathansohn, Ingrid Dobloug Roede, Melissa G. Soto, Nitzan Zilberman, *Card Game*, October 2018. Produced as part of Agit Arch Experiments workshop Dimensions of Citizenship with Ann Lok Lui and Mimi Zeiger, October 12–14, 2018, organized by Ana Miljački and the Critical Broadcasting Lab.
P 344: Alexander Bodkin, Stratton Coffman, Jaya Alba Eyzaguirre, Sarah Wagner, *RealKinn*, Agit Arch Experiments, Exhibit in MIT Keller Gallery, October 2018. Photo by Sarah Wagner.
P 345: Jaya A. Eyzaguirre, Sebastian Kamau, and Taeseop Shin, *Fukushima 2100*, Earth on Display: The Anthropocene Museum of Natural History, Exhibit at the Harvard Museum of Natural History, November 4, 2018. Photo by Pavlo Kryvozub.
P 346–347: Sara Hendren and Wendy Jacob in conversation as part of Architectural Access: Code and Care, November 6, 2018. Photo by Sarah Wagner.

S2 : caesium mineral

S6 : emergency iodine pills

S3 : rice in house

S1 : Safecast geiger counter

Architecture and Urbanism (A+U)
Fabrizio Barozzi, Visiting Professor
Lorena Bello, Visiting Lecturer
Yung Ho Chang, Professor of the Practice
Brandon Clifford, Assistant Professor
Linna Choi, Visiting Lecturer
Marcelo Coelho, Design Lecturer
Alexander D'Hooghe, Visiting Professor
Yolande Daniels, Lecturer
Michael Dennis, Professor Emeritus
Christopher Dewart, Technical Instructor; Shop
    Manager
Rami el Samahy, Visiting Lecturer
Philip Freelon, Professor of the Practice
Benjamin Fry, Design Lecturer
Antón García-Abril, Professor
Sam Ghantous, Teaching Fellow
Rania Ghosn, Associate Professor
Reinhard Goethert, Principal Research Associate
Mark Goulthorpe, Associate Professor
Christophe Guberan, Design Minor Visiting Lecturer
Florian Idenburg, Sullivan Visiting Professor
Mariana Ibañez, Assistant Professor
Jeremy Jih, Visiting Lecturer
Zain Karsan, Teaching Fellow
Sheila Kennedy, Professor
Axel Kilian, Visiting Assistant Professor
John Klein, Research Scientist
Jennifer W. Leung, Visiting Lecturer
Miho Mazereeuw, Associate Professor
Ana Miljački, Associate Professor
Robert Mohr, Visiting Lecturer
Lee Moreau, Design Lecturer
Jennifer O'Brien, Technical Instructor; Shop
    Manager
William O'Brien Jr., Associate Professor
Tarik Oualalou, Visiting Lecturer
Cristina Parreño, Lecturer
Pratik Ravel, Visiting Lecturer
Jessica Rosenkrantz, Design Minor Lecturer
Roi Salgueiro, Research Associate; Lecturer
Adèle Naudé Santos, Professor
Hashim Sarkis, Professor; Dean
Susanne Schindler, Visiting Lecturer
Andrew Scott, Professor; Department Head
Rafi Segal, Associate Professor
Rosalyne Shieh, Marion Mahony Fellow
Maya Shopova, Teaching Fellow
Marc Simmons, Associate Professor of the Practice
Danniely Staback, Teaching Fellow
Hans Tursack, Pietro Belluschi Fellow

Anne Whiston Spirn, Professor
Dan Wood, Visiting Lecturer
J. Meejin Yoon, Professor

Art, Culture and Technology (ACT)
Azra Akšamija, Associate Professor
Lara Ramez Baladi, Lecturer
Judith Barry, Professor; Director
Mario Caro, Lecturer
Renée Green, Professor
Marisa Jahn, Lecturer
Sung Hwan Kim, Lecturer
Matthew Mazzotta, Lecturer
Tobias Putrih, Lecturer
Rasa Smite, Lecturer
Raitis Smits, Lecturer
Nida Sinnokrot, Assistant Professor
Gediminas Urbonas, Associate Professor

Building Technology (BT)
Josephine Carstensen, Visiting Lecturer
John Fernández, Professor
Leon Glicksman, Professor
Caitlin Mueller, Associate Professor
Les Norford, Professor
John Ochsendorf, Professor
Christoph Reinhart, Professor; Director

Design and Computation (DCG)
Maroula Bacharidou, Teaching Fellow
Terry Knight, Professor
Takehiko Nagakura, Associate Professor
Lawrence Sass, Associate Professor; Director
George Stiny, Professor
Skylar Tibbits, Assistant Professor
Andrzej Zarzycki, Lecturer

History, Theory and Criticism of Architecture and Art
(HTC)
Arindam Dutta, Associate Professor
David H. Friedman, Professor Emeritus
Timothy Hyde, Associate Professor
Lauren Jacobi, Associate Professor
Mark Jarzombek, Professor
Caroline A. Jones, Professor
Nasser Rabbat, Professor; Director, Aga Khan
    Program for Islamic Architecture
Kristel Smentek, Associate Professor; Director
James Wescoat, Professor

Staff
Sable Aragon, ACT Group Assistant
José Luis Argüello, Aga Khan Program Assistant
Darren Bennett, Admissions Coordinator;
    Webmaster
Kathaleen Brearley, HTC Group Assistant
Erin Buckley, BT Group Assistant
Renée Caso, Academic Programs Manager
Irina Chernyakova, Publications and Exhibitions
Marion Cunningham, ACT Administrative Officer
Patricia Driscoll, Assistant to the Department Head
Marissa Friedman, ACT Communications and Public
    Programs Coordinator
Eduardo Gonzalez, Network Administrator
Gina Halabi, HTC Group Assistant
Jim Harrington, Director, Facilities
Lisa Hersh, HR and Finance Assistant
Christopher Jenkins, A+U Group Assistant
Duncan Kincaid, Director, Computer Resource
    Network
Douglas Le Vie, Fiscal Officer
Inala Locke, Computation Group Assistant
Kevin McLellan, ACT Financial Assistant
Tonya Miller, Student Services Assistant
Jesi Nishibun, A+U Group Assistant
Andreea O'Connell, Administrative Officer
Bryan O'Keefe, Senior Financial Associate
Paul Pettigrew, Director, Undergraduate Recruitment,
    Career Development, and Alumni Outreach
Chelsea Polk, ACT Media Assistant
Alan Reyes, Administrative Assistant
John Steiner, ACT Media Associate
Cynthia Stewart, Graduate Administrator
Thera Webb, ACT Project Archivist
Graham Yeager, ACT Fabrication Associate

Ammar Ahmed is a designer from Pakistan. He acquired his M.Arch degree from MIT Department of Architecture. His interests lie at the intersection of photography and architecture.

Irina Chernyakova manages communications and public programs at the MIT Department of Architecture, from which she graduated with a master's degree in the history, theory, and criticism of architecture and art.

Sam Ghantous is a Teaching Fellow in the Department of Architecture at MIT, where he works on issues of new media in architecture.

Maya Shopova is a Teaching Fellow in the Department of Architecture at MIT, where she received her M.Arch degree. Her work focuses on questions of collectivity and collaboration.

J. Meejin Yoon is an architect, designer, and educator. Yoon taught at MIT for seventeen years and served as the Head of the Department of Architecture from 2014–2018.

Thank you to Dean Hashim Sarkis and Melissa Vaughn, Director of Communications, for their advocacy and support on this project. We are grateful to Ana Miljački for her constructive feedback; to alumnae Jess Jorge and Jessica Pace, who worked on its earliest iterations; to Patsy Baudoin and Susan Spilecki for their thoughtful edits; and to Lucas Freeman for a final attentive and vital review of the materials.

Special thanks to Andreea O'Connell, Administrative Officer, and Douglas Le Vie, Fiscal Officer, for their administrative support throughout the project. And thank you to Department staff Darren Bennett, Kathaleen Brearley, Erin Buckley, Renée Caso, Patricia Driscoll, Gina Halabi, Lisa Hersh, Chris Jenkins, Inala Locke, Tonya Miller, Jesi Nishibun-Dunaway, Bryan O'Keefe, Paul Pettigrew, Kathleen Ross, and Cynthia Stewart for keeping everything running, always.

Lastly, thank you to student archivists Ammar Ahmed, Dalma Földesi, Daniel Marshall, Jung In Seo, and Jaehun Woo; to CRON and Duncan Kincaid for working with us on archiving student work; to photographers Andy Ryan and Sarah Wagner; and especially all the students, faculty, and staff who contributed work, responded to all of our requests, and supported the project.

This volume is made possible with funding from the MIT Department of Architecture.

The *Agendas in Architecture* series features student and faculty design, research, and scholarship from the MIT Department of Architecture.

Certain Agendas in Architecture
Alexander D'Hooghe and Sarah Dunbar, Editors
2006

Uncertain Futures
Ana Miljački with Lisa Pauli, Morgan Pinney, and Buck Sleeper, Editors
2009

Testing to Failure
Sarah Hirschman, Editor
2011

Building Discourse
Irene Hwang, Editor
2014